Ethics: Contemporary Readings

"I am very impressed with this collection. It seems to me to have great pedagogical value on its own, and it would work splendidly with Gensler's [text] book. The selections are well chosen – both accessible and interesting. The inclusion of Continental writers is particularly to be applauded."

Robert Arrington, Georgia State University

Ethics: Contemporary Readings is designed to lead any student into the subject and does so through carefully selected classic and contemporary articles. The book includes articles by the leading figures in the field and provides an excellent entry to the topic. The book complements Harry Gensler's *Ethics: A Contemporary Introduction* (Routledge 1998). Articles are arranged under the following headings:

- Initial Approaches to Morality
- Further Approaches to Morality
- Ethical Methodology
- Normative Theory
- Applied Ethics

Articles by the following thinkers are included:

Aristotle	Habermas	Mackie	Ross
Ayer	Hare	Mill	Sartre
Benedict	Hetzler	Moore	P. Singer
Brandt	Hume	Nagel	Slote
Callahan	Kant	Ni	
Callicott	M.L. King	Nc	
Finnis	Kohlberg	O'	
Frankena	C.S. Lewis	Ra	
Gensler	MacIntyre	Ri	

The volume is prefaced by two extensive introductions by the . . . . ele is also situated by an explanatory passage. This volume will be ideal for any student taking a course or module in ethics.

Harry J. Gensler, S.J., is Professor of Philosophy at John Carroll University, Cleveland. He is author of *Ethics: A Contemporary Introduction* (Routledge 1998), *Formal Ethics* (Routledge 1996), and *Introduction to Logic* (Routledge 2002). **Earl W. Spurgin** is Associate Professor of Philosophy at John Carroll University and author of several articles in ethics and business ethics. **James C. Swindal** is Associate Professor and Chair of Philosophy at John Carroll University and author of *Reflection Revisited: Jürgen Habermas's Discursive Theory of Truth* (1999).

Routledge Contemporary Readings in Philosophy

Series Editor: Paul K. Moser
Loyola University of Chicago

Routledge Contemporary Readings in Philosophy is a major new series of philosophy anthologies aimed at undergraduate students taking core philosophy disciplines. It is also a companion series to the highly successful *Routledge Contemporary Introductions to Philosophy*. Each book of readings provides an overview of a core general subject in philosophy, offering students an accessible transition from introductory to higher-level undergraduate work in that subject. Each chapter of readings will be carefully selected, edited, and introduced. They will provide a broad overview of each topic and will include both classic and contemporary readings.

Philosophy of Science
Yuri Balashov and Alex Rosenberg

Metaphysics
Michael J. Loux

Epistemology
Michael Huemer with introduction by Robert Audi

Philosophy of Mind
Timothy O'Connor and David Robb

Ethics
Harry J. Gensler, Earl W. Spurgin, and James C. Swindal

ETHICS
Contemporary Readings

Edited by

Harry J. Gensler, Earl W. Spurgin,
and James C. Swindal

Routledge
Taylor & Francis Group
NEW YORK AND LONDON

First published 2004
by Routledge
29 West 35th Street, New York, NY 10001

Simultaneously published in the UK
by Routledge
11 New Fetter Lane, London EC4P 4EE

Routledge is an imprint of the Taylor & Francis Group

Typeset in Sabon by Harry J. Gensler
Printed and bound in Great Britain by MPG books Ltd,
Bodmin, Cornwall

Publisher's Note
This book has been prepared from camera-ready
copy provided by the editors

Library of Congress Cataloging in Publication Data
A catalog record for this book has been requested

British Library Cataloguing in Publication Data
A catalogue record for this book is available from the British Library

ISBN 0–415–25680–1 (hbk)
ISBN 0–415–25681–x (pbk)

CONTENTS

CONTENTS

PART IV: NORMATIVE THEORY: CONSEQUENTIALISM, NONCONSEQUENTIALISM, DISTRIBUTIVE JUSTICE, AND VIRTUE

PART V: APPLIED ETHICS: ABORTION AND OTHER ISSUES

PREFACE

This anthology can be used either as a companion to Harry Gensler's *Ethics: A Contemporary Introduction* (Routledge 1998) or as a stand-alone textbook (with or without further materials).

The anthology begins with two substantial introductions – one on general issues of ethical theory and one on the history of ethics. Then there are thirty-five selections, roughly arranged to follow the order of topics in Gensler's book. So the readings move from views about the nature and methodology of morality to views defending specific moral norms.

Most of our readings are about moral theory and were written by major analytic philosophers of the last hundred years. But we also included some applied ethics, some continental philosophers, some non-philosophers, and some earlier thinkers.

The anthology is intended for those who have studied some philosophy but are focusing on ethics for the first time. So we searched for readings that beginners can grasp. To further promote understanding, we pruned the readings carefully and added brief introductions, section headings, explanatory endnotes, study questions, and suggestions for further study.

How we ought to live is an important question – indeed, one that has increasing importance for us. We hope that this book may help some people to deal with this topic in a clearer and wiser way.

Harry J. Gensler
Earl W. Spurgin
James C. Swindal

ACKNOWLEDGMENTS

PART I: INITIAL APPROACHES TO MORALITY

Benedict, Ruth, from "Anthropology and the abnormal" in the *Journal of General Psychology* 10 (1934).

Gensler, Harry J., and Tokmenko, Mary Grace, from "Are values relative to culture?" in *Dialogue* (Scotland) 14 (2000).

Hume, David, from *Treatise of Human Nature* (1739) and *Enquiry Concerning the Principles of Morals* (1751).

Nagel, Thomas, from *What Does it All Mean?* ©1987 Oxford University Press.

Lewis, C. S., from *Mere Christianity* ©1952 Geoffrey Bles.

The Bible, from *The New American Bible* ©1992 Catholic Book Publishing.

PART II: FURTHER APPROACHES TO MORALITY

Moore, G. E., from *Principia Ethica* ©1903 Cambridge University Press.

Ross, W. D., from *The Right and the Good* ©1930 Oxford University Press.

Ayer, A. J., from *Language, Truth and Logic* ©1946 Dover.

Mackie, J. L., from *Ethics: Inventing Right and Wrong* ©1977 Penguin.

Hare, R. M., from *Freedom and Reason* ©1963 Clarendon Press.

Sartre, J-P., from *Existentialism and Human Emotions*, Frechtman, B. (trans.) ©1957 Philosophical Library.

PART III: ETHICAL METHODOLOGY

Frankena, William K., from *Ethics* ©1972 Prentice-Hall.

Habermas, Jürgen, from "Discourse Ethics: notes on a program of philosophical justification" in *Moral Consciousness and Communicative Action*, Lenhardt and Weber Nicholson (trans.) ©1990 MIT Press.

Hertzler, Joyce, from "On Golden Rules" in the *International Journal of Ethics* 44 (1934).

Ricoeur, Paul, from "The Golden Rule" in *New Testament Studies* 36 (1990).

Nietzsche, Friedrich, from *Beyond Good and Evil* and *Thus Spoke Zarasthustra*, both from *The Philosophy of Nietzsche*, Zimmern, H. and Common, T. (trans.) ©1954 Modern Library.

Kohlberg, Lawrence, from "A cognitive-developmental approach to moral education" in the *Humanist* 32 (1972).

PART IV: NORMATIVE THEORY

Smart, J. J. C., from *Utilitarianism: For and Against* ©1973 Cambridge University Press.
Williams, Bernard, from *Utilitarianism: For and Against* ©1973 Cambridge University Press.
Brandt, Richard B., from "Toward a credible form of utilitarianism" in *Morality and the Language of Conduct*, Castaneda, H-N., and Nakhnikian, G. (eds) ©1960 Wayne State University Press.
Finnis, John, from *Natural Law and Natural Rights* ©1980 Oxford University Press.
Rawls, John, from *A Theory of Justice* (second edition) ©1999 Harvard University Press.
Nozick, Robert, from *Anarchy, State and Utopia* ©1974 Basic Books.
MacIntyre, Alasdair, from *After Virtue* ©1981 Notre Dame University Press.
Slote, Michael, from *From Morality to Virtue* ©1992 Oxford University Press.

PART V: APPLIED ETHICS

Thomson, Judith Jarvis, from "A defense of abortion" in *Philosophy and Public Affairs* 1 (1971).
Callahan, Sydney, from "Abortion and the sexual agenda: A case for pro-life feminism" in *Commonweal* 113 (1986).
Singer, Peter, from *Animal Liberation* (revised edition) ©1975 and 1990 Avon Books.
O'Neill, Onora, from "The moral perplexities of famine relief" in *Matters of Life and Death,* Tom Regan (ed.) ©1980 Temple University Press.
Callicott, J. Baird, from "The conceptual foundations of the land ethic" in *Companion to a Sand County Almanac* ©1987 University of Wisconsin Press.

While reasonable effort has been put into obtaining permission prior to publication, there are some cases where it has been impossible to trace the copyright holder or to secure a reply. The editors and the publishers apologize for any errors and omissions and, if notified, the publisher will endeavor to rectify these at the earliest possible opportunity.

HARRY J. GENSLER
Moral Philosophy

Racism was rampant not long ago. I can recall when black Americans and black South Africans were routinely denied access to voting, to the better public education, and to the better jobs. My parents can remember when six million Jews were put in concentration camps and killed by the Nazis. When my great grandparents lived, most black Americans were slaves.

Such racist actions are wrong. That is my belief, and I expect most readers to agree. Today most people believe that such actions are, not only wrong, but *obviously* wrong. Yet not long ago such beliefs were controversial; the morality of racist actions was widely debated, with intelligent people on both sides of the debate.

To reflective people, these facts raise many questions. Some of these questions involve the history of racism – why it existed and how things changed. There are further questions about psychological causes of racism – about literary portrayals of racism – and about theological responses. And there are philosophical questions about the morality of racism and the nature of morality; here we will focus on philosophical questions.[1]

Is there a right and a wrong in any objective sense? If we say "Racism is wrong," are we just making a claim about our cultural standards or personal feelings – or are we making an objective claim that is true or false regardless of what anyone may think or feel? Are there objective ethical truths? If there are, how can we know them? Is there any way to reason against those who have opposing views about what is right and wrong? These questions are about "metaethics" – which studies the nature and methodology of moral judgments. Metaethics is one of the two main branches of moral philosophy.

The other branch of moral philosophy is called "normative ethics." This branch tries to defend norms about what is right or wrong, worthwhile, virtuous, or just. You do normative ethics if you defend norms like "Racism is wrong" or "We ought always to do whatever maximizes the pleasure of sentient beings." You do metaethics if you defend ideas like "There are objective moral truths based on God's will" or "Moral beliefs express, not objective truths, but only our personal feelings."

Metaethics is more basic, since it studies the nature of morality and the method for selecting moral principles and doing normative ethics. This book begins with metaethics and ends with normative ethics. The book has five parts, each having readings from several authors:

Initial approaches to morality	three metaethical views that particularly appeal to beginning students: cultural relativism, subjectivism, supernaturalism
Further approaches to morality	three metaethical views that appeal more to philosophers: intuitionism, emotivism, prescriptivism
Ethical methodology	justifying moral claims, the golden rule, racial segregation, moral education
Normative theory	utilitarianism, nonconsequentialism, distributive justice, virtue ethics
Applied ethics	abortion, animal rights, famine relief, environmental ethics

These divisions roughly follow those of the companion book, my *Ethics: A Contemporary Introduction* (London: Routledge, 1998), which may be consulted for a longer treatment of most of the views.[2]

1. Initial approaches to morality

Part I considers three views that particularly appeal to students: that "good" makes a claim about social conventions (cultural relativism), personal feelings (subjectivism), or God's will (supernaturalism).

Cultural relativism, our first view, holds that "good" means what is "socially approved" by the majority in a given culture. Racism, for example, is not good or bad objectively; instead, it is good in a society that approves of it, but bad in one that disapproves of it. Cultural relativists see morality as a product of culture. They think that societies disagree widely about morality, and that we have no clear way to resolve the differences. They conclude that there are no objective values. Cultural relativists view themselves as tolerant; they see other cultures, not as "wrong," but as "different."

Despite its initial plausibility, cultural relativism has many problems. Imagine that you lived in a society that approved of racism. Then, according to cultural relativism, you would have to agree that racism is good (since "good" just means "socially approved"). You could not think for yourself and say "Racism is socially approved but bad" (since this would be self-contradictory). Cultural relativism imposes conformity and an uncritical acceptance of social norms; it denies us the freedom to think for ourselves on moral issues.

Another problem is that we all belong to various overlapping groups. I am part of a specific nation, state, city, and neighborhood; and I am also part of various family, professional, religious, and peer groups. These groups often have conflicting values. According to cultural relativism, when I say "Racism is wrong" I mean "My society disapproves of racism." But *which* society does this refer to? Maybe most in my national and religious societies disapprove of racism, while most in my professional and family societies approve of it. Cultural relativism could give us clear guidance only if we belonged to just one society; but the world is more complicated than that. We are all multicultural to some extent.

Many social scientists oppose cultural relativism. The psychologist Lawrence Kohlberg,[3] for example, claimed that people of all cultures go through roughly the same stages of moral thinking. Cultural relativism represents a relatively low stage in which we simply conform to society. At more advanced stages, we reject cultural relativism; we become critical of accepted norms and think for ourselves about moral issues. How to do that is a central issue of moral philosophy.

Subjectivism, our second view, says that moral judgments describe our personal feelings: "X is good" means "I like X." We are to pick out our moral principles by following our feelings. This view allows us to think for ourselves – since we need not agree with society; it bases ethics, not on what society feels, but on what we personally feel.

Subjectivism has problems. It holds, implausibly, that the mere fact that we like something (such as getting drunk and hurting others) would make it good. It gives a weak basis for dealing with areas like racism (which would be good if I liked it) and moral education (since children would be taught to follow their likes and dislikes). And it tells us to follow our feelings but gives us no guide on how to develop rational and wise feelings.

Supernaturalism, our third view, holds that moral judgments describe God's will: "X is good" means "God desires X." Ethics is based on religion; God's will creates the moral order. Supernaturalism can be defended as a Biblical teaching, as a consequence of belief in God (who is viewed as the source of all basic laws), and as the only plausible source of objectively binding duties. As to how we can know God's will, supernaturalists have suggested sources like the Bible, the church, prayer, and reason.

Supernaturalism, despite being initially plausible (at least to religious people), has some problems. Supernaturalism seems to make it impossible for atheists to make moral judgments – an implausible result. And the ancient Greek philosopher Socrates asked a penetrating question: "Is a good thing good *because* God desires it? Or does God desire it *because* it is already good?" Most people would go with the latter view, which says that God desires kindness because it is already good; but this requires that we recognize a good and bad independent of God's will – and thus that we give up supernaturalism. The supernaturalist has to say, less plausibly, that kindness is good just because God desires it – and that cruelty would be good if God desired it.

Some are led to supernaturalism because they want to connect ethics and religion. But the two could connect closely without supernaturalism. Even if good and bad are independent of God's will, religion still gives us additional way to know moral truths, additional motives to be moral, and a world view that better supports morality.

This chart summaries the three views of Part I:

	"Good" means	Moral truths are	To form your moral beliefs, follow
Cultural relativism	"socially approved"	relative	your society
Subjectivism	"what I like"	relative	your feelings
Supernaturalism	"what God desires"	objective	God's will

Part I has six readings:

Cultural relativism	Ruth Benedict Harry Gensler and Mary Grace Tokmenko (a criticism)
Subjectivism	David Hume Thomas Nagel (a criticism)
Supernaturalism	C. S. Lewis Key Biblical passages

2. Further approaches to morality

Part II considers three views about the meaning of "good" that have appealed to philosophers of the last hundred years: intuitionism, emotivism, and prescriptivism.

Intuitionism claims that "good" is indefinable, that there are objective moral truths, and that the basic moral truths are self-evident to a mature mind. Let me explain these claims.

First, intuitionists claim that "good" is a simple, indefinable notion – not to be confused with notions like "socially approved" or "what I like" or "what God desires." Intuitionists had a procedure for attacking definitions of "good." Suppose that someone claimed that "good" means "socially approved." Intuitionists would ask, "Are socially approved things necessarily good?"; the answer seems to be "no," which would refute the definition. Other definitions of "good" can be criticized in a similar way. If you claim that "good" means "…" (some descriptive phrase), intuitionists would object that it is consistent to say that things that are … are sometimes not good – which refutes the definition.

A corollary is Hume's law, that we cannot deduce an "ought" from an "is": we cannot prove moral conclusions from non-moral premises alone. The only way we could deduce moral conclusions from purely factual premises, intuitionists argue, is if we could define moral terms like "good" in descriptive terms – which they claim to be impossible. According to Hume's law, we cannot give facts about society (or evolution, or God, or desires, or whatever) – and then from these alone logically deduce a moral conclusion; we could always consistently accept the facts and yet reject the moral conclusion. But then neither science nor religion can establish the basic principles of morality.

Second, intuitionists claim that there are moral truths that are objective, in the sense that they do not depend on human thinking or feeling. "Hatred is wrong" is an example. Hatred is wrong in itself; it would still be wrong even if everyone approved of it. It is an objective truth that hatred is wrong. This is what mature common sense believes – and so we should go with it, intuitionists argue, so long as it is not disproved.

Third, intuitionists hold that the basic moral principles are self-evident truths – known truths that require no further proof or justification. When we deliberate about moral issues, we appeal to moral principles that we cannot further justify; we accept or reject these principles depending on how they accord with our moral intuitions. The test of such principles is, not their initial plausibility, but whether a careful examination uncovers implications that clash with our intuitions. To arrive at the self-evident first principles of morality requires reflection and intellectual maturity.

The American Declaration of Independence argues from an intuitionist standpoint. It claims certain moral truths to be self-evident – for example that everyone has a right to life, liberty, and the pursuit of happiness. It sees morality as based on objective truths that are present inside of us, in our own minds and reason; any mature person should be able to grasp the basic moral truths.

Intuitionism, despite its popularity in the history of philosophy, has problems. It is much more plausible to claim self-evident principles in mathematics than in ethics. Mathematical principles claimed to be self-evident are precise and largely agreed on by the experts. Ethical principles claimed to be self-evident are vague and widely disputed. Intuitionists themselves disagree widely about what is self-evident.

Moral intuitions come largely from social conditioning, and can vary greatly between cultures; for example, infanticide (or slavery) is seen in some cultures as "self-evidently right" and in others as "self-evidently wrong." It is hard to imagine that such variable intuitions are a reliable guide to objective moral truths. And appealing to intuitions can lead to an early stalemate on moral issues – as when we argue with someone who thinks it self-evident that whites have a right to enslave blacks.

Emotivism, our next view, says that moral judgments express positive or negative feelings. "X is good" means "Hurrah for X!" – and "X is bad" means "Boo on X!" Since moral judgments are exclamations, they are not true or false; so there cannot be moral truths or moral knowledge.

Emotivists say that we can reason about moral issues if we assume a system of values. Suppose we assume that everyone has a right to life, liberty, and the pursuit of happiness; then we can conclude that racism is wrong. Or suppose we assume (with some of the Nazis) that that we should be honest, decent, loyal, and comradely to members of our own blood – but not care what happens to anyone else; then we can conclude that racism is right. So we can reason about morality if we assume a system of values. But we cannot reason about the basic moral principles themselves; in fact, there is no sense in which any system of basic values is objectively more correct than any other system.

Some emotivists base their view on logical positivism, which holds (roughly) that any genuine truth claim must be able to be tested by sense experience. Moral judgments, since they cannot be tested by sense experience, cannot be genuine truth claims but can only express feelings; thus logical positivism leads to emotivism. But logical positivism has largely been rejected by philosophers, since it is self-refuting; the view is not itself testable by sense experience and hence would not be a legitimate truth claim on its own grounds.

Others base emotivism on this principle, which is an important part of scientific method: "A view is better if it is simpler and explains more." These emotivists claim that their view is simpler and explains more. What could be simpler than the idea that evaluative judgments express positive or negative feelings? Emotivists do not have to bring in things that are difficult to defend – like God, self-evident moral truths, and non-empirical properties of goodness. And the emotional nature of "good" seems to explain various aspects of morality: why we cannot define "good" in purely descriptive terms, why we cannot prove moral conclusions from factual premises, and why people disagree so much about morality. Morality becomes more understandable once we see it as a matter of feelings and not of truths.

However, it is not clear that emotivism explains morality adequately; by rejecting moral knowledge and moral truths, it seems to water down what morality is. Another problem is that moral judgments, instead of being essentially emotional, go from "very emotional" to "not very emotional." And in complicated sentences (like "Hurrah for good people!") we often cannot plausibly replace "good" with an exclamation.

Another problem is that emotivism would seem to destroy the objectivity of scientific method. Consider this norm that is crucial to scientific reasoning and that emotivists appeal to: "A view is *better* if it is simpler and explains more." On emotivism, "better" translates into an exclamation; and so this norm would mean "Hurrah for a view that is simpler and explains more!" – and thus could not express a truth.

Emotivism claims that, in disputes about basic moral principles, we cannot appeal to reason but only to emotion. This could easily lead to social chaos and to propaganda wars in which each side, unable to resort to reason, simply tries to manipulate the feelings of the other side. It would be preferable if people could rationally deliberate about basic moral differences and perhaps resolve some of them.

Some emotivists add a stronger rationality component. While admitting that ethics is based on feelings, they insist that our feelings can be more or less rational to the extent that we are informed and impartial. This view works somewhat like prescriptivism.

Prescriptivism, our next view, sees moral judgments as a type of prescription, or imperative. Moral judgments, like the simple imperative "Close the door," do not state facts and are not true or false; instead, they express our will, or our desires. Ought judgments are *universalizable* prescriptions; "you ought to do this" means "Do this and let everyone do the same in similar cases." Moral beliefs express our desire that a kind of act be done in the present case and in all similar cases – including ones where we imagine ourselves in someone else's place.

Prescriptivism tries to show how moral beliefs can be both free and rational. Moral beliefs can be *free* because they express our desires and are not provable from facts. Moral beliefs can be *rational* because the logic of "ought" leads to a method of moral reasoning that engages our rational powers to their limits.

Moral beliefs are subject to two basic logical rules:

U   To be logically consistent, we must make similar evaluations about similar cases.

P   To be logically consistent, we must keep our moral beliefs in harmony with how we live and want others to live.

Rule U holds because moral judgments are universalizable: it is part of their meaning that they apply to similar cases. So I am inconsistent if I accept "I ought to steal Detra's bicycle" without also accepting "If the situation were reversed then Detra ought to steal my bicycle." Rule P holds because moral judgments are prescriptions (imperatives), and thus express our will, or our desires, about how we and others are to live. So I am inconsistent if I accept "If then situation were reversed then Detra ought to steal my bicycle" without also desiring that my bicycle be stolen in this situation.

A golden-rule consistency condition follows from these logical rules:

> This combination is logically inconsistent:
>
> • I believe that I *ought* to do something to another.
> • I do not desire that this be done to me in the same situation.

This consistency condition is a more precise version of the traditional golden rule ("Treat others as you want to be treated"). We violate it if we think we ought to do something to another (like steal their bicycle or enslave them), but do not desire that this would be done to us in the same situation.

To think rationally about ethics, we need to be informed, imaginative, and consistent; and the most important part of consistency is to follow the golden rule. To see how this applies to racism, think of the Nazis who believed this: "We ought to put Jews into concentration camps." To be rational in this moral belief, the Nazis would have to get their facts straight (especially the facts about racism and about the impact of their actions on the Jews) – imagine themselves in the place of their victims – and be consistent (which involves desiring that they would be treated the same way if they were in the same situation). Very few Nazis would come out as rational. So prescriptivism gives a way to argue against racism – a way that is much more powerful than just appealing to moral intuitions or to feelings.

Prescriptivism, while it has important insights about the golden rule and moral rationality, has been criticized as resting on a questionable foundation. It says that ought judgments are universalizable prescriptions (or imperatives), and not truth claims. This leads it to deny the possibility of moral knowledge and moral truths – which seems to conflict with how we approach ethics in our daily lives.

Prescriptivism's rejection of moral truths makes it easier for Nazis to escape the golden-rule argument. Prescriptivism's consistency conditions tell us what we have to do, if we choose to use "ought" and other moral terms consistently. But we might avoid using moral terms. If we do so, we do not violate any moral truths and do not violate golden-rule consistency. On prescriptivism, none of these is a moral truth:

- We ought to make moral judgments about our actions.
- We ought to be consistent.
- We ought to follow the golden rule.

Moral truths would make it harder to escape the golden-rule argument.

This chart summaries the three views of Part II:

	"Good"	Are there moral truths?	To form your moral beliefs, follow
Intuitionism	is indefinable but objective	yes	your moral intuitions
Emotivism	is emotional – like "Hurrah!"	no	your feelings
Prescriptivism	expresses how we want people (ourselves and others) to live	no	what you can consistently will, after you get the facts and use your imagination

Part II has six readings:

Intuitionism	G. E. Moore W. D. Ross
Emotivism	A. J. Ayer J. L. Mackie (who held the related error theory)
Prescriptivism	R. M. Hare Jean-Paul Sartre (who held a related existentialist ethics)

3. Ethical methodology

Part III considers four areas that are dealt with in Chapters 7–9 of the accompanying *Ethics* textbook:

- a practical method of forming moral beliefs that does not rely on a specific analysis of moral terms,
- the golden rule,
- racism, and
- moral education.

The method of forming moral beliefs emphasizes the golden rule and is applied to racism and moral education.

How should we select a method for picking our moral principles? One approach is to build on what we take moral terms to mean. So we follow a religious method if we take "good" to be about God's will; we get other methods if we take it to be about social conventions, personal feelings, or independent objective truths. The problem here is that people continue to disagree on how to understand moral terms; this would seem to lead to a permanent stalemate on how to reason about morality.

One way out of the difficulty is to defend a method that makes sense from various views about the meaning of moral terms. I propose roughly this method (which I call "the golden-rule consistency approach"):

> When you form your moral beliefs, try to be informed on the facts, imagine yourself in the place of the various parties involved, be consistent, and treat others only as you are willing to be treated yourself in the same situation.

This method emphasizes four elements: (1) information, (2) imagination, (3) consistency, and (4) the golden rule. For our ethical thinking to be fully rational, we need all four elements working together. We are "rational" (or "wise") in our ethical beliefs to the extent that we satisfy a variety of considerations. Only God (knowing everything, imagining vividly the inner life of each person, being consistent in every way, and so on) could satisfy them completely. We humans find practical rationality difficult, and we satisfy its requirements only to a lesser or greater degree.

Our method might be defended from various views about the nature of moral judgments – for example:

> Cultural relativism: I accept these as demands of my own society. Practically every society, to survive, has to make similar demands on its members. The golden rule, for example, is endorsed by practically every society on planet earth.

> Subjectivism and emotivism: I accept this method because it fits my feelings – which favor being informed, imaginative, and consistent, and following the golden rule. Most people I know have

similar feelings; when I meet someone with different feelings, I try to show them that they will be more satisfied with their lives if they live this way.

Supernaturalism: I accept these demands as God's will; my religion (and practically every religion of the world) teaches us to follow the golden rule and to strive to imitate the wisdom of God, who alone is perfectly informed, consistent, and loving.

Intuitionism: It is self-evidently true that we ought to follow the golden rule and to strive to be informed, imaginative, and consistent. By following these self-evident truths, our minds can be led to discover other moral truths.

Prescriptivists can hardly disagree with the method, since it comes from them – even though I freed the method from their assumption that ought judgments are prescriptions instead of truth claims.

Let me now explain these four elements further.

Factual understanding requires that we know the facts of the case: circumstances, alternatives, consequences, and so on. To the extent that we are misinformed or ignorant, our moral thinking is flawed. Of course, we can never know *all* the facts; and often we have no time to research a problem and must act quickly. But we can act out of greater or lesser knowledge. Other things being equal, a more informed judgment is a more rational one.

We also need to understand ourselves, and how our feelings and moral beliefs originated; this is important because we can to some extent neutralize our biases if we understand their origin. For example, some people are hostile toward a group because they were taught this when they were young. Their attitudes might change if they understood the source of their hostility and broadened their experience; if so, their attitudes are less rational, since they exist because of a lack of self-knowledge and experience.

Imagination (role reversal) is a vivid and accurate awareness of what it would be like to be in the place of those affected by our actions. This differs from just knowing facts. So in dealing with poor people, besides knowing facts about them, we also need to appreciate and envision what these facts mean to their lives; movies, literature, and personal experience can help us to visualize another's life. We also need to appreciate future consequences of our actions on ourselves; knowing that drugs would have harmful effects on us differs from being able to imagine these effects in a vivid and accurate way.

Consistency demands a coherence among our beliefs, between our ends and means, and between our moral judgments and how we live; it also, I argue, includes golden-rule consistency – that we not act toward another in a way that we are unwilling to be treated in the same situation. I will focus on these four consistency norms:[4]

> Basic consistency in beliefs: do not believe logically incompatible things; and do not believe something while rejecting what logically follows from it.
>
> Conscientiousness: keep your actions, resolutions, and desires in harmony with your moral beliefs.
>
> Impartiality: make similar evaluations about similar actions, regardless of the individuals involved.
>
> The golden rule: treat others only as you consent to being treated in the same situation.

We often appeal to what I call "basic consistency in beliefs" when we argue about ethics. You say that such and such is *wrong*, and I ask "Why?" You respond with an argument consisting in a factual premise, a moral premise, and a moral conclusion. Your factual premise could perhaps be challenged on grounds of factual accuracy. Your moral premise could perhaps be challenged on grounds of consistency; we look for cases where you would reject the implications of your own principle – perhaps cases where the principle applies to how we should treat you.

Here is a concrete example. When I was ten years old, I heard a racist argue something like this: "Blacks ought to be treated poorly, because they are inferior." How can we respond? Should we dispute the racist's factual premise and say "All races are genetically equal"? Or should we counter with our own moral principle and say "People of all races ought to be treated equally"? Either strategy will likely lead to a stalemate, where the racist has his premises and we have ours, and neither side can convince the other.

I suggest instead that we formulate the racist's argument clearly and then watch it explode in his face. First we need to clarify what the racist means by "inferior." Is "being inferior" a matter of IQ, education, wealth, physical strength, or what? Let us suppose that he defines "inferior" as "having an IQ of less than 80." Since the racist's conclusion is about how *all* blacks ought to be treated, his premises also have to use "all." So his argument goes:

> All blacks have an IQ of less than 80.
> All who have an IQ of less than 80
> ought to be treated poorly.
> ∴ All blacks ought to be treated poorly.

While this is valid, we can appeal to factual accuracy against the first premise and to consistency against the second premise. Regarding consistency, we can ask the racist whether he accepts what his second premise logically entails about whites:

> All who have an IQ of less than 80
> ought to be treated poorly.
> ∴ All *whites* who have an IQ of less
> than 80 ought to be treated poorly.

The racist will not accept this conclusion. But then he inconsistently believes a premise but refuses to believe what follows from it. To restore consistency, he must either give up his principle or else accept its implications about whites. It would be very difficult for the racist to reformulate his argument to avoid such objections; he needs some criterion that crisply divides the races (as IQ does not) and that he applies consistently to people of his own race.

Appealing to consistency is often useful in moral disputes. The appeal is powerful, since it does not presume material moral premises (which the other party may reject) but just points out problems in one's belief system.

Our next two species of consistency are conscientiousness and impartiality. Conscientiousness says "Keep your actions, resolutions, and desires in harmony with your moral beliefs." This forbids inconsistencies between my moral judgments and how I live or how I want others to live. Here's an example of a combination that violates conscientiousness:

- I believe that all short people ought to be beat up – just because they are short.
- I do not desire that if I were short then I be beat up.

Here your principle logically entails "If I were short then I ought to be beaten up." If you do not accept this or do not desire that it would be followed, then you are inconsistent and your moral thinking is flawed.

Impartiality says "Make similar evaluations about similar actions, regardless of the individuals involved." I violate this if I make conflicting evaluations about actions that I regard as exactly or relevantly similar – for example, if I make these two judgments:

- It would be all right for me to hurt this person.
- In the reversed situation, it would be wrong for this person to hurt me.

To test my impartiality, it can be useful to ask whether I would make the same evaluation about a similar case in which the parties are in different places – in which, for example, I am on the receiving end of the action.

The golden rule is the most important consistency norm. In its simplest formulation, the rule says "Treat others as you want to be treated." In Matthew 7:12, Jesus gave the rule as the summary of the Jewish Bible. The Rabbi Hillel had earlier said much the same thing. Even earlier, Confucius had used the rule to summarize his teachings. All the major religions and many nonreligious thinkers teach the rule as being of central importance; and it is practically universal among the different cultures of the world. All this suggests that the rule may be an important moral truth.

To avoid some of the common objections to the golden rule, it is important to formulate it carefully. I suggest this formulation:

Golden rule:	*GR forbids this combination*:
Treat others only as you consent to being treated in the same situation.	• I do something to another. • I am unwilling that this be done to me in the same situation.

This formulation has a don't-combine form (forbidding a combination) and has you imagine an exactly reversed situation. To apply GR, you imagine yourself in the exact place of the other person on the receiving end of the action. If you act in a given way toward another, and yet are unwilling that you be treated that way in the same circumstances, then you violate the rule.

The golden rule is best seen as a consistency principle. It does not replace regular moral norms. It is not an infallible guide on which actions are right or wrong. It does not give all the answers. It only prescribes consistency – that we not have our actions (toward another) be out of harmony with our desires (toward a reversed situation action). To apply the golden rule adequately, we need knowledge and imagination. We need to *know* what effect our actions have on the lives of others. And we need to be able to *imagine* ourselves, vividly and accurately, in the other person's place on the receiving end of the action. With knowledge, imagination, and GR, we can progress far in our moral thinking.

The golden rule follows from the requirements to be conscientious and impartial. Suppose that you want to steal Detra's bicycle. And suppose that you are *conscientious* (keep your actions and desires in harmony with your moral beliefs) and *impartial* (make similar evaluations about similar actions). Then you will not steal her bicycle unless you also are willing that your bicycle be stolen in the same situation. This chart shows the steps in the derivation:

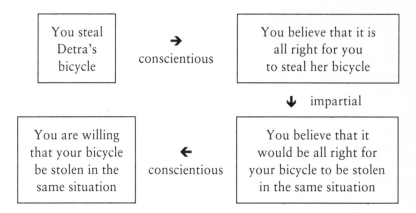

Here is a less graphical argument. If we are conscientious and impartial, then:

> We will not *act* to do something to another unless we *believe* that this act is all right.
> We will not *believe* that this act is all right unless we *believe* that it would be all right for this to be done to us in the same situation.
> We will not *believe* that it would be all right for this to be done to us in the same situation unless we are *willing* that this be done to us in the same situation.
> ∴ We will not *act* to do something to another unless we are *willing* that this be done to us in the same situation.

So if we are conscientious and impartial, then we will follow GR: we will not do something to another unless we are willing that it be done to us in the same situation.

So GR follows from the requirements to be conscientious and impartial. But why be conscientious and impartial? Why care about consistency at all?

As I mentioned before, different views could answer differently. Maybe we ought to be consistent because this is inherently right; our minds grasp the duty to be consistent as the first duty of a rational being. Or maybe we accept the consistency norms because they are commanded by God, are useful social conventions, or accord with how we want to live (perhaps because inconsistency brings painful "cognitive dissonance" and social sanctions). And perhaps demands to be conscientious and impartial are built into our moral language (so violating them involves a strict logical inconsistency), or perhaps not. Different views could accept the consistency norms for different reasons.

Now let us apply our method to racism. Imagine that you were brought up in a society that practiced Nazism or slavery or apartheid – and that the correctness of racism was so built into your moral intuitions that it seemed "self-evident" to you. Is there any way that you could use your intelligence to criticize racist norms? If so, how?

Let us consider parallel cases in other areas. Suppose that your society taught you that there was a highest prime number – or that the earth was flat. You could in principle use your intelligence to criticize these beliefs. There is a good argument going back to Euclid that there is no highest prime; and there are indirect signs that the earth is round – or you could build a space ship and go out and look at the earth. In practice, few people will have the independence, energy, and intelligence to pursue such ideas; but eventually someone will, and the word will spread. The morality case is similar.

To rationally criticize inherited racist norms requires the things we mentioned before: *factual accuracy* (understanding facts about race and how the victims suffer – and understanding how you came to have your present feelings and attitudes about race), *imagination* (role reversal – visualizing what it would be like for ourselves and our families to be treated in like manner), and *consistency* (especially the golden rule – which tells us to treat others only as we are willing to be treated ourselves in the same situation). Historically, people who criticized racist norms often appealed to the golden rule and to these other factors.

A speech by President Kennedy in 1963 illustrates how to apply GR to racism. Kennedy appealed to the golden rule in an anti-segregation speech during the first black enrollment at the University of Alabama. He asked whites to consider what it would be like to be treated as second class citizens because of skin color. He asked them to imagine themselves being black – and being told that they could not vote, or go to the best public schools, or eat at most public restaurants. He asked whether they would be content to being treated that way in such circumstances. He was sure that they would not – and yet this is how they treated others. He said the "heart of the question is ... whether we are going to treat our fellow Americans as we want to be treated."

How would our method apply to the moral education of children? Obviously, an important part of moral education is to teach adult values to children – by words, by example, by reward and punishment, and by praise and blame. But this is not enough, since the same approach could teach racist values to children. Nazi parents who teach their values to children (by words, by example, by reward and punishment, and by praise and blame) will likely produce racist children who later will regard the correctness of racism as self-evident.

I suggest that, besides teaching moral content, we also need to teach moral rationality; helping children to be more rational in their moral thinking is an important part of moral education. While moral rationality has many aspects, I would emphasize these "five commandments" of rational moral thinking:

- Information: Make informed decisions.
- Imagination: Put yourself in the other person's place.
- Conscientiousness: Live in harmony with your moral beliefs.
- Impartiality: Make similar evaluations about similar actions.
- Golden rule: Treat others as you want to be treated.

Adults can teach these by personal example; adults need to deal with a child in an informed way, imagine themselves in the child's place, follow principles consistently, and treat the child in accord with the golden rule. In addition, adults can promote the corresponding skills and attitudes in the child; adults can encourage the child to get the facts before making a decision, to put oneself in the place of the other person, to follow principles consistently, and to treat others in accord with the golden rule.

Part III has eight readings:

Justifying moral claims	William K. Frankena Jürgen Habermas Immanuel Kant
The golden rule	Joyce Hertzler Paul Ricoeur Friedrich Nietzsche (a criticism of "love thy neighbor")
Two applications	Martin Luther King (racial segregation) Lawrence Kohlberg (moral education)

4. Normative theory

Part IV is about normative theory – which defends basic norms about what is right or wrong, worthwhile, virtuous, or just. We will consider four areas:

- consequentialist (especially utilitarian) approaches to right and wrong,
- nonconsequentialist approaches to right and wrong,
- human rights and distributive justice, and
- virtue and vice (virtue ethics).

Consequentialist (or teleological) views hold we ought to do whatever maximizes good consequences. On such views, it does not in itself matter what kind of thing we do; what matters is that we maximize good results. Consequentialism comes in various flavors. These differ on whether to maximize good results for ourselves only (egoism) or for everyone affected by our action (utilitarianism) – and on whether to evaluate consequences solely in terms of pleasure and pain (hedonism) or in terms of a variety of goods (pluralism) or in terms of whatever people in fact desire (preference satisfaction).

Egoism is difficult to hold in a consistent way. Egoism says "Everyone ought to do whatever maximizes their own self-interest, regardless of how this affects others." To hold this consistently, we would have to want other people to live that way toward us. So we would have to desire that X harm us greatly (even paralyze us for life) if this would maximize X's self-interest. Assuming that we cannot desire this, then we cannot consistently accept egoism. So it would be difficult to accept egoism as a rational view about how we ought to live.

Classical (hedonistic) utilitarianism is a popular kind of consequentialism. This view says that we ought always to do whatever maximizes the balance of pleasure over pain for everyone affected by our action. This view could be defended by the golden rule, which leads us to be concerned about the happiness and misery of others. Or it could be based on God's will, self-evident truths, or our own personal feelings.

We can apply utilitarianism directly (by estimating the likely consequences of each option and then picking the option with the best consequences) or indirectly (by applying a "rule of thumb" about what kinds of action tend to have good or bad results). Many utilitarians reject exceptionless rules. They think any rule should be broken when this has better consequences; so they see moral rules only as loose "rules of thumb."

Critics of utilitarianism object that the view has bizarre implications which make it difficult to hold the view in a consistent way. For example, imagine a town where the lynch mob enjoys hangings so much that it maximizes pleasure to hang you for a crime that you did not commit. Would it then be right to hang you – as utilitarianism would imply? Utilitarians can respond to such objections by biting the bullet (accepting the implausible result), denying that such cases are possible, or modifying utilitarianism.

Pluralistic rule utilitarianism is a modified form of utilitarianism. It rejects hedonism (that only pleasure is intrinsically good). Instead, it accepts a pluralistic view of value (that many things are intrinsically good, including things like virtue, knowledge, pleasure, life, and freedom). This view also says that we ought to do what would be prescribed by the *rules* with the best consequences for people in society to try to follow. It says that we will live better if we follow strict rules in areas like killing or drugs. Without strict rules, we will too often talk ourselves into doing foolish things. Rule utilitarians claim that their approach avoids the bizarre implications and produces better consequences.

Critics object that rule utilitarianism, even if it would lead to the right judgments, would do so for the wrong reasons. Rule utilitarianism opposes killing the innocent on the grounds that socially useful rules would forbid such actions. But what if socially useful rules permitted such actions? Then would killing the innocent be right? Rule utilitarians would have to say yes. Nonconsequentialists prefer to hold that killing the innocent is *wrong in itself*.

Nonconsequentialist views hold that some kinds of action (such as breaking promises or killing the innocent) are wrong in themselves, and not just wrong because they have bad consequences. Such things may be exceptionlessly wrong, or may just have some independent moral weight against them.

Ross's prima facie view is a popular nonconsequentialist approach. Ross focuses on our duty to keep promises. This duty does not hold in an exceptionless way, since it can be overridden by other duties. And yet it is not just a rule of thumb that we can break whenever it has good consequences to do so. Instead, the duty to keep promises is an independent duty. It binds us, other things being equal, but may sometimes have to yield to other duties.

Ross's basic moral principles say that we ought, other things being equal, to do or not to do certain kinds of things. There are duties of fidelity, reparation, gratitude, justice, beneficence, self-improvement, and nonmaleficence. When these duties conflict, we have to weigh one duty against another and see which is stronger in the situation.

Nonmaleficence is stronger than beneficence; in general, it is not right to harm one person to help another or to promote social usefulness. Many of our duties are relational; we have a specific duty to a person because of how that person is related to us (as, for example, someone to whom we have made a promise).

There are other forms of nonconsequentialism besides that of Ross. John Finnis's nonconsequentialism defends exceptionless norms and is based on the "natural law" approach of St Thomas Aquinas (an important medieval philosopher). Onora O'Neill's nonconsequentialism[5] is based on the "respect for persons as ends as themselves" approach of Immanuel Kant (an important philosopher of the eighteenth century).

Our next area is human rights and distributive justice. Here we find a classic controversy between two Harvard professors, John Rawls and Robert Nozick.

Rawls suggests that the basic rules of justice for a society are the rules that we would agree to under certain hypothetical conditions ("the original position"). Imagine that we are free and rational, but do not know our own place in society (whether rich or poor, black or white, male or female). The knowledge limitation is meant to insure impartiality; if we do not know our race, for example, then we cannot manipulate the rules to favor our race. The principles of justice are those we would agree to under these conditions. Rawls argues we would agree to the "equal liberty principle" (which insures things like freedom of religion and freedom of speech) and the "difference principle" (which promotes the equal distribution of wealth, except for inequalities that serve as incentives to benefit everyone and are open to everyone on an equal basis). So a Rawlsian society would be fairly egalitarian, but with some inequalities; doctors would get more money, for example, if we needed to pay doctors more in order to have enough qualified doctors.

Nozick, on the other hand, says that whatever you earn fairly is yours – and society has no right to take it away from you in order to redistribute wealth or help the poor. So a Rawlsian society would be unjust, since it could not be brought about without violating our rights of ownership.

Our last area of normative theory deals with virtue, which is seen as the central topic of normative ethics by Aristotle (an important philosopher of ancient Greece) and by his recent "ethics of virtue" followers.

A virtue is a good habit – a disposition to act and feel in certain ways, a disposition that corresponds with and internalizes a correct principle of action. A good person is a virtuous person. The ancient Greeks emphasized four cardinal (basic) virtues:

- *wisdom:* rationally understanding how we ought to live
- *courage:* facing danger and fear with proper confidence
- *temperance:* having reason control our emotions
- *justice:* dealing fairly with others.

To these natural virtues, Christianity added three theological virtues – and claimed that the greatest of these is love:

- *faith:* believing in God and in what he has revealed
- *hope:* emotionally trusting in God and in his promises
- *love:* unselfishly striving to serve God, and to do good and not harm to his creatures.

We have indirectly talked about three of these virtues – wisdom (forming our moral beliefs wisely and rationally), justice (impartiality and distributive justice), and love (the golden rule). But we talked about them in a different way. The virtue approach focuses on them as character traits or practices rather than as principles of action.

Part IV has eleven readings:

	John Stuart Mill
Utilitarianism	J. J. C. Smart
	Bernard Williams (a criticism)
	Richard B. Brandt (rule-utilitarianism)
Nonconsquentialism	W. D. Ross
	John Finnis
Distributive justice	John Rawls
	Robert Nozick
Virtue ethics	Aristotle
	Alasdair MacIntyre
	Michael Slote

5. Applied ethics

While this book emphasizes ethical theory, we thought it good to include a few readings about specific topics in Part V. Our readings deal with abortion, animal rights, famine relief, and environmental ethics.

Abortion, our first topic, is one of the most important and controversial moral issues of our time. How we approach abortion will be greatly influenced by our wider views about ethics.

Many who are pro-abortion argue on consequentialist grounds (either egoist or utilitarian). They claim that abortions often have the best consequences. An abortion can avoid the disgrace to an unwed mother, the disruption of schooling or a career, and financial burdens. The child-to-be has less chance for happiness when these problems or probable birth defects exist. And abortion provides a second chance to prevent a birth when contraceptives fail.

Opponents say that we can have equally good results without abortion; we need better social support toward unwed mothers and poor families, better adoption practices, wiser use of contraceptives, artificial wombs, and so on. Children born with handicaps can lead happy and productive lives, if we show them love; such handicaps can bring families together and give them a sense of purpose. And abortions can harm women psychologically and promote callous attitudes toward human life.

Others object that we mostly rely on guesses when we apply utilitarianism – since we can't really know whether having or not having the baby would produce better consequences. Still others object that utilitarianism is a very questionable view, since it justifies killing any innocent human (whether a fetus or infant – or the sick, handicapped, or elderly) when this produces even a tiny increase in good consequences.

Rule utilitarianism would apply a bit differently, since it asks what *rule* about killing (including abortion) would have the best consequences for society to adopt and try to follow. Some claim that it would have the best long-range consequences if society adopted a strict rule against killing (including against abortion); but others dispute this claim.

Nonconsequentialists typically appeal to some general principle about killing – and then draw conclusions about abortion from this. Here are a few of the nonconsequentialist principles that have been proposed:

- Killing innocent human life from the moment of conception is seriously wrong – and is never to be permitted.
- Killing innocent human life from the moment of conception is seriously wrong – and is to be permitted only in cases of rape or to save the life of the mother.
- The wrongness of killing a fetus depends on its stage of development; a very young fetus can be killed for almost any reason, while it is more seriously wrong to kill a developed fetus.
- It is permissible to kill a fetus at any stage of development for almost any reason; but it is seriously wrong to kill an infant.
- It is not in itself wrong to kill a fetus or infant; the right to life begins when the child develops self-awareness and strong desires about its future.[6]
- One who has voluntarily assumed no special obligation toward another person has no obligation to do any thing requiring great personal cost to preserve the life of the other.[7]

These principles are typically defended by appealing to moral intuitions – despite the fact that people's moral intuitions on this issue vary greatly.

Thus we come to a more basic question: "How should we pick out our moral principles?" How we answer this depends on our metaethical perspective. Cultural relativists, for example, will go by what their society says; so if most people favor a moderately anti-abortion stance (that abortion is wrong in most cases – but perhaps not very early abortions or in cases of rape), then they will go along with this. Subjectivists and emotivists, on the other hand, will go with their feelings; for them, you just think about the issue and then follow what you feel.

Supernaturalists will appeal to religion and to God's will. The Bible does not directly mention abortion and can be interpreted either way on this issue; but the first Christian source after the Bible, the Didache, is explicitly against both abortion and infanticide. Catholic teaching has strongly condemned abortion, but many other churches are more divided on this issue.

Intuitionists will appeal to their moral intuitions on this issue. But we have seen that the moral intuitions of different people seem to favor radically different norms about abortion.

In the last chapter of my *Ethics* book, I argue that the golden-rule consistency view and prescriptivism favor the belief that abortion is wrong in at least most cases. While the details here are complicated, I basically argue that most people will not be consistent if they hold that abortion is normally permissible – since they will not consent to the idea of themselves having been aborted in normal circumstances. But this argument, even if it succeeds at what it tries to do, will still leave some details fuzzy.

Our last three topics are animal rights, famine relief, and environmental ethics. These raise questions like the following:

- Should our moral concern extend to animals too? Is it a kind of racism to regard interests of animals as less important than similar interests of humans? Does an animal have the same right to life as a small child, if both have the same mental level?
- Is there a morally relevant difference between directly killing someone and just allowing someone to die? If not, then are we murderers if we do not contribute heavily to famine relief?
- Should our moral concern extend to non-sentient parts of nature (like plants and mountains)? If so, then should we be concerned about these for their own sake, or just for the sake of humans and other sentient creatures?

Part V has five readings:

Abortion	Judith Jarvis Thomson (a defense)
	Sydney Callahan (a criticism)
Other issues	Peter Singer (animal rights)
	Onora O'Neill (famine relief)
	J. Baird Callicott (environmental ethics)

Notes

1   Racism, the example I use here, is representative of a larger group of issues about how to treat others who are different from us (perhaps in terms of religion, or sex, or sexual orientation, or ethnic background, or whatever). Most of the same questions and principles apply to these other issues.

2   Part I corresponds to Chapters 1–3 of *Ethics*, Part II to Chapters 4–6, Part

III to Chapters 7–9, Part IV to Chapters 10–11, and Part V to Chapter 12. Sometimes the divisions between the parts of this present book are not strict; often a given reading could plausibly be put in various places.

3   See the reading from Lawrence Kohlberg in Part III of the book.

4   Let me make three general remarks about these consistency norms. (1) There are other consistency norms, including ends–means consistency ("Keep your means in harmony with your ends") and the formula of universal law ("Act only as you're willing for anyone to act in the same situation – regardless of imagined variations of time or person"). (2) I do not insist that all violations of these norms commit a strict "logical inconsistency"; it suffices if there is some reason (from whatever perspective we accept) to avoid violating these norms. (3) These norms are subject to implicit restrictions; for example, the "basic consistency in beliefs" norm is subject to the proviso that we are or should be aware of the logical relations involved. For further discussions of these consistency norms, see Chapters 7–9 of my *Ethics: A Contemporary Introduction* (London: Routledge, 1998), or my more technical *Formal Ethics* (London: Routledge, 1996), or the logical formalization in Chapter 11 of my *Introduction to Logic* (London: Routledge, 2002).

5   See the reading from Onora O'Neill in Part V of the book.

6   The reading from Peter Singer assumes this principle, which he sees as having a utilitarian justification. Singer holds that infanticide is in itself no greater an evil than abortion – and that both are often justified.

7   The reading from Judith Jarvis Thomson assumes this principle. She applies it to a woman who is pregnant from rape or from contraceptive failure.

JAMES C. SWINDAL and EARL W. SPURGIN
The History of Ethics

Ethics has a history that both is illuminating in its own right and can help us to understand contemporary approaches. Accordingly, we decided to include a short sketch of the history of ethics. Our sketch divides very roughly into three main periods of thought:

Ancient	Socrates and Plato Aristotle Epicureans and Stoics
Medieval	St Augustine St Thomas Aquinas Duns Scotus and William of Ockham
Modern	Thomas Hobbes David Hume Immanuel Kant John Stuart Mill

Philosophers use the term "modern" to refer to the enlightenment period, which is roughly the seventeenth and eighteenth centuries; here we stretched that into the nineteenth century.[1] In contrast, "contemporary" covers roughly the last hundred years – the twentieth and twenty-first centuries.

Socrates and Plato

In the West, philosophical inquiry into ethics – the study of what we ought to do – began with the ancient Greeks. Greek ethicists inquired into how a person could use reason to achieve "the good life." But they disagreed about both what the good life is and the nature of the practical reason that can reach it.

Life in Greece and Asia Minor in the fifth century BC was a time of relative peace. This enabled trade and commerce to increase among diverse peoples in the region. Such interaction brought increased awareness of social differences. This led philosophers both to question their own way of doing things and to notice positive features in social practices other than their own. In his *Histories*, Herodotus (485–430 BC) defended the view that what is good is relative to a specific culture. This respect for custom inspired the Sophist Protagoras (480–410 BC) to claim, "man is the measure of all things." The Sophists stressed the difference between subjective values and objective facts, holding that decisions should be based not on stable natures (*phusis*) but on conventional rules (*nomos*). The Athenian Socrates (470–399 BC) was in fact considered a relativist by some, though his student Plato saw him in a different light.

According to Plato (427–348 BC), Socrates believed in the existence of objective ethical standards while noting how difficult it was for us to specify them. In the early dialogue the *Euthyphro*, Socrates inquires into the meaning of piety with Euthyphro, a young man who was going to report his father for having killed a slave. Socrates asks Euthyphro whether something is good because the gods love it, or whether the gods love it because it is good. The dialogue reaches the conclusion that human reasoning about what is good has a certain independence from the vagaries of the gods' determination of the rightness of our actions and mores. Then in the *Gorgias*, Socrates indicates that pleasure and pain fail to furnish an objective standard for determining right from wrong since they never exist apart from one another, while good and evil do.

In the *Republic*, a dialogue Plato wrote later, Socrates considers the nature of a just life. He first attacks common conceptions of justice. Some Sophists claimed that anyone, left to one's own devices, would be unjust. Moreover, the unjust tend to be happier than the just. Socrates replies with an analogy: just as in good society, each person has a specific function that is ordered harmoniously with the functions of all, so just persons have a proper balance among the rational, spirited, and appetitive aspects of their souls. A person with such a well ordered soul is happy. Then the dialogue gives a systematic underpinning of this view of justice. Plato held that all things in the visible realm, *qua* intelligible, participate in separate forms that are invisible, unchanging, and perfect. Thus there is a form even for moral predicates, such as justice and happiness. The highest of all forms, and one very difficult to grasp, is the form of the Good. To know the Good requires an ascetic and intellectually rigorous way of life. People who grasp the Good will always do good actions. Bad actions are performed solely out of ignorance of the Good. Bad actions thus are not blameworthy in the strict sense, though in the *Laws* Plato does allow societies to punish persons for doing them.

The upshot for Plato is that practical action, guided by the form of the Good, takes precedence over theoretical thinking about things. Ethical prescriptions are not general deductions from self-evident principles but are particular judgments issuing from one's ordering of three parts of one's soul.

Aristotle

Aristotle (384–322 BC), a student of Plato, modified a number of his mentor's idealistic and quasi-religious ethical views. Aristotle was not only a philosopher, but also an encyclopedist and natural scientist. He served as the tutor to Alexander the Great for three years. Aristotle's *Nicomachean Ethics* was the first systematic treatment of ethics in the West. It is the basis for all subsequent development of *aretaic*, or virtue, ethics. Whereas act-oriented ethics is concerned primarily with what we *do*, a virtue ethics is interested ultimately in who we *are*.

Aristotle rejected Plato's metaphysical claim that separated forms exist apart from things in which they participate. Instead he argued that forms combine with matter to form composite things. So there is not one separate form of the Good, but many "goods," each of which is a quality of a particular thing or function. Thus there is also a basic good for humans.

Observing human activity, Aristotle found that wise persons seek an end that is self-sufficient, final, and attainable over one's life. This end is happiness, achievable only by a life of virtue. He pointed out how neither pleasure, wealth, nor honor can be an ultimate end. To be virtuous one must perform the actions that habitually bring virtue. Though this sounds circular, it indicates that one needs to be trained or educated to be virtuous – virtue does not come naturally. Virtue is of two types: moral, which deals in part with the irrational part of the soul, and intellectual, which involves only the rational part of the soul. The bulk of Aristotle's argument deals with how we go about developing a moral character on the basis of which we can habitually choose the actions that lead to our happiness.

Aristotle describes in some detail several examples of moral virtues, such as temperance, courage, and justice. But he also provides a formal description of a moral virtue. Each emerges from the habitual choosing of a mean, relative to us, between extremes in certain types of situations. This is often called his doctrine of the "golden mean." Courageous persons, for example, always choose the action that is intermediate for them between cowardliness and foolhardiness. The determination of the mean does refer to pleasure and pain, since we tend to do actions that bring pleasure and avoid actions that bring pain. The virtuous person is brought up to find pleasure in virtuous actions and pain in vices. Despite the importance of the golden mean, Aristotle insists that some actions, such as adultery, theft, and murder, do not admit of a mean and are always wrong.

Aristotle also insists on the importance of friendship in the life of a virtuous person. Though a virtuous person is to a large degree self sufficient, he needs to share his life with those with whom he shares a good deal in common. But friendships can be based neither on pleasure nor utility alone. The highest form of virtue is found not in enjoying friends, but in contemplating truth.

Epicureans and Stoics

After Alexander the Great's death in 323 BC, Greece fell into a significant decline. Numerous generals battled for parts of the empire. Philosophers became interested in the practicalities of dealing with political and social instability. Many urged that one ought to refrain from participation in the world, turning instead to the solace of philosophical thought and conversation.

Epicurus (341–270 BC) taught that happiness involves a serenity that emerges from simple physical and mental pleasures. Thus he founded his Garden, a place of ideal hedonism apart from the woes of the world. Much of his thought was inspired by the Cyrenaic doctrine of Aristippus (435–356 BC), who claimed that pleasure was the supreme good. Both held that humans necessarily seek what they perceive to be pleasurable: a doctrine often referred to as psychological hedonism. These pleasures are, however, to be pursued with prudence. But unlike Aristippus, Epicurus argued that since life affords so few intense pleasures, one should choose an enduring pleasure over an intense one. After all, intense pleasures take a great deal of pain to procure – and pain often follows them. So Epicurus endorsed *ataraxia*, the avoidance of trouble in the mind and pain in the body. One ought to seek moderate and natural pleasures: gentle motions of the body. The maintenance of such pleasure requires, in turn, only the obligation to restrain from harming one another. Epicurus also sought to dispel the mental pain incumbent upon fear of divine retribution. He argued that since God is truly blessed, he does not subject us to irrational punishments in this life.

Epicurus undergirded his ethical claims with a metaphysical atomism. While Democritus (460–360 BC) had developed a deterministic view of the movement of atoms, Epicurus held atoms in motion swerve at times, bestowing some novelty to nature. Thus humans have a modicum of freedom and control over their lives. But at death, the atoms that constituted a person swerve into entirely new configurations, annihilating the individual entirely.

In marked contrast to these atomistic views, the Stoics, beginning with Zeno (336–264 BC), depicted the cosmos as an organic unity in which the form and purpose of each part is determined by God. Anyone can grasp that God is a rational principle immanent in the whole. Each individual is a "fragment" of God. A grasp of this rational principle enables individuals to live in harmony with the cosmos as "citizens of the universe." But like followers of Epicurus, many Stoics nonetheless remained detached from the struggles and sufferings of the world.

Epictetus (50–130 AD), a late Stoic, argued that one ought to be as self-sufficient as possible. One's will must be disciplined to conform to reason. If successful in this endeavor, a person never wills anything unattainable. We cannot control physical events that affect us, but we can control our *attitudes* towards them. One simply accepts what one cannot attain. Like Epicurus, Epictetus argued that death is nothing to be feared. We live our lives by stable rules, not momentary pleasures. But we also realize that each of us is a part of the whole and can as such recognize a duty to all others. Given his emphasis on the importance of both moral rules and the autonomy of the will, Epictetus was a distant precursor of Kant.

St Augustine

The arrival of Christianity in the West changed ethical thinking markedly. It introduced as normative for its adherents Jesus's command to love God. Thus Christian ethicists, starting with St Paul, outlined the way to achieve not an earthly "good life," as the Greeks did, but heavenly beatitude with God. Christianity's doctrine of personal salvation also reinforced the importance of free will and individual responsibility for actions. But Christian ethicists nonetheless retained a number of earlier ideas, particularly neo-Platonic views about the emanation of various orders of creation from a divine principle and Stoic ideas about reason.

St Augustine of Hippo (354–430) was the first major Christian ethical philosopher. He distinguished between the two cities in which one can dwell: the City of God or the City of Man. Good men and good angels dwell in the former; evil men and bad angels in the latter. In the City of Man, men use temporal goods to find earthly peace, while in the City of God they use them to enjoy eternal peace. Thus the Greek virtues are nothing more than prideful vices unless they are used in service of the enduring virtues of faith, hope, and love. Augustine illustrates the virtue of love by the "double love" command found in the gospels. Jesus commanded each of us to love God with our whole heart, soul, and mind, and our neighbor as ourselves. Since this command presupposes that one first love oneself, Augustine assumes that each has a natural propensity to love oneself, both mind and body. To love neighbors requires that we not only refrain from injuring them, but also promote their good when we can. In the end, God will judge us on the basis of our response to this double love command, though he will also do so with mercy.

Despite his focus on the centrality of the love of God, Augustine also took account of factors within an agent that influence whether its action is good or bad. In his *Confessions*, he makes it clear that the quality of one's intention and resolve has ethical import. The deficiencies of the will stem not from its objects, but from the will itself. For example, he insists that "avarice is not a fault inherent in gold, but in the man who inordinately loves gold." Many subsequent ethical thinkers took up this internalism.

St Thomas Aquinas

St Thomas Aquinas (1224–74), a medieval philosopher, moved Christian philosophy beyond its preoccupation with neo-Platonic thought. Educated as a Dominican monk in Cologne and Paris, he came under the influence of the reemergence of Aristotelian thought – primarily in Jewish and Islamic philosophy – that was taking place in Europe.

Like Augustine, Aquinas built his ethical thinking upon the foundation of Christian revelation, particularly its claim that each individual person is created in God's image and likeness. But under the influence of Aristotle's conviction that philosophy ought to begin with careful observation of the physical world, Aquinas drew a sharp distinction between the disciplines of philosophy and theology. He held that philosophical analysis of the world is independent from, though never a rival to, revelation.

Aquinas borrowed heavily from Aristotelian ethics. He adopted four of its core principles: that all actions are directed towards determinate ends and ultimately a final end; that happiness is the final end inasmuch as it is desirable for its own sake, self-sufficient, and attainable; that choice involves selecting means for this final end; and that an agent needs a moral character developed through the habits of choice to realize this happiness. He also agreed with Aristotle that the will is always directed to what appears good to it, even if this good is not truly good. But like Augustine, Aquinas argued that the ultimate happiness is not realizable in this life, as Aristotle assumed, but found only in beatitude with God. Moreover, Aristotle's account of virtues was incomplete since it lacked reference to the Christian virtues of faith, hope, and love.

Thomas underpinned his normative ethics with an account of the natural law. This is knowable by natural reason apart from revelation. The natural law is the part of God's governance of creation applicable to us. Our practical reason grasps as its first principle that good is to be done and promoted and evil is to be avoided. But since good has the characteristic of an end, those things to which we have a natural inclination can be apprehended by reason as goods. Thomas lists three sets of these inclinations: to survive, to reproduce and educate offspring, and to know the truth about God and to live in society. These principles are timeless and invariant. However, Aquinas realized that the application of these principles to specific situations is often very difficult.

Aquinas analyzed actions on the basis not only of their conformity to the natural law but also of their specific features. The *object* of an action defines the action (e.g. talking to a person), the *circumstances* consider the context in which the action takes place (in a lecture hall during a lecture), and the *end* is the act's purpose (to ask the person a question about the lecture). But like Aristotle, he claims that any suboptimal end is in turn a means to the ultimate end. All three aspects of action must be proper for the act to be considered good. But the end has a particular priority: it defines the nature of the person doing the act. Aquinas thus is a modified internalist about ethics since he bases the goodness of an action not on its consequences but upon the rightness of the reason determining it. But unlike Augustine, he believes that human freedom stems not from the lack of causal influences, but from the internal deliberation that causes our actions. Like Aristotle, Aquinas held that one's moral character is integral to this causal production of actions.

Duns Scotus and William of Ockham

The fourteenth century was significantly more socially and political tumultuous than Aquinas's thirteenth. Franciscan philosophers, such as John Duns Scotus (1265–1308) and William of Ockham (1285–1349) gained prominence over their Dominican rivals. The Franciscans, for the most part, rejected Aquinas's intellectualism and argued that the will is independent both of causal influences and of strict determination by the intellect's knowledge of what is good. Scotus had continued to defend much of Aquinas's natural theology: the capacity of reason to discover God in nature without the aid of revelation. But Ockham argued for a much more limited role for reason in such matters. Both Scotus and Ockham held that matters of moral judgment were settled ultimately not by reason, but by faith. Their views reinforced a stronger sense of individual autonomy both in moral and political matters. They foreshadowed the humanistic ethics of the modern age to follow.

Ockham in particular was affected by the political instability of the time. He was accused of heresy and summoned to the Papal residence at Avignon. But after a few years there he fled, acquiring protection from the emperor Ludwig in Germany. Ockham wrote treatises defending the emperor, arguing that political power comes not through God but through the secular authorities themselves. His political philosophy limits the Pope's authority and power relative to the natural rights and liberties of persons.

Ockham's ethical thought is based on the principle that the world is radically contingent. In it exist only individuals. Universals, if they existed, would limit God's omnipotence to order the world as He wills. As Hume will later hold, Ockham claims that we discover the natural order of these individuals not by a priori deductive reasoning, but by experience. Ockham thus complements the radical contingency of the world with the conviction that God's goodness is purely spontaneous and not necessitated. God freely bestows on us the gifts of existence and freedom of choice. Moreover, we can be confident, owing to God's love, that He will maintain the contingent natural sequences of events so we can discern order and survive.

Though he dedicated no specific treatise to ethics, Ockham did suggest a number of ethical guidelines. Since morality is knowledge of what is to be done under particular circumstances, it is act-centered. But morality cannot be a positive science since it depends on human and divine precepts that can be known neither *per se* nor empirically. It is focused not on outward behaviors, but on intentions. Human dignity, moral goodness, and responsibility stem less from the power of intellect than from the will. Only the act of will bestows upon humans a means of escape from the causality of nature. All other acts, whether bodily or mental, can be called virtuous only extrinsically. But Ockham does claim that the dictates of right reason (*recta ratio*) are proper guides for behavior. For a Christian, these prudential dictates cannot be independent of the content of the faith. Right reason leads a person to fulfill moral obligations solely for the love of God. This entails that the ultimate foundation of ethics is God's will. Ockham thus develops a kind of divine command ethics, though he never denies the autonomy of the dictates of right reason as such.

Thomas Hobbes

Ethics in the modern age began with a movement away from the other-worldly focus that dominated medieval ethics. Although the principal figures of early modern ethics generally did not openly reject the existence of God, they rejected the medieval idea that we should look to God for a guide to our actions. Likewise, they rejected the medieval idea that eternal salvation should be the motivation for ethical behavior. Instead of looking to God's design of the world in order to understand the purpose of ethics, we should employ what was then the burgeoning scientific method. The purpose of ethics is not to instruct humans how best to love God, but, rather, to show humans how best to live together in this world.

The modern move away from the medieval other-worldly focus began with the English philosopher Thomas Hobbes (1588–1679). He lived through some difficult times for England that undoubtedly influenced his ethical views. The Spanish Armada invaded the year he was born, and the English Civil War occurred during his lifetime. He was also greatly influenced by the scientific method and Euclid's geometrical proofs. He sought to employ those methods in ethics in his major work *Leviathan*. The result was a theory of ethics that was based on a methodical argument that begins with assumptions about the nature of humans and the world, and follows those assumptions to their logical conclusion.

The state of nature is the backdrop for Hobbes's argument. This is a presocietal condition where humans live with no common rules or power over them. The state of nature contains neither arts, nor agriculture, nor any of things we associate with cooperative life. Hobbes uses the idea of the state of nature as a tool to uncover the natural traits of humans and the natural condition of the world.

Examination of the state of nature reveals that humans are relatively equal. In terms of physical strength and mental powers, we are close enough in abilities that no one can rely on being able to overpower or outwit another person should the need arise. And, in the state of nature, the need will arise. Without agriculture and the other benefits of cooperative life, resources such as food and shelter will be in short supply. Inevitably, one will need to take what one needs from others. Because of the equality among humans, each person is in jeopardy of attack from others over scarce resources.

This jeopardy in which natural humans find themselves matters greatly to them. Hobbes is an egoist. He thinks humans are by nature motivated solely by self-interest. Whenever a person acts voluntary, the act is motivated by some good for that person. Self-preservation is one important good to humans. When this concern for self-preservation is combined with Hobbes's assumption that humans are rational, he concludes that persons in the state of nature recognize the insecurity of their lives and seek to change it. Self-interested beings seek to live long and well, but life in the state of nature precludes that.

A secure life for all can be accomplished, however, only through the social contract. The social contract is a covenant where each person agrees to follow the will of a sovereign with absolute power. Such a leader is necessary to place a check on the self-interested motivations of humans. Without such a leader, each person will continue to act in a purely self-interested manner. The result is a continuation of the insecure state of nature. The absolute sovereign becomes a common power over humans that provides just the threat they need to motivate them to live by certain rules that allow cooperation. The threat of the sovereign's sword appeals to their self-interest. Since persons wish to live long and well, it is in their interests to avoid the sovereign's punishment by following the rules. By doing so, they can cooperate in ways that produce greater resources and a more secure life for all. In short, only with an absolute sovereign, can humans live together peacefully in this world.

Hobbes's theory changes the course of ethics. Ethics is, simply, whatever the sovereign says it is. The sovereign receives his right to rule and make laws through the consent of the governed people. When they give their consent, they agree to do whatever the sovereign wishes. Until that time, there is no moral authority over humans. Once the social contract is made, however, the sovereign has sole moral authority. Obeying him is just and disobeying him is unjust. This is a marked departure from the medievals. Hobbes does not look to God for the source of ethics. Instead, he looks to an earthly authority, the sovereign, whose laws enable us to cooperate in ways that help us to meet our needs.

Hobbes also changes our motivation to act ethically. For the medievals, the motivation is to earn salvation in the afterlife. For Hobbes, however, the motivation is to avoid the punishment of the sovereign. The sovereign's authority includes the power to punish in any fashion he sees fit. Ethics consists of following the sovereign's will, and the motivation to do so is to avoid the sovereign's sword.

David Hume

Although modern ethics, in general, builds on Hobbes's worldly focus, much of it departs from Hobbes's bleak picture of human nature. We can see evidence of this in David Hume (1711–76). Hume was born in Edinburgh, Scotland. He took up philosophy in his late teens, and by his late twenties had published his major work, *A Treatise of Human Nature*. Like Hobbes, Hume was greatly influenced by the scientific method. He, too, sought to infuse ethics with a worldly focus that does not look to God as the guide for our actions nor to salvation for the motivation to act ethically. He saw humans, however, as naturally more sympathetic to others than did Hobbes. This led him away from Hobbes's conclusion that an absolute sovereign is necessary in order for us to live together peacefully.

For Hume, the source of ethical judgments is our sentiments. When one deems an act virtuous, it is because one has a feeling of approval from the view or contemplation of the act. When one deems an act vicious, it is because one has a feeling of disapproval from the view or contemplation of the act. Reason plays a secondary role in our ethical judgments. We use reason to collect data about acts such as their possible consequences, their relations to other acts, and their possible conflicts with the various goals that we have. Reason, however, does not deem acts virtuous or vicious. Sentiments perform this primary role. Reason merely collects the data on which the sentiments operate. Reason is relegated to this secondary role because it lacks the capacity to move us to act. Only sentiments have this capacity. Since ethical judgments have the capacity to move us to act, they must be based on sentiments instead of reason.

Although sentiments are the source of moral judgments, sympathy drives the sentiments. We have a natural sympathy for other humans. The closer another person is, the stronger one's sympathy for that person. One feels a stronger sympathy for one's family than for a stranger in another country, yet one still has a fellow-feeling even for humans one has never met. As I write this, I hear news accounts of a terrible earthquake in India that killed thousands of people. Although I know no one in India, my sympathy is engaged by the news and I feel saddened by the loss of fellow humans. My feelings would be even stronger had I friends or family in India, but, nevertheless, my feelings are affected by the natural sympathy I have for humans that I do not even know.

Our natural sympathy for others explains our feelings of approval for acts that Hume calls the natural virtues. When one views or contemplates a natural virtue, such as an act of charity, beneficence, or generosity, one's sympathy for others directly drives the feeling of approval. The act's positive effect on another person moves one's sympathy which gives rise to the feeling of approval. Because one has sympathy for others, even those one does not know, and the good from such acts is produced by each occurrence, no other consideration is necessary in order for the feeling of approval to arise.

The same is not true, however, for acts that Hume calls the artificial virtues. The view or contemplation of an artificial virtue, such as an act of justice, keeping a promise, or obeying the government, does not move one's sympathy directly. Not every occurrence of such acts produces good. In fact, a particular instance of, say, justice, may well engage one's sympathy in a way that produces a feeling of disapproval for the act. Suppose the accused in a criminal trial is acquitted because of a technicality. One's sympathy for the victim or the victim's family may drive one to have a feeling of disapproval for the acquittal. One develops feelings of approval for the artificial virtues only after one contemplates the entire scheme with which they are associated. Once one considers the usefulness of the system of justice and its accompanying rules, one develops a feeling of approval for acts such as the acquittal. After one sees such acts as part of a beneficial scheme, one's sympathy is moved and one develops feelings of approval for particular acts of justice.

Through his use of our natural sympathy, Hume is able to produce an ethical theory that carries on Hobbes's move away from the other-worldly focus of medieval ethics. He looks to something in this world, our sentiments, to guide our acts. Although he certainly thinks we need governments and systems of justice so that we can cooperate and live together successfully, he sees no need for an absolute sovereign to check our self-interest. Our sympathy does that for us. It produces in us feelings of approval and disapprobation that deem acts virtuous or vicious. These virtues and vices guide our acts.

This, however, raises the issue of our motivation to act ethically. By carrying on Hobbes's worldly focus, Hume loses salvation as a motivation for ethical behavior. By dropping Hobbes's absolute sovereign, he loses the threat of the sovereign's sword as the motivation for ethical behavior. It appears he has nothing to offer as a motivation, but he can offer our sentiments. Among the sentiments is, at least, for most of us, a desire to feel good about ourselves when we examine our characters and reflect on the kind of people we are. One can feel good about who one is only if one can examine one's life and determine that one has the kind of character that leads one to ethical behavior. The desire for that good feeling motivates one to perform the virtues and avoid the vices. If one lacks that desire, however, then Hume can offer one no motivation to act ethically. Fortunately, he believes, few people lack that desire.

Immanuel Kant

Hume instigated one of the great debates in modern ethics. He clearly staked out the position that ethical judgments are based on feelings. This position was rejected by the German philosopher Immanuel Kant (1724–1804). Kant lived his entire life in Königsberg, East Prussia. His parents had a strong religious influence on him, and his studies were greatly influenced by mathematics and science. He was a man who lived an extremely ordered life, and this order is evident in his writings. His early works were scientific, but in 1785 he published the *Groundwork of the Metaphysics of Morals*. In this work and others, Kant produced an ethical theory that attacked Hume directly. His theory bases ethical judgments on reason alone. Feelings are not the source of ethical judgments, and, in fact, they are an obstacle to our understanding of right and wrong.

For Kant, ethical principles are discoverable a priori, without experience of the world. When one seeks to discover the ethical status of an act, one consults reason. Reason deems the act ethical or unethical, while feelings and experience merely cloud the issue. Kant's theory is a nonconsequentialist theory in that an act is right or wrong in and of itself, independent of its consequences. It is normative in that it provides a principle that is meant to tell one how one should act. An act either accords with reason or it does not, no matter how desirable or undesirable its consequences. If it accords with reason, one should perform it. If it does not accord with reason, one should avoid it. This is a departure from Hume who sees the consequences of an act as an important part of the data that reason collects so that sentiments can pass judgment on the act.

Kant's categorical imperative functions as the test of reason that an act must pass in order for it to be ethical. An imperative is a command of reason.

Hypothetical imperatives command one to act in certain ways on the condition that one seeks certain goals, such as: if you wish to be a good student, then study hard. A hypothetical imperative is how reason directs one to achieve one's particular ends. The categorical imperative, on the other hand, directs one to act in certain ways regardless of what goals one seeks or what one's ends may be. Kant provides three different formulations of the categorical imperative, but the two most famous are the universalizability and end-in-itself formulations.

The universalizability formulation tells one to act only according to that maxim that one can will to become a universal law. A maxim is a principle of volition, or guide, to action. A universal law is a law that applies to all rational agents. If one is contemplating acting in a particular manner, one must determine one's maxim and let reason judge whether one can will the maxim to be a law for all rational agents to follow. One's preferences are not at issue. Whether one would like for the maxim to be a universal law for all rational agents to follow is beside the point. What matters is whether one's reason can will it. This is a matter of logic.

Kant illustrates the point with the example of a lying promise. A man in need of money wishes to borrow it on the strength of his promise to return it even though he knows he will not be able to do so. He must determine his maxim and put it to the test. His maxim is as follows: when in need of money I will borrow it by making a lying promise. Reason cannot will such a maxim to be a universal law for all rational agents as it encounters a contradiction. If such a law were universal, then promises would come to mean nothing to those to whom they are made. Persons could not borrow on the strength of promises. This is a bad consequence, but it is not this consequence that causes the act to fail the test. One can will bad consequences. One cannot will, however, a law that destroys the system of promises and at the same will that there be such a system for one to use. This is the contradiction that prevents this maxim from passing the universalizability test.

The lying promise fails to pass the test provided by the end-in-itself formulation as well. According to this formulation, one should always act so that one treats humanity as an end-in-itself, never simply as a means. A means is a tool or instrument. We are never to treat other persons or ourselves as mere tools to achieve our goals. To treat a person as an end-in-itself is to recognize the person as a rational agent with his or her own goals and ends. In short, it means to treat that person with respect and dignity. Clearly, the lying promise treats another person as a means only. The promisor does not treat the promisee with dignity, but, rather, as a mere tool to achieve the promisor's goal of obtaining the needed money.

The categorical imperative results in a very strict set of ethical rules. For example, Kant derives exceptionless prohibitions against lying and suicide. These acts are wrong regardless of the circumstances and the consequences they produce. Exceptionless rules such as these give rise to staunch criticism of Kant's ethics. Many suggest that it is a rule-bound theory that places a higher value on rules than persons. They claim that the idea that lying is always wrong regardless of its consequences is surely misguided. If I can protect another person from great harm only by lying, lying is what I should do.

John Stuart Mill

This criticism sets the stage for another of the great debates in modern ethics. This is the debate between the two most noted schools of normative ethical theory: nonconsequentialist and consequentialist. Unlike nonconsequentialists, consequentialists judge the rightness and wrongness of acts by their consequences. The English utilitarians Jeremy Bentham (1748–1832) and John Stuart Mill (1806–73) provided the most famous consequentialist theories, and Mill's utilitarianism has had the most lasting influence.

Mill's childhood included a very formal education that was supervised by his father, a friend and follower of Bentham. The younger Mill began his studies of philosophy by age twelve. This was after he had studied Latin by age eight and Greek by age three. Throughout his education, he was able to spend time with Bentham's disciples. The result was his acceptance of Bentham's utilitarianism with almost religious fervor. By the time he was twenty, however, he had broken from his worship of Bentham's ideas and began to develop his own utilitarianism known as the greatest happiness principle. He was also a political reformer who sought greater equality among the sexes and races. This was an attitude that found its way into his utilitarianism.

According to Mill's utilitarianism, one should act so as to produce the greatest balance of happiness over unhappiness for everyone affected by the action. When one must decide how to act, one must determine which of the various possible courses of action will produce the greatest balance of happiness for society. In practical terms, this means one must determine which course of action will produce the most happiness for all those affected. One's own happiness is merely one of the happiness levels that must be considered. It counts no more and no less than the happiness level of any other person affected. In fact, no person's happiness counts more or less than another's regardless of one's race, sex, or religion. In this way, Mill's theory advocates the kind of equality that he sought in the political realm.

Mill's theory provides a striking contrast to Kant's. Consider a lie to protect another from considerable harm. Kant sees such an act as violating an exceptionless rule. Mill, however, says that such an act is justified by the happiness that it produces. One must determine that the lie is the possible course of action that will produce the greatest balance of happiness, but Mill does not rule out the act by virtue of it being a lie.

Several criticisms are often made against utilitarianism, and Mill sought to overcome many of them. Two are of particular interest here. First, many suggest that utilitarianism promotes the more base side of human nature. Utilitarians generally hold that one's happiness is merely the difference between one's pleasures and one's pains. By maximizing happiness, we promote those pleasures that are beneath us. We are taught to promote pleasures regardless of the kind of pleasures they are.

Mill neutralized this criticism by arguing that happiness is made up of higher and lower pleasures. The lower pleasures are those that humans and other animals alike can experience, such as those from food, drink, and sex. The higher pleasures are those that only humans can experience because they require intellect to attain them. Only humans can experience the pleasure that accompanies reading a good novel or solving a difficult scientific problem. Since the higher pleasures are greater than the lower, a happiness that is made up predominantly of higher pleasures is likely to be greater than one that is made up predominantly of lower pleasures. The result is that Mill's utilitarianism tends to promote those pleasures that are worthy of us. It should be noted, however, that many think this has the effect of turning Mill's utilitarianism into an elitist theory that promotes the happiness of the upper class. They, after all, are the ones who have the leisure to pursue most of the higher pleasures.

Second, many argue that utilitarianism requires one to perform a calculation that one generally does not have time to perform before acting. In most cases, it is impossible for one to determine in advance all who might be affected by one's possible courses of actions, how they will be affected, and to what degree they will be affected before one must act. It is simply too demanding a calculation.

In his response to this criticism, Mill illuminates the sharp difference between his theory and Kant's. Whereas Kant is suspicious of experience in ethics, Mill embraces it. He argues that such a demanding calculation need not be made every time one acts because it has already been made. Experience has taught us what types of acts tend to promote happiness and what types of acts tend to promote unhappiness. One has access to secondary principles that are based on the entire history of human experience. If one contemplates committing willful murder, one need not determine who would be affected by the act, how, and to what degree. The secondary principle do not commit willful murder tells one not to do it, and the principle is justified by the greatest happiness principle itself.

Mill's utilitarianism has had lasting influence for two primary reasons. First, his distinction between higher and lower pleasures removed a troubling stigma that was attached to utilitarian theories. Second, his use of secondary principles set the stage for what has become the dominant form of utilitarianism in contemporary ethics. That form, rule utilitarianism, is the subject of some of the selections in this anthology.

The works of Hobbes, Hume, Kant, and Mill are indicative of the important moves that have been made in modern ethics. They are not the only modern philosophers who made important contributions to ethics. Indeed, there are many more. The works of these philosophers, however, represent significant departures from medieval ethics as well as some of the major ethical debates in the modern era. An understanding of these works is essential for understanding contemporary approaches to ethics.

For further study

Aristotle's *Nicomachean Ethics* and Plato's dialogues (including *Euthyphro, Gorgias, Republic*, and *Laws*) are available in many translations. See also *Epicurus: The Extent Remains* (edited by C. Bailey, Oxford: Clarendon, 1926) and *The Works of Epictetus* (edited by T. Higginson, Boston: Little Brown, 1866).

St Augustine's *Confessions* and *City of God* are available in various translations; see also his *On Christian Teaching* (translated by R. Green, Oxford: Oxford University Press, 1997). St Thomas Aquinas's writings are available in many versions, including *Aquinas: Selected Works* (edited by R. McInerney, New York: Penguin, 1998). See also Duns Scotus's *Philosophical Writings* (translated by A Wolter, Indianapolis: Hackett, 1987) and *Collected Articles of Ockham* (edited by P. Boehner, St Bonaventure, NY: The Franciscan Institute, 1958).

Modern ethical treatises include Thomas Hobbes's *Leviathan*, David Hume's *Treatise of Human Nature* and *Enquiry Concerning the Principles of Morals*, Immanuel Kant's *Groundwork of the Metaphysic of Morals* (sometimes called *Fundamental Principles of the Metaphysics of Morals*), and John Stuart Mill's *Utilitarianism*. These are available in various translations and editions.

Many articles on the history of ethics and individual figures are available in the *Encyclopedia of Philosophy* (edited by P. Edwards, New York: Macmillan, 1967) and the *Routledge Encyclopedia of Philosophy* (edited by E. Craig, New York: Routledge, 1998). The many anthologies on the history of ethics include *Great Traditions in Ethics* (edited by Theodore Denise, Sheldon Peterfreund, and Nicholas White, Belmont, CA: Wadsworth, 1996). This present anthology has short readings on Aristotle, Hume, Kant, and Mill. Many of these sources point to further literature on the history of ethics and individual figures.

Note

1   We also stretched "medieval" back to include Augustine (who lived a few centuries before the start of the Middle Ages).

PART I

INITIAL APPROACHES TO MORALITY: CULTURAL RELATIVISM, SUBJECTIVISM, AND SUPERNATURALISM

RUTH BENEDICT
Defending Cultural Relativism

Ruth Benedict, an influential American anthropologist who lived from 1887 to 1948, specialized in the study of native American cultures.

Benedict claimed that what is considered "normal" varies greatly between societies. For example, trances and homosexuality, while considered "abnormal" in many cultures, are tolerated and have important social functions in some other cultures. What a culture considers "normal" is encouraged to continue; in time, it becomes a cultural "good."

Benedict claims that ethics is relative to culture and that "morally good" is synonymous with "socially approved." As you read the selection, ask yourself how plausible you find this view. How would you think about racism or other ethical issues if you followed it? Does Benedict herself completely endorse this relativism?

Abnormality in a culture

Social anthropology has become a study of the varieties and common elements of cultural environment and the consequences of these in human behavior. In the higher cultures the standardization of custom and belief has given a false sense of the inevitability of the particular forms that gained currency, and we need to turn to a wider survey to check the conclusions we hastily base upon this near-universality of familiar customs. Modern civilization, from this point of view, becomes not a necessary pinnacle of human achievement but one entry in a long series of possible adjustments.

These adjustments, whether in mannerisms like ways of showing anger, or joy, or grief, or in human drives like sex, prove to be far more variable than experience in any one culture would suggest. In certain fields, such as religion or marriage, these wide limits of variability are well known and can be fairly described. In others it is not yet possible to give a generalized account.

One problem relates to the normal-abnormal categories. How far are such categories culturally determined, or how far can we with assurance regard them as absolute?

One of the most striking facts is the ease with which our abnormals function in other cultures. It does not matter what kind of "abnormality" we choose for illustration – those which indicate extreme instability, or those like sadism or delusions of grandeur or of persecution – there are well-described cultures in which these abnormals function at ease and with honor, and apparently without danger or difficulty to the society.

The Kwakiutl people

An extreme example is that of the North Pacific Coast of North America. The civilization of the Kwakiutl, at the time when it was first recorded in the last decades of the nineteenth century, was one of the most vigorous in North America. It was built up on an ample economic supply of goods, the fish which furnished their food staple being practically inexhaustible and obtainable with comparatively small labor, and the wood which furnished the material for their houses, their furnishings, and their arts being always procurable. They lived in coastal villages that compared favorably in size with those of any other American Indians and they kept up communication by means of sea-going canoes.

It was one of the most vigorous and zestful of the aboriginal cultures of North America, with complex crafts and ceremonials, and elaborate and striking arts. It certainly had none of the earmarks of a sick civilization. The tribes of the Northwest Coast had wealth in our terms. That is, they had not only a surplus of economic goods, but they made a game of the manipulation of wealth.

The details of this manipulation of wealth are in many ways a parody on our own economic arrangements, but it is with the motivations that were recognized in this contest that we are concerned. The drives were those which in our own culture we should call megalomaniac. There was an uncensored self-glorification and ridicule of the opponent that it is hard to equal in other cultures.

All of existence was seen in terms of insult. Not only derogatory acts performed by a neighbor or an enemy, but all untoward events, like a ducking when one's canoe overturned, were insults. All threatened one's ego security, and the first thought was how to get even, how to wipe out the insult. Until he had resolved upon a course of action by which to save his face after any misfortune, an Indian of the Northwest Coast retired with his face to the wall and neither ate nor spoke. He rose from it to follow out some course which according to the traditional rules should reinstate him in his own eyes and those of the community: to distribute property enough to wipe out the stain, or to go head-hunting in order that somebody else should be made to mourn. His activities in neither case were specific responses to the bereavement he had just passed through, but were elaborately directed toward getting even. If he had not the money to distribute and did not succeed in killing someone to humiliate another, he might take his own life. He had staked everything, in his view of life, upon a certain picture of the self, and, when the bubble of his self-esteem was pricked, he had no interest, no occupation to fall back on, and the collapse of his inflated ego left him prostrate.

Behavior honored upon the Northwest Coast is one which is recognized as abnormal in our civilization, and yet it is sufficiently close to the attitudes of our own culture to be intelligible to us. The megalomaniac paranoid trend is a definite danger in our society. It is encouraged by some of our major preoccupations, and it confronts us with a choice of two possible attitudes. One is to brand it as abnormal and reprehensible, and is the attitude we have chosen in our civilization. The other is to make it an essential attribute of ideal man, and this is the solution in the culture of the Northwest Coast.

Normality is defined by culture

Normality is culturally defined. An adult shaped to the drives and standards of these cultures, if he were transported into our civilization, would fall into our categories of abnormality. In his own culture, he is the pillar of society, the end result of socially inculcated mores.

No one civilization can utilize in its mores the whole potential range of human behavior. Just as there are great numbers of possible phonetic articulations, and the possibility of language depends on a selection and standardization of a few of these, so the possibility of organized behavior of every sort, from the fashions of local dress and houses to a people's ethics and religion, depends upon a similar selection among the possible behavior traits. In the field of economic obligations or sex taboos this selection is as nonrational and subconscious a process as it is in the field of phonetics. It is a process which goes on in the group for long periods of time and is historically conditioned by accidents of isolation or of contact of peoples.

Most organizations of personality that seem to us abnormal have been used by civilizations in the foundations of their institutional life. Conversely the most valued traits of our normal individuals have been looked on in differently organized cultures as aberrant. Normality, in short, within a very wide range, is culturally defined.

Normality and the good

It is a point that has been made more often in relation to ethics. We do not any longer make the mistake of deriving the morality of our own locality and decade directly from the inevitable constitution of human nature. We do not elevate it to the dignity of a first principle. We recognize that morality differs in every society, and is a convenient term for socially approved habits. Mankind has always preferred to say, "It is a morally good," rather than "It is habitual," and the fact of this preference is matter enough for a critical science of ethics. But historically the two phrases are synonymous.

The concept of the normal is a variant of the concept of the good. It is that which society has approved. A normal action is one which falls well within the limits of expected behavior for a particular society.

On the Northwest Coast the person who finds it difficult to read life in terms of an insult contest will be the person upon whom fall all the difficulties of the culturally unprovided for. The person who does not find it easy to humiliate a neighbor, who is genial and loving, may find some unstandardized way of achieving satisfactions, but not in the major patterned responses that his culture requires of him.

The vast majority of the individuals in any group are shaped to the fashion of that culture. In other words, most individuals are plastic to the molding force of the society into which they are born. In a society that values trance, as in India, they will have supernormal experience. In a society that institutionalizes homosexuality, they will be homosexual. In a society that sets the gathering of possessions as the chief human objective, they will amass property. The deviants, whatever the type of behavior the culture has institutionalized, will remain few in number. The majority of mankind quite readily take any shape that is presented to them.

A hint of a non-relativist perspective

Western civilization allows and culturally honors gratifications of the ego which according to any absolute category would be regarded as abnormal. The portrayal of unbridled and arrogant egoists as family men, as officers of the law, and in business has been a favorite topic of novelists, and they are familiar in every community. Such individuals are probably mentally warped to a greater degree than many inmates of our institutions.

Our picture of our own civilization is no longer in terms of a changeless and divinely derived set of categorical imperatives. In this matter of mental ailments, we must face the fact that even our normality is man-made. Just as we have been handicapped in dealing with ethical problems so long as we held to an absolute definition of morality, so too in dealing with the problems of abnormality we are handicapped so long as we identify our local normalities with the universal sanities. No society has yet achieved self-conscious and critical analysis of its own normalities and attempted rationally to deal with its own social process. But the fact that it is unachieved is not therefore proof of its impossibility. It is a faint indication of how momentous it could be in human society.

Understanding abnormal human behavior in any absolute sense independent of cultural factors is still far in the future. The study of the neuroses and psychoses of our civilization give much information about the stresses of Western civilization, but no final picture of inevitable human behavior. Any conclusions about such behavior must await the collection by trained observers of psychiatric data from other cultures. Since no adequate work of the kind has been done at the present time, it is impossible to say what core of definition of abnormality may be found valid from the comparative material. It is as it is in ethics: all our local conventions of moral behavior and of immoral are without absolute validity, and yet it is quite possible that a modicum of what is considered right and what wrong could be disentangled that is shared by the whole human race.

Did Benedict follow her own theory?

After defining "good" as "socially approved," what will Benedict do when she sees that racial discrimination is "socially approved"? Will she conclude that it is "good" – and come to favor it? Surprisingly, in this passage written ten years later, she saw racial discrimination as both socially *approved* and as *bad* (like a sickness).

As Americans of the 1940's we have important resources which we can use to reduce race prejudice. We shall be more successful the more realistically we use them and the less we hope for miracles. However much we hesitate to acknowledge it, race prejudice is deeply entrenched in our routine life and probably, measured by any objective standards, only South Africa goes further in segregation, discrimination, and humiliation. We do not seem, in the eyes of other nations, to be good exemplars of democratic equality. Our race prejudice is the great enemy within our gates. Our whole country is very sick.

Apparently against her own views, Benedict claimed that things that are socially approved, like racial discrimination, can still be *bad* (in some non-relative sense). In this next passage, she draws on her expertise as an anthropologist to argue against racist attitudes.

As an anthropologist, I know the studies on the superiority and inferiority of racial groups. No scientific study gives any basis for thinking that all the healthy people, the intelligent people, the imaginative people, are segregated in one race or born in certain countries and not in others. If you could choose the top third of the human race for their physical stamina, their brains and their decent human qualities, all races of the world would be represented in this top group.

We are always more complicated than we need to be when we explain race prejudice. We justify race prejudice by referring over and over to the poverty, illiteracy, and shiftlessness of the people we segregate – the bad effects of making anybody a second-class citizen. Why not try the experiment of offering every opportunity freely to all Americans, with no ifs and buts? We know from experience that people from every racial group in America and from every country of origin respond to education, become healthy when they have good food and good medical care, and can learn to perform the tasks our civilization offers.

When we succumb to race prejudice we don't see the "man from outside" as a person in his own right, with eyes, ears, hands like ours. We classify him like a piece of merchandise by outward signs of color or face or gestures or language. We don't judge him on his personal merits. The cure for race prejudice is as simple as that: to treat people on their merits, without reference to any label of race or religion or country of origin. There would he one effect: race prejudice would die of malnutrition.

America needs the help of all her citizens to ensure human dignity to all Americans.

Study questions

1   What motivates Benedict to study, in particular, cultures that are not "higher" cultures?
2   Which accepted practices of the Kwakiutl would be considered abnormal in most Western cultures?
3   What parallels does Benedict draw between social practices and language?
4   What problem does she raise regarding the "objectivity" of any observer of culture?
5   Does Benedict see the fact of cultural diversity as itself establishing that "good" means "socially approved"?
6   Explain the paragraph that mentions the possibility of universal values. Some think that Benedict here violates her own view. Do you agree?
7   When Benedict saw that racial discrimination was "socially approved," did she conclude that it was therefore good?
8   On what grounds does Benedict criticize claims asserting the superiority or inferiority of any race?

For further study

The main selection has excerpts, which are sometimes simplified in their wording, from Ruth Benedict's "Anthropology and the abnormal" in the *Journal of General Psychology* 10 (1934): 59–82. This essay is also in *An Anthropologist at Work: Writings of Ruth Benedict*, edited by Margaret Mead (Boston: Houghton Mifflin, 1959); the selections about racism are from pages 367–8 and 359–60. See also her study of Japanese culture, entitled *The Chrysanthemum and the Sword* (New York: World Publishing, 1967). For recent monographs on her work, see Hilary Lapsley, *Margaret Mead and Ruth Benedict: The Kinship of Women* (Amherst: University of Massachusetts Press, 1999); Judith Modell, *Ruth Benedict: Patterns of a Life* (Philadelphia: University of Pennsylvania Press, 1983); and Margaret Caffrey, *Ruth Benedict: Stranger in this Land* (Austin: University of Texas Press, 1989). For a recent defense of ethical relativism, see Richard Rorty, "Postmodernist bourgeois liberalism," in his *Objectivity, Relativism, and Truth* (Cambridge: Cambridge University Press, 1991), pages 197–202. Harry Gensler's *Ethics: A Contemporary Introduction* (London and New York: Routledge, 1998) discusses cultural relativism in Chapter 1.

Related readings in this anthology include Hertzler and Kohlberg (social scientists who defend trans-cultural norms); Gensler and Tokmenko, Lewis, and Nagel (who attack cultural relativism); Ayer and Mackie (who attack the objectivity of ethics); and Hare, King, and Singer (who criticize racial discrimination).

HARRY J. GENSLER and
MARY GRACE TOKMENKO
Against Cultural Relativism

Harry J. Gensler is an editor of this book and Mary Grace Tokmenko was
one of his students. Together they wrote this fictional piece on cultural
relativism. The core of this view is the claim that "good" means what is
"socially approved" in a given culture. The article tries to show that this
view has unacceptable consequences.

As you read the selection, ask yourself if you find cultural relativism initially plausible. How strong do you find the objections to this view?

A defense of cultural relativism

Hi, my name is Vera. I'm a student at Camford University, near my home in
Liverpool. I recently got back from a term abroad in South Africa. My
younger sister Relativa was especially happy to see me and asked if I'd like to
proof-read an essay she was writing for school. I agreed and retreated to a
back room to read her paper.

My sister's essay defended cultural relativism (CR), which says that moral
judgments merely describe social conventions. She expressed CR's central
claim in a definition:

"Good" means what is "socially approved" in a given culture.

If I say "Racism isn't *good*," I'm saying it isn't *socially approved* in my
culture. Each society has its own values. Things are good or bad, not objectively, but only relative to the values of a given society.

I read Relativa's essay a couple of times, trying to get clear on what she
was claiming and why. She rested her case on (a) the diversity of values
between cultures and (b) the impossibility of resolving moral disputes
between cultures.

Regarding diversity, Relativa recounted that she had been brought up to
believe that morality is about objective facts. Just as snow is white, so also

infanticide is wrong. But she gave this up when she learned how cultures disagree about morality. I highlighted these words in her paper:

> Our values come from our upbringing. Mom and Dad teach us that it's wrong to kill infants, and society later reinforces this teaching. These values become part of us. So we see "Infanticide is wrong" as an objective fact. But later we learn about other cultures. We discover that the norms we were taught are the norms of our own society; other societies have different ones. Just as societies create different styles of food and clothing, so too they create different moral codes. Morality is a cultural construct. In some societies, like ancient Rome, killing infants was perfectly acceptable.

From this diversity of values, Relativa concluded that values are relative to culture:

> Right and wrong are relative. Think of it this way: a thing cannot be "below" absolutely; it's always below *something else*. The same story goes for values; something isn't "wrong" absolutely, but only "wrong *in*" this or that society. Infanticide might be wrong in one society but right in another. So when *I* call infanticide "wrong," this just means that *my* society disapproves of it.

So a value judgment always has an implicit reference to a given society. Now some dispute this and claim there's an objective truth about the morality of infanticide. Relativa rejected this, since she thought there was no neutral standpoint for resolving moral disputes between cultures:

> The myth of objectivity says that things can be good or bad "absolutely" – not relative to this or that culture. But how can we know what is good or bad absolutely? How can we argue about infanticide or other things without just presupposing the standards of our own society? People who speak of good or bad absolutely are absolutizing the norms of their own society. They take the norms they were taught to be objective facts.

Relativa then talked about tolerance:

> As I've come to accept cultural relativism, I've become more tolerant of other cultures. I've given up the attitude that "we're right and they're wrong." I've come to realize that the other side isn't "wrong" in its values; it's just "different." We have to see others

from their point of view; if we criticize them, we're just imposing the standards of our own society. We cultural relativists are more tolerant.

She ended by saying that those who believe in the "myth of objectivity" need to study anthropology or perhaps "live for a time in another culture." That last point struck home, since I had just spent several months immersed in another culture; and yet I did not believe in cultural relativism.

I was impressed with my sister's essay. Little Relativa was starting to struggle with important issues. I had similarly found cultural relativism attractive a few years earlier; but I came to see problems with the view when I focused on it more clearly.

Problems with cultural relativism

When Relativa asked how I liked her essay, I smiled and said: "You're addressing important issues; but let me ask you a few questions. First, do you ever disagree with your society about values?" Relativa answered, "Not much; like everyone else, I'm a child of my culture." I pushed her further, "But even children can rebel. Don't we all at times disagree with group norms? If everyone else approved of getting drunk and driving off a cliff, would you have to agree?" Relativa paused a few moments while the idea sank in; then she responded:

> Okay, I see your point. If "good" means "socially approved," then I can't disagree with my society about values. If I saw that something was *socially approved*, I'd have to say it was *good*. I couldn't think for myself and disagree. I'd have to be a conformist about values – even if I saw that my society's values were based on ignorance.

I asked, "Don't you think it's important to think for yourself about values?" She said, "Yes, of course; but I see that cultural relativism prevents this."

I then told her about South Africa, which until recently had legally enforced race segregation, an "apartheid" policy that mistreated blacks. A cultural relativist living there years ago would have to see apartheid as good, since it was socially approved. But even then a minority disagreed. At this point, Relativa broke in:

> I see the problem here. With CR, "good" by definition is what the majority approves; so minority views (like those opposing apartheid) are always wrong. But then how can we change the values of

society – if we can't disagree with the majority? Sometimes social values *need* to change, as in South Africa. But with CR we can't express disagreement with accepted values without contradicting ourselves. So CR would stifle social change.

As I nodded in agreement, I reflected how intolerant CR is toward minority views.

Relativa's face turned to puzzlement as yet another problem came to her mind. She asked me in a halting way:

But how on earth could people who had been brought up to believe one thing (like the acceptability of apartheid) *come to think* something else – something that went against the teaching of their society? What could possibly bring them to do this?

I told her that there may be moral ideas common to all cultures that would lead people to criticize apartheid – ideas like the golden rule, "Treat others as you want to be treated." Perhaps people, after imagining themselves in the place of their victims, saw that they were treating others as they were themselves unwilling to be treated in the same circumstances. I asked Relativa if the golden rule was widely held throughout the world. She replied:

Yes, I learned in anthropology that most cultures accept the golden rule. Now that I think about it, I guess I've over-emphasized how cultures differ. While there are disagreements over details, most cultures are in broad agreement on most aspects of morality. This is natural, since cultures couldn't survive unless they had *some* rules (and somewhat similar ones) about things like killing, stealing, and lying.

I added that, even if societies disagreed widely about morality, that wouldn't show that there was no truth of the matter. Cultures disagree widely about anthropology or religion or even physics. Yet there still may be correct and incorrect ideas on these subjects. So, despite the disagreements, there still may be some truth of the matter about whether it's right to treat people badly because of their race.

Attractions of cultural relativism

I asked Relativa why she and others find CR so attractive. She responded:

I guess I liked cultural relativism because (1) it promotes tolerance, (2) it gives clear guidelines (you just follow what your society says), and (3) it seems to be the view of sophisticated social
scientists.

I suggested that we go through these ideas one by one.

First, I asked Relativa whether CR *could* promote intolerance and ridicule
toward others (whether in our own culture or in another). She replied:

Yes, if such intolerance were socially approved. If society favored
imprisoning people or burning them at the stake for their beliefs,
then these forms of intolerance would have to be good. Now that
I see this, it troubles me.

I added, "If we value tolerance, then maybe we need a better basis for it than
CR."

Next I turned to the "clear guidelines" idea. I asked Relativa what group
she considered to be "her society." Since she was puzzled about how to
respond, I told her that I belong to various groups with different values. At
Camford, for example, I'm part of the dressage team; I enjoy the horseback
competition, but the group is very elitist and constantly looks down on
people who are poor or of other races. But I'm also part of the Service Club,
which respects and tries to help poor people of any race. If I defined my
personal values by what each of those groups approved of, I'd be in conflict.
Relativa broke in:

Okay, I see the problem. According to CR, when I say that something is "good" I mean that it's "socially approved in my group."
But which group is "my group"? I'm part of many groups with
conflicting values. Suppose that my family and my religious group
disapprove of racism, while my friends and my neighbors approve.
What would CR tell me to believe?

"That's the point," I said. "CR would give us clear guidelines only if we
belonged to just one society; but we don't – instead, we belong to various
overlapping societies."

Since Relativa saw CR as "the view of sophisticated social scientists," I
told her that many important social scientists oppose CR. The famous
psychologist Lawrence Kohlberg, for example, claimed that people of all
cultures go through the same stages of moral thinking. CR represents a
relatively low stage in which we simply conform to society. At more advanced stages, we reject CR; we become critical of accepted norms and think
for ourselves about moral issues. Kohlberg's view suggests that there's more

to moral thinking than just absorbing the values of our culture; there's also a critical level where we start to think for ourselves and perhaps disagree with what society taught us.

Learning from other cultures

We were both enjoying the conversation; at long last, the two of us were discussing something serious in a constructive way. Yet little sister was becoming tired from my questioning. So, to put the discussion more on my shoulders, Relativa asked me to talk about my experiences in South Africa and how these might shed light on cultural relativism. I, in turn, was eager to share my experiences with my sister.

So I talked about my experiences. I recounted how I passed the Study Abroad office at Camford one day and spied a poster about a college in Cape Town. For the rest of the day, all I could think about was how great it would be to get away for a term and immerse myself in another culture. What a great learning experience! When I returned the next day, I discovered that the college in Cape Town had an internship program in social work, which was my area. I was very happy about this, since it would help me in my future work to understand how another culture dealt with social problems.

After I arrived in Cape Town several months later, I wasn't sure that I had made the right choice. I felt uncomfortable in this new culture and longed to be back home. I had trouble, for example, adjusting to how casual and unstructured things were; I was used to a very structured life at Camford, where I loved to type out a weekly schedule for myself. Eventually, though, I opened myself up to the Cape Town lifestyle and began to enjoy it.

The greatest part of my experience was getting to know my host family, which consisted of a doctor and his wife, and two wonderful children. The family helped me learn about the food and music and other customs of South Africa. And the daughter let me use her computer to keep in touch with my friends back home by e-mail, which helped me not to feel so isolated.

I had long discussions about values with the doctor, who was very intelligent and had studied in Britain and America. We often compared life in Britain with life in South Africa. He was critical, for example, of how older people were treated in Britain, so often being isolated from younger folks. He preferred the common South African practice, whereby grandparents lived with the family and helped raise the children; he thought this was better for everyone. I wasn't sure this would work as well in Britain, but his comments made me think. Now when I consider social problems in my own country, I try to learn from how other cultures deal with the same problems.

Since my host family was colored, we often talked about race relations. I was especially interested in what life was like under the old apartheid system;

the wife told me how painful it was to live under a system that made her children feel that they weren't as good as white people. Of course, we both condemned the old practice of apartheid and welcomed the changes. But the doctor emphasized that people still had a long way to go, and that subtle forms of racism still exist in South Africa – as well as in Britain and America.

When I discussed values with intelligent and open-minded people in South Africa, I found that we tended to agree more than disagree. This was so even when we were discussing defects in my society or in their society. Seldom was there a conflict between "British values" (values that nearly all British accept) and "South African values" (values that nearly all South Africans accept). The one exception was when the English cricket team played South Africa; only then did we line up neatly on opposite sides.

One big problem with cultural relativism is that it divides people. CR simplistically sees each group as having its own unified system of values. So "we" (as in "we British") have our values, and "they" (as in "those South Africans") have theirs. This "we versus they" mentality may have worked reasonably well when cultures were isolated from each other. But we live in a shrinking world where technology tears down fences between cultures; think of transcontinental flights, global news agencies, multinational corporations, and the Internet. Today we need ways to mediate disputes between societies and to establish some common norms. Since CR helps very little with such problems, it gives a poor basis for life in the twenty-first century.

Cultural relativism also limits our ability to learn from other cultures. CR says "Our culture's norms are okay, and so are yours." But our culture's norms might not be okay. Our norms might have biases and blind spots that we won't recognize unless we dialogue with others. Societies, since they deal in differing ways with the same life problems, can learn much from each other. Our growth demands that we experience other ways of thinking and acting – and that we be open to change how we do things on the basis of this experience.

CR says that whatever is socially approved must thereby be good. So if it's socially approved to value money above all else, then this must be good. And if it's socially approved to put Jews in concentration camps, then this too must be good. To live as a cultural relativist is to live as an uncritical conformist. But cultural relativism is an error: "good" doesn't mean "socially approved." What is socially approved may sometimes be very bad.

Study questions

1 Explain the cultural relativist's view about the meaning of "good" and its relativity to culture.

2 What reasons does Relativa give for holding cultural relativism?

3 How would Vera respond to these reasons for holding cultural relativism? What is her main objection to cultural relativism?
4 In what ways would cultural relativism promote or not promote tolerance for other moral beliefs?
5 Explain the subgroup problem.
6 Do all social scientists support cultural relativism?
7 Why does Vera think that cultural relativism divides people?
8 How does Vera think that we can learn from other cultures? How would cultural relativism limit our ability to do this?

For further study

This selection is from "Are Values Relative to Culture?" which appeared in the Scottish journal *Dialogue* 14 (April 2000): 3–6. Be careful of terminology if you do outside reading; what is here called "cultural relativism" is sometimes called "ethical relativism." To sort out the different types of "relativism" in ethics, see Richard Brandt's "Ethical Relativism" in the *Encyclopedia of Philosophy* (edited by Paul Edwards, London and New York: Macmillan and the Free Press, 1967). For a defense of cultural relativism by a prominent anthropologist, see William Sumner's longer *Folkways* (Boston: Ginn & Co., 1911). Harry Gensler's *Ethics: A Contemporary Introduction* (London and New York: Routledge, 1998) discusses cultural relativism in Chapter 1; this essay is in part derived from ideas in that chapter.

Related readings in this anthology include Benedict (who defends cultural relativism); Ayer and Mackie (who attack the objectivity of ethics); Lewis, Kohlberg, and Nagel (who attack cultural relativism and defend the objectivity of ethics); Hertzler and Ricoeur (who discuss the golden rule); and Hare, King, and Singer (who criticize racial segregation).

DAVID HUME
Ethical Claims Describe Feelings

David Hume, a British philosopher who lived from 1711 to 1776, has had a great influence on contemporary ethics. For this reason, we thought it helpful to include some short excerpts from his writings.

Hume's ethical thinking had two phases. The first phase saw ethics as based on feelings instead of reason; here Hume is close to classic subjectivism: "X is good" means "I like X." His second phase saw ethics as based on a combination of reason and feelings; we first use reason to get our facts straight and then we see what our other-regarding feelings move us to do. Here Hume is closer to the ideal observer view: "X is good" means "We would desire X if we were informed and impartially concerned for everyone."

As you read the selection, ask yourself whether Hume's early view gave a satisfactory approach to morality. Can you understand why he tried to incorporate more rationality and altruistic sentiment in his later view?

Morality is not from reason (his early view)

Some affirm that virtue is a conformity to reason, that there are eternal fitnesses of things which are the same to every rational being that considers them. All these systems concur in the opinion that morality, like truth, is discerned merely by ideas. In order to judge these systems, we need only consider whether it is possible, from reason alone, to distinguish between moral good and evil.

Since morals have an influence on the actions and affections, it follows, that they cannot be derived from reason; and that because reason alone can never have any such influence. Morals excite passions, and produce or prevent actions. Reason of itself is utterly impotent in this particular. The rules of morality, therefore, are not conclusions of reason.

As long as it is allowed that reason has no influence on our passions and actions, 'tis in vain to pretend that morality is discovered only by a deduction of reason. An active principle can never be founded on an inactive.

Reason and feelings

Reason is the discovery of truth or falsehood. Truth or falsehood consists in an agreement or disagreement either to the real relationship of ideas, or to real existence and matter of fact.[1] Whatever, therefore, is not susceptible of this agreement or disagreement, is incapable of being true or false, and can never be an object of our reason. Now 'tis evident our passions, volitions, and actions, are not susceptible of any such agreement or disagreement. 'Tis impossible, therefore, they can be pronounced either true or false, and be either contrary or conformable to reason.

Reason, in a strict sense, can only have an influence on our conduct in two ways: Either it excites a passion by informing us of the existence of something which is a proper object of it; or it discovers the connection of causes and effects, so as to afford us means of exerting any passion.[2] These judgments may often be false and erroneous. A person may suppose a pain or pleasure to lie in an object, which has no tendency to produce either of these sensations. A person may also take false measures for attaining his end, and may retard instead of forwarding his project.

Reason is and ought only to be the slave of the passions, and can never pretend to any other office than to serve and obey them. When a passion is neither founded on false suppositions, nor chooses means insufficient for the end, the understanding can neither justify nor condemn it. 'Tis not contrary to reason to prefer the destruction of the whole world to the scratching of my finger. 'Tis not contrary to reason for me to choose my total ruin, to prevent the least uneasiness of a person wholly unknown to me. 'Tis as little contrary to reason to prefer even my own acknowledged lesser good to my greater.

Morality is from feelings

Thus on the whole 'tis impossible that the distinction between moral good and evil can be made by reason; since that distinction has an influence upon our actions, of which reason alone is incapable. But reason and judgment may be the mediate cause of an action, by prompting or directing a passion.

If the thought and understanding were alone capable of fixing the boundaries of right and wrong, the character of virtuous and vicious either must lie in some relations of objects, or must be a matter of fact. This consequence is evident. As the operations of human understanding divide themselves into two kinds, the comparing of ideas and the inferring of matters of fact, were virtue discovered by the understanding it must be an object of one of these relations.[3]

Take any action allowed to be vicious: Willful murder, for instance. Examine it in all lights, and see if you can find that matter of fact, or real existence, which you call vice. In whichever way you take it, you find only certain passions, motives, volitions and thoughts. There is no other matter of fact in the case. The vice entirely escapes you, as long as you consider the object. You never can find it, till you turn your reflection into your own breast, and find a sentiment of disapprobation, which arises in you, towards this action. Here is a matter of fact; but 'tis the object of feeling, not of reason. It lies in yourself, not in the object. So that when you pronounce any action or character to be vicious, you mean nothing, but that from the constitution of your nature you have a feeling or sentiment of blame from the contemplation of it.[4]

Thus the course of the argument leads us to conclude that, since virtue and vice are not discoverable by reason, it must be by means of some sentiment that we are able to mark the difference between them. Morality, therefore, is more properly felt than judged of.

Hume's later thinking

I am apt to suspect that reason and sentiment concur in almost all moral determinations and conclusions. The final sentence, it is probable, which pronounces characters and actions amiable or odious, praiseworthy or blamable, depends on some internal sense or feeling, which nature has made universal in the whole species. But in order to pave the way for such a sentiment, and give a proper discernment of its object, it is often necessary that much reasoning should precede and general facts fixed and ascertained.

The notion of morals implies some sentiment common to all mankind, which recommends the same object to general approbation, and makes every man, or most men, agree in the same opinion or decision concerning it. This is the sentiment of humanity.[5]

When a man denominates another his enemy, he is understood to speak the language of self-love, and to express sentiments, peculiar to himself, and arising from his particular circumstances. But when he bestows on any man the epithets of vicious or depraved, he speaks another language, and expresses sentiments, in which he expects all his audience to concur with him. He must here, therefore, depart from his private and particular situation, and must choose a point of view, common to him with others; he must move some universal principle of the human frame, and touch a string to which all mankind have an accord and symphony. If he mean, therefore, to express that this man possesses qualities, whose tendency is pernicious to society, he has chosen this common point of view, and has touched the principle of humanity, in which every man, in some degree, concurs.[6]

Study questions

1   Hume thinks that morality influences our conduct. Explain how he uses this idea to argue that morality cannot be from reason.
2   What does Hume mean by "reason"? With what two kinds of truth does reason deal?
3   How can reason influence conduct? Can feelings and actions go against reason?
4   Explain Hume's statement that "Reason is and ought only to be the slave of the passions."
5   Hume thinks that there are only two kinds of truth. Explain how he uses this idea to argue that moral beliefs do not express truths.
6   What is the point of his "willful murder" example? What do we mean when we call the murder "bad"?
7   In Hume's later thinking, how do reason and feeling cooperate as we make moral judgments?
8   In what way do agents making moral judgments try to be "impartial"? How can this help people to reach agreement on moral issues?

For further study

This selection has excerpts, which are sometimes simplified in their wording, from two of David Hume's books. Our earlier sections are from *A Treatise of Human Nature* (1739); our excerpts are mostly from the beginning of Book 3, but the "reason is the slave" paragraph is from Section 3 of Part 3 of Book 2. Our last section is from *An Enquiry Concerning the Principles of Morals* (1751); the first paragraph is from Section 1 while the rest is from Part 1 of Section 9. For more on Hume's approach, see Antony Flew's *David Hume: Philosopher of Moral Science* (Oxford: Oxford University Press, 1986), J. L. Mackie's *Hume's Moral Theory* (London: Routledge and Kegan Paul, 1980), and Barry Stroud's *Hume* (London: Routledge and Kegan Paul, 1977). Harry Gensler's *Ethics: A Contemporary Introduction* (London and New York: Routledge, 1998) discusses subjectivism and the ideal observer view in Chapter 2.

Related readings in this anthology include Ayer and Mackie (who give contemporary versions of Hume's view); Kant (the major historical opponent of Hume); Nagel (a recent opponent of subjectivism); Smart (who uses Hume's approach to defend utilitarianism); and Callicott (who uses Hume's approach to defend environmental ethics).

Notes

1   This principle, which is central to Hume's thought, is often called "Hume's fork." Hume's fork says that every truth is about either abstract ideas (like "2+2=4") or empirical facts (like "It's raining outside"). Unless we have feelings, neither of these sorts of truth can incite us to action; in this sense, reason is inert.

2   Here is an example to clarify Hume's point. Suppose that I desire to eat. "There is an apple on the tree" and "To get the apple I must climb the tree" can then influence my conduct, by telling me how to satisfy my desires. So, assuming a previous desire, reason can influence my conduct.

3   Hume again appeals to "Hume's fork," this time to argue that moral judgments cannot be truths.

4   Contemporary philosophers who are inspired by Hume on this point go in one of two ways. Subjectivists see "X is bad" as a truth claim about the speaker's feelings, along the lines of "I dislike X." Emotivists see "X is bad" as an exclamation (not a truth claim), like "Boo on X!" While these views are fairly close in practice, they differ in some important ways; Ayer's defense of emotivism in this anthology claims that subjectivism is much easier to refute.

5   Hume's "sentiment of humanity" involves concern for others – a sentiment that we all share to some degree (although it may be weaker than our desire for self-interest). Moral judgments appeal to this sentiment.

6   Some see Hume here as anticipating the ideal observer theory. This view sees "X is good" as a truth claim about what we would desire under certain conditions: "We would desire X if we were fully informed and had impartial concern for everyone."

THOMAS NAGEL
Ethical Claims Are Objective

Thomas Nagel, an American philosopher born in 1937, has contributed much to the study of ethics. His influence extended to the governmental arena in 1981, when he defended affirmative action in testimony before a US Senate subcommittee.

Nagel argues for objective values. He claims that some actions, like causing needless harm to others, can be judged as wrong or bad from a general standpoint that everyone should be able to understand. He appeals to consistency and to the resentment that we all feel when others cause needless harm to us.

As you read the selection, keep in mind why some people see ethical claims as subjective. Ask yourself whether Nagel answers these objections and whether he provides a satisfactory objective basis for ethics.

Ethics and reasons

Suppose you work in a library, checking people's books as they leave, and a friend asks you to let him smuggle out a hard-to-find reference work that he wants to own.

You might hesitate to agree for various reasons. You might be afraid that he'll be caught, and that both you and he will then get into trouble. You might want the book to stay in the library so that you can consult it yourself.

But you may also think that what he proposes is wrong – that he shouldn't do it and you shouldn't help him. If you think that, what does it mean, and what, if anything, makes it true?

To say it's wrong is not just to say it's against the rules. There can be bad rules which prohibit what isn't wrong – like a law against criticizing the government. A rule can also be bad because it requires something that *is* wrong – like a law that requires racial segregation in hotels and restaurants. The ideas of wrong and right are different from the ideas of what is and is not against the rules. Otherwise they couldn't be used in the evaluation of rules as well as of actions.

If you think it would be wrong to help your friend steal the book, then you will feel uncomfortable about doing it: in some way you won't want to do it, even if you are also reluctant to refuse help to a friend. Where does the desire not to do it come from; what is its motive, the reason behind it?

There are various ways in which something can be wrong, but in this case, if you had to explain it, you'd probably say that it would be unfair to other users of the library who may be just as interested in the book as your friend is, but who consult it in the reference room, where anyone who needs it can find it. You may also feel that to let him take it would betray your employers, who are paying you precisely to keep this sort of thing from happening.

These thoughts have to do with effects on others – not necessarily effects on their feelings, since they may never find out about it, but some kind of damage nevertheless. In general, the thought that something is wrong depends on its impact not just on the person who does it but on other people. They wouldn't like it, and they'd object if they found out.

But suppose you try to explain all this to your friend, and he says, "I know the head librarian wouldn't like it if he found out, and probably some of the other users of the library would be unhappy to find the book gone, but who cares? I want the book; why should I care about them?"

The argument that it would be wrong is supposed to give him a reason not to do it. But if someone just doesn't care about other people, what reason does he have to refrain from doing any of the things usually thought to be wrong, if he can get away with it: what reason does he have not to kill, steal, lie, or hurt others? If he can get what he wants by doing such things, why shouldn't he? And if there's no reason why he shouldn't, in what sense is it wrong?

Reasons and self-interest

There have been many attempts to answer this question. One type of answer tries to identify something else that the person already cares about, and then connect morality to it.

For example, some people believe that even if you can get away with awful crimes on this earth, and are not punished by the law or your fellow men, such acts are forbidden by God, who will punish you after death (and reward you if you didn't do wrong when you were tempted to). So even when it seems to be in your interest to do such a thing, it really isn't.

This is a rather crude version of the religious foundation for morality. A more appealing version might be that the motive for obeying God's commands is not fear but love. He loves you, and you should love Him, and should wish to obey His commands in order not to offend Him.

But however we interpret the religious motivation, there are three objections to this type of answer. First, plenty of people who don't believe in God still make judgments of right and wrong, and think no one should kill another for his wallet even if he can be sure to get away with it. Second, if God exists, and forbids what's wrong, that still isn't what *makes* it wrong. Murder is wrong in itself, and that's *why* God forbids it (if He does).[1] God couldn't make just any old thing wrong – like putting on your left sock before your right – simply by prohibiting it. If God would punish you for doing that it would be inadvisable to do it, but it wouldn't be wrong. Third, fear of punishment and hope of reward, and even love of God, seem not to be the right motives for morality. If you think it's wrong to kill, cheat, or steal, you should want to avoid doing such things because they are bad things to do to the victims, not just because you fear the consequences for yourself, or because you don't want to offend your Creator.

This third objection also applies to other explanations of the force of morality which appeal to the interests of the person who must act. For example, it may be said that you should treat others with consideration so that they'll do the same for you. This may be sound advice, but it is valid only so far as you think what you do will affect how others treat you. It's not a reason for doing the right thing if others won't find out about it, or against doing the wrong thing if you can get away with it (like being a hit and run driver).

Reasons and universality

There is no substitute for a direct concern for other people as the basis of morality. But morality is supposed to apply to everyone: and can we assume that everyone has such a concern for others? Obviously not: some people are very selfish, and even those who are not selfish may care only about the people they know, and not about everyone. So where will we find a reason that everyone has not to hurt other people, even those they don't know?

Well, there's one general argument against hurting other people which can be given to anybody who understands English (or any other language), and which seems to show that he has *some* reason to care about others, even if in the end his selfish motives are so strong that he persists in treating other people badly anyway. It's an argument that I'm sure you've heard, and it goes like this: "How would you like it if someone did that to you?"

It's not easy to explain how this argument is supposed to work. Suppose you're about to steal someone else's umbrella as you leave a restaurant in a rainstorm, and a bystander says, "How would you like it if someone did that to you?" Why is it supposed to make you hesitate, or feel guilty?

Obviously the direct answer to the question is supposed to be, "I wouldn't like it at all!" But what's the next step? Suppose you were to say, "I wouldn't like it if someone did that to me. But luckily no one *is* doing it to me. I'm doing it to someone else, and I don't mind that at all!"

This answer misses the point of the question. When you are asked how you would like it if someone did that to you, you are supposed to think about all the feelings you would have if someone stole your umbrella. And that includes more than just "not liking it" – as you wouldn't "like it" if you stubbed your toe on a rock. If someone stole your umbrella you'd *resent* it. You'd have feelings about the umbrella thief, not just about the loss of the umbrella. You'd think, "Where does he get off, taking my umbrella that I bought with my hard-earned money and that I had the foresight to bring after reading the weather report? Why didn't he bring his own umbrella?" and so forth.

When our own interests are threatened by the inconsiderate behavior of others, most of us find it easy to appreciate that those others have a reason to be more considerate. When you are hurt, you probably feel that other people should care about it: you don't think it's no concern of theirs, and that they have no reason to avoid hurting you. That is the feeling that the "How would you like it?" argument is supposed to arouse.

Because if you admit that you would *resent* it if someone else did to you what you are now doing to him, you are admitting that you think he would have a reason not to do it to you. And if you admit that, you have to consider what that reason is. It couldn't be just that it's *you* that he's hurting, of all the people in the world. There's no special reason for him not to steal *your* umbrella, as opposed to anyone else's. There's nothing so special about you. Whatever the reason is, it's a reason he would have against hurting anyone else in the same way. And it's a reason anyone else would have too, in a similar situation, against hurting you or anyone else.

But if it's a reason anyone would have not to hurt anyone else in this way, then it's a reason *you* have not to hurt someone else in this way. Therefore it's a reason not to steal the other person's umbrella.

This is a matter of simple consistency. Once you admit that another person would have a reason not to harm you in similar circumstances, and once you admit that the reason he would have is very general and doesn't apply only to you, or to him, then to be consistent you have to admit that the same reason applies to you now. You shouldn't steal the umbrella, and you ought to feel guilty if you do.

Someone could escape from this argument if, when he was asked, "How would you like it if someone did that to you?" he answered, "I wouldn't resent it at all. I wouldn't *like* it if someone stole my umbrella in a rainstorm, but I wouldn't think there was any reason for him to consider my feelings about it." But how many people could honestly give that answer? I think most people, unless they're crazy, would think that their own interests and harms matter, not only to themselves, but in a way that gives other people a reason to care about them too. We all think that when we suffer it is not just bad for *us,* but *bad, period.*

The basis of morality is a belief that good and harm to particular people (or animals) is good or bad not just from their point of view, but from a more general point of view, which every thinking person can understand. That means that each person has a reason to consider not only his own interests but the interests of others in deciding what to do. And it isn't enough if he is considerate only of some others – his family and friends, those he specially cares about. Of course he will care more about certain people, and also about himself. But he has some reason to consider the effect of what he does on the good or harm of everyone. If he's like most of us, that is what he thinks others should do with regard to him, even if they aren't friends of his.

Ethics and impartiality

Even if this is right, it is only a bare outline of the source of morality. It doesn't tell us in detail how we should consider the interests of others, or how we should weigh them against the special interest we all have in ourselves and the particular people close to us. It doesn't even tell us how much we should care about people in other countries in comparison with our fellow citizens. There are many disagreements among those who accept morality in general, about what in particular is right and what is wrong.

For instance: should you care about every other person as much as you care about yourself? Should you in other words love your neighbor as yourself (even if he isn't your neighbor)? Should you ask yourself, every time you go to a movie, whether the cost of the ticket could provide more happiness if you gave it to someone else, or donated the money to famine relief?

Very few people are so unselfish. And if someone were that impartial between himself and others, he would probably also feel that he should be just as impartial *among* other people. That would rule out caring more about his friends and relatives than he does about strangers. He might have special feelings about certain people who are close to him, but complete impartiality would mean that he won't *favor* them – if for example he has to choose between helping a friend or a stranger to avoid suffering, or between taking his children to a movie and donating the money to famine relief.

This degree of impartiality seems too much to ask of most people: someone who had it would be a kind of terrifying saint.[2] But it's an important question in moral thought, how much impartiality we should try for. You are a particular person, but you are also able to recognize that you're just one person among many others, and no more important than they are, when looked at from outside. How much should that point of view influence you? You do matter somewhat from outside – otherwise you wouldn't think other people had any reason to care about what they did to you. But you don't matter as much from the outside as you matter to yourself, from the inside – since from the outside you don't matter any more than anybody else.

Not only is it unclear how impartial we should be; it's unclear what would make an answer to this question the right one. Is there a single correct way for everyone to strike the balance between what he cares about personally and what matters impartially? Or will the answer vary from person to person depending on the strength of their different motives?

Study questions

1 Why does Nagel reject the idea that what is wrong is what goes against accepted rules – or what goes against God's commands?
2 What is Nagel's general argument against hurting other people? Explain the role of consistency and resentment in his argument.
3 Does Nagel think that some things are wrong from a general point of view that everyone can understand? How does he defend his answer?
4 How does Nagel evaluate the idea that we should care about every person as much as we care about ourselves, our family, and our friends?
5 What kinds of issues does the idea of impartiality raise for ethics?

For further study

This selection is from Thomas Nagel's *What Does It All Mean?* (New York: Oxford University Press, 1987), pages 59–69. See also his *The View From Nowhere* (New York: Oxford University Press, 1986) and *Equality and Partiality* (New York: Oxford University Press, 1991). Harry Gensler's *Ethics: A Contemporary Introduction* (London and New York: Routledge, 1998) discusses related views in Chapters 2 and 8.

Related readings in this anthology include Ayer, Benedict, Hume, Mackie, and Sartre (who oppose objective values); Lewis (who defends a religious basis for moral objectivity); Kant (who defends objective values); and Hare, Frankena, and Hertzler (who defend impartiality).

Notes

1 For more on this point, see Plato's *Euthyphro* or Chapter 3 of Harry Gensler's *Ethics: A Contemporary Introduction* (London and New York: Routledge, 1998).
2 To appreciate his point, imagine how you would feel if your parents cared as much about a child they just met on the subway as they do for you.

C. S. LEWIS

The Moral Law Is from God

C. S. Lewis, a British scholar and novelist who lived from 1898 to 1963, was one of the most popular and influential religious writers of the last hundred years. He wrote much in defense of Christianity. Here he argues that there is an objective moral law, that this moral law must have a source, and that this source must be God.

As you read the selection, ask yourself how you would respond to this argument if you were an atheist. Is Lewis's defense of an objective moral law convincing? Could someone reasonably accept an objective moral law without believing in God?

The objectivity of the moral law

Everyone has heard people quarreling. Sometimes it sounds funny and sometimes it sounds merely unpleasant; but however it sounds, I believe we can learn something very important from listening to the kind of things they say. They say things like this: "How'd you like it if anyone did the same to you?" – "That's my seat, I was there first" – "Leave him alone, he isn't doing you any harm" – "Give me a bit of your orange, I gave you a bit of mine" – "Come on, you promised."

Now what interests me about all these remarks is that the man who makes them is not merely saying that the other man's behavior does not happen to please him. He is appealing to some standard of behavior which he expects the other man to know about. And the other man very seldom replies: "To hell with your standard." Nearly always he tries to make out that what he has been doing does not really go against the standard, or that if it does there is some special excuse. He pretends there is some special reason in this particular case why the person who took the seat first should not keep it, or that things were quite different when he was given the bit of orange, or that something has turned up which lets him off keeping his promise. It looks, in fact, very much as if both parties had in mind some kind of Law or Rule of fair play or decent behavior or morality or whatever you like to call it, about which they really agreed. Quarreling means trying to show that the other man is in the wrong. And there would be no sense in trying to do that unless you and he had some sort of agreement as to what Right and Wrong are.

Now this Law or Rule about Right and Wrong used to be called the Law of Nature. Nowadays, when we talk of the "laws of nature" we usually mean things like gravitation, or heredity, or the laws of chemistry. But when the older thinkers called the Law of Right and Wrong "the Law of Nature," they really meant the Law of Human Nature. The idea was that, just as all bodies are governed by the law of gravitation and organisms by biological laws, so the creature called man also had his law – with this great difference, that a body could not choose whether it obeyed the law of gravitation or not, but a man could choose either to obey the Law of Human Nature or to disobey it.

This law was called the Law of Nature because people thought that everyone knew it by nature and did not need to be taught it. They did not mean, of course, that you might not find an odd individual here and there who did not know it, just as you find a few people who are color-blind or have no ear for a tune. But taking the race as a whole, they thought that the human idea of decent behavior was obvious to everyone. And I believe they were right. If they were not, then all things we said about the war [World War II] were nonsense. What was the sense in saying the enemy were in the wrong unless Right is a real thing which the Nazis at bottom knew as well as we did and ought to have practiced? If they had had no notion of what we mean by right, then, though we might still have had to fight them, we could no more have blamed them for that than for the color of their hair.

Is morality relative to culture?

I know that some people say the idea of a Law of Nature or decent behavior known to all men is unsound, because different civilizations and different ages have had quite different moralities.

But this is not true. There have been differences between their moralities, but these have never amounted to anything like a total difference. If anyone will take the trouble to compare the moral teaching of, say, the ancient Egyptians, Babylonians, Hindus, Chinese, Greeks and Romans, what will really strike him will be how very like they are to each other and to our own. Some of the evidence for this I have put together in the appendix of another book called *The Abolition of Man*; but for our present purpose I need only ask the reader to think what a totally different morality would mean. Think of a country where people were admired for running away in battle, or where a man felt proud of double-crossing all the people who had been kindest to him. You might just as well try to imagine a country where two and two made five. Men have differed as regards what people you ought to be unselfish to – whether it was only your own family, or your fellow countrymen, or everyone. But they have always agreed that you ought not to put yourself first. Selfishness has never been admired. Men have differed as to whether you should have one wife or four. But they have always agreed that you must not simply have any woman you liked.

Whenever you find a man who says he does not believe in a real Right and Wrong, you will find the same man going back on this a moment later. He may break his promise to you, but if you try breaking one to him he will be complaining "It's not fair." A nation may say treaties do not matter; but then, next minute, they spoil their case by saying that the particular treaty they want to break was an unfair one. But if treaties do not matter, and if there is no such thing as Right and Wrong – in other words, if there is no Law of Nature – what is the difference between a fair treaty and an unfair one? Have they not let the cat out of the bag and shown that, whatever they say, they really know the Law of Nature just like anyone else?

It seems, then, we are forced to believe in a real Right and Wrong. People may be sometimes mistaken about them, just as people sometimes get their sums wrong; but they are not a matter of mere taste and opinion any more than the multiplication table. Now if we are agreed about that, I go on to my next point, which is this. None of us are really keeping the Law of Nature. If there are any exceptions among you, I apologize to them. They had much better read some other work, for nothing I am going to say concerns them.

Is the moral law a human invention?

Some people object to me saying, "Isn't what you call the Moral Law just a social convention, something that is put into us by education?" I think there is a misunderstanding here. The people who ask that question are usually taking it for granted that if we have learned a thing from parents and teachers, then that thing must be merely a human invention. But, of course, that is not so. Some of the things we learn are mere conventions which might have been different – we learn to keep to the left of the road, but it might just as well have been the rule to keep to the right – and others of them, like mathematics, are real truths. The question is to which class the Law of Human Nature belongs.

There are two reasons for saying it belongs to the same class as mathematics. The first is, as I said before, that though there are differences between the moral ideas of one time or country and those of another, the differences are not really very great – not nearly so great as most people imagine – and you can recognize the same law running through them all: whereas mere conventions, like the rule of the road or the kind of clothes people wear, may differ to any extent.

The other reason is this. When you think about these differences between the morality of one people and another, do you think that the morality of one people is ever better or worse than that of another? Have any of the changes been improvements? If not, then of course there could never be any moral progress. Progress means not just changing, but changing for the better. If no set of moral ideas were truer or better than any other, there would be no sense in preferring civilized morality to savage morality, or Christian morality to Nazi morality. In fact, of course, we all do believe that some moralities are better than others.

Very well then. The moment you say that one set of moral ideas can be better than another, you are, in fact, measuring them both by a standard, saying that one of them conforms to that standard more nearly than the other. You are, in fact, comparing them both with some Real Morality, admitting that there is such a thing as a real Right, independent of what people think, and that some people's ideas get nearer to that real Right than others. Or put it this way. The reason why your idea of New York can be truer or less true than mine is that New York is a real place, existing quite apart from what either of us thinks. If when each of us said "New York" each meant merely "The town I am imagining in my own head," how could one of us have truer ideas than the other? There would be no question of truth or falsehood at all. In the same way, if the Rule of Decent Behavior meant simply "whatever each nation happens to approve," there would be no sense in saying that any one nation had ever been more correct in its approval than any other; no sense in saying that the world could ever grow morally better or morally worse.

I conclude then, that though the differences between people's ideas of Decent Behavior often make you suspect that there is no real natural Law of Behavior at all, yet the things we are bound to think about these differences really prove just the opposite.

But one word before I end. I have met people who exaggerate the differences, because they have not distinguished between differences of morality and differences of belief about facts. For example, one man said to me, "Three hundred years ago people in England were putting witches to death. Was that what you call the Rule of Human Nature or Right Conduct?" But surely the reason we do not execute witches is that we do not believe there are such things. If we did – if we really thought that there were people going about who had sold themselves to the devil and received supernatural powers in return and were using these powers to kill their neighbors or drive them mad – surely we would all agree that if anyone deserved the death penalty, then these filthy quislings did? There is no difference of moral principle here: the difference is simply about matter of fact.

In the case of stones and trees and things of that sort, what we call the Laws of Nature may not be anything except a way of speaking. When you say that nature is governed by certain laws, this may only mean that nature does, in fact, behave in a certain way. The so-called laws may not be anything real – anything above and beyond the actual facts which we observe. But in the case of Man, we saw that this will not do. The Law of Human Nature, or of Right and Wrong, must be something above and beyond the actual facts of human behavior. In this case, besides the actual facts, you have something else – a real law which we did not invent and which we know we ought to obey.

Two views of the universe

I now want to consider what this tells us about the universe we live in. Ever since men were able to think, they have been wondering what this universe really is and how it came to be there. And, very roughly, two views have been held. First, there is what is called the materialist view. People who take that view think that matter and space just happen to exist, and always have existed, nobody knows why; and that the matter, behaving in certain fixed ways, has just happened, by a sort of fluke, to produce creatures like ourselves who are able to think. By one chance in a thousand something hit our sun and made it produce the planets; and by another thousandth chance the chemicals necessary for life, and the right temperature, occurred on one of these planets, and so some of the matter on this earth came alive; and then, by a very long series of chances, the living creatures developed into things like us. The other view is the religious view. According to it, what is behind the universe is more like a mind than it is like anything else we know. That is to say, it is conscious, and has purposes, and prefers one thing to another. And on this view it made the universe, partly for purposes we do not know, but partly, at any rate, in order to produce creatures like itself – I mean, like itself to the extent of having minds. Please do not think that one of these views was held a long time ago and that the other has gradually taken its place. Wherever there have been thinking men both views turn up.

You cannot find out which view is the right one by science in the ordinary sense. Science works by experiments. It watches how things behave. Every scientific statement in the long run, however complicated it looks, really means something like, "I pointed the telescope to such and such a part of the sky at 2:20 a.m. on January 15th and saw so-and-so," or "I put some of this stuff in a pot and heated it to such-and-such a temperature and it did so-and-so." Do not think I am saying anything against science: I am only saying what its job is. And the more scientific a man is, the more (I believe) he would agree with me that this is the job of science – and a very useful and necessary job it is too. But why anything comes to be there at all, and whether there is anything behind the things science observes – something of a different kind – this is not a scientific question. If there is "Something Behind," then either it will have to remain altogether unknown to men or else make itself known in some different way. The statement that there is any such thing, and the statement that there is no such thing, are neither of them statements that science can make. Supposing science ever became complete so that it knew every single thing in the whole universe. Is it not plain that the questions, "Why is there a universe?" "Has it any meaning?" would remain just as they were?

The moral law is from God

Now the position would be quite hopeless but for this. There is one thing, and only one, in the whole universe which we know more about than we could learn from external observation. That one thing is Man. We do not merely observe men, we are men. In this case we have, so to speak, inside information; we are in the know. And because of that, we know that men find themselves under a moral law, which they did not make, and cannot quite forget even when they try, and which they know they ought to obey.

The position of the question, then, is like this. We want to know whether the universe simply happens to be what it is for no reason or whether there is a power behind it that makes it what it is. Since that power, if it exists, would be not one of the observed facts but a reality which makes them, no mere observation of the facts can find it. There is only one case in which we can know whether there is anything more, namely our own case. And in that one case we find there is.

Or put it the other way round. If there was a controlling power outside the universe, it could not show itself to us as one of the facts inside the universe. The only way in which we could expect it to show itself would be inside ourselves as an influence or a command trying to get us to behave in a certain way. And that is just what we do find inside ourselves. Surely this ought to arouse our suspicions? In the only case where you can expect to get an answer, the answer turns out to be Yes; and in the other cases, where you do not get an answer, you see why you do not.

Suppose someone asked me, when I see a man in a blue uniform going down the street leaving little paper packets at each house, why I suppose that they contain letters? I should reply, "Because whenever he leaves a similar little packet for me I find it does contain a letter." And if he then objected, "But you've never seen all these letters which you think the other people are getting," I should say, "Of course not, and I shouldn't expect to, because they're not addressed to me. I'm explaining the packets I'm not allowed to open by the ones I am allowed to open." It is the same about this question. The only packet I am allowed to open is Man. When I do, especially when I open that particular man called Myself, I find that I do not exist on my own, that I am under a law; that somebody or something wants me to behave in a certain way. I do not, of course, think that if I could get inside a stone or a tree I should find exactly the same thing, just as I do not think all the other people in the street get the same letters as I do. I should expect, for instance, to find that the stone had to obey the law of gravity – that whereas the sender of the letters merely tells me to obey the law of my human nature, He compels the stone to obey the laws of its stony nature. But I should expect to find that there was, so to speak, a sender of letters in both cases, a Power behind the facts, a Director, a Guide.

I have got to a Something which is directing the universe, and which appears in me as a law urging me to do right and making me feel responsible and uncomfortable when I do wrong. I think we have to assume it is more like a mind than it is like anything else we know – because after all the only other thing we know is matter and you can hardly imagine a bit of matter giving instructions.

Study questions

1 According to Lewis, why should we think there is an objective moral law?
2 Lewis considers two objections to his belief that there is an objective right and wrong. What are the objections? How does Lewis answer them?
3 What is the difference between a "mere convention" and a "real truth"? Give an example of each.
4 What are the two basic ways to view the world? What is the key to deciding between the two views?
5 Formulate Lewis's argument for God's existence.

For further study

This selection has excerpts from Clive Staples Lewis's *Mere Christianity* (London: Geoffrey Bles, 1952), pages 3–20; the rest of this book defends basic Christian beliefs. His many other books include The *Abolition of Man* (London: Oxford University Press, 1943), which he refers to in this selection, and *The Problem of Pain* (New York: Macmillan, 1944), which defends the reasonableness of believing that this world (which includes much pain and suffering) was created by an all-good and all-powerful God. Plato's *Euthyphro* raised an important objection to basing ethics on religion; for a recent debate on this objection, see "Is God the source of morality?" by Sharon M. Kaye and Harry J. Gensler, in *God Matters: Readings in the Philosophy of Religion* (New York: Longman Press, 2003), edited by Raymond Martin and Christopher Bernard, pages 481–7. Immanuel Kant gave a somewhat different moral argument for the existence of God in his *Critique of Practical Reason* (New York: Library of Liberal Arts, 1956), translated by L. W. Beck. Harry Gensler's *Ethics: A Contemporary Introduction* (London and New York: Routledge, 1998) discusses whether ethics is based on religion in Chapter 3.

Related readings in this anthology include Moore, Nagel, and Ross (who also accept moral objectivity but don't base it on religion); Mackie and Sartre (non-believers who reject moral objectivity because they think it requires belief in God); Ayer (whose approach excludes both God and an objective ethics); and King and Ricoeur (who connect ethics with religion but don't deny the possibility of a non-religious ethics).

THE BIBLE

Love of God and Neighbor

The Judeo-Christian Bible has had an important influence on moral thinking. Here are a few of the passages that relate to morality.

The ten commandments

Then God delivered all these commandments: "I, the Lord, am your God, who brought you out of the land of Egypt, that place of slavery. You shall not have other gods besides me. You shall not carve idols for yourselves in the shape of anything in the sky above or on the earth below or in the waters beneath the earth; you shall not bow down before them or worship them. You shall not take the name of the Lord, your God, in vain. Remember to keep holy the sabbath day. Six days you may labor and do all your work, but the seventh day is the sabbath of the Lord, your God. No work may be done then.

"Honor your father and your mother, that you may have a long life in the land which the Lord, your God, is giving you. You shall not kill. You shall not commit adultery. You shall not steal. You shall not bear false witness against your neighbor. You shall not covet your neighbor's house. You shall not covet your neighbor's wife nor anything else that belongs to him." (Exodus 20:1–17)[1]

God desires justice

What care I for the number of your sacrifices? says the Lord. Trample my courts no more! Bring no more worthless offerings; your incense is loathsome to me. When you spread out your hands, I close my eyes to you. Though you pray the more, I will not listen.

Wash yourselves clean! Put away your misdeeds; cease doing evil; learn to do good. Make justice your aim: redress the wronged, hear the orphan's plea, defend the widow. (Isaiah 1:11–7)

Judge similar cases similarly

[The prophet Nathan told King David this story.] "Judge this case for me! In a certain town there were two men, one rich, the other poor. The rich man had flocks and herds in great numbers. But the poor man had nothing at all except one little ewe lamb that he had bought. He nourished her, and she grew up with him and his children. She was like a daughter to him. Now, the rich man received a visitor, but he would not take from his own flocks and herds to prepare a meal for the wayfarer who had come to him. Instead he took the poor man's ewe lamb and made a meal of it for his visitor."

David grew very angry with that man and said to Nathan: "As the Lord lives, the man who has done this merits death!"

Then Nathan said to David: "You are the man! Thus says the Lord God of Israel: 'I anointed you king of Israel. I gave you the house of Israel and of Judah. Why have you spurned the Lord and done evil in his sight? You have cut down Uriah the Hittite with the sword; you took his wife as your own.'"

Then David said to Nathan, "I have sinned against the Lord." (2 Samuel 12:1–13)

Imagine yourself in the other person's place

You shall not oppress an alien; you well know how it feels to be an alien, since you were once aliens yourselves in the land of Egypt. (Exodus 23:9)

The beatitudes

Blessed are the poor in spirit, for theirs is the kingdom of heaven. Blessed are they who mourn, for they will be comforted. Blessed are the meek, for they will inherit the land. Blessed are they who hunger and thirst for righteousness, for they will be satisfied. Blessed are the merciful, for they will be shown mercy. Blessed are the clean of heart, for they will see God. Blessed are the peacemakers, for they will be called children of God. Blessed are they who are persecuted for the sake of righteousness, for theirs is the kingdom of heaven. (Matthew 5:3–10)

The golden rule

- Do to no one what you yourself dislike. (Tobit 4:15)
- Do to others whatever you would have them do to you. This is the law and the prophets.[2] (Matthew 7:12)

• Do to others as you would have them do to you. (Luke 6:31)

Love of God and neighbor

Jesus was asked, "Teacher, which commandment in the law is the greatest?" He replied, "You shall love the Lord, your God, with all your heart, with all your soul, and with all your mind. This is the greatest and the first commandment. The second is like it: You shall love your neighbor as yourself. The whole law and the prophets depend on these two commandments." (Matthew 22:36–40)[3]

The good Samaritan

[A scholar of the law asked Jesus to clarify "love your neighbor."] He said to Jesus, "And who is my neighbor?"

Jesus replied, "A man fell victim to robbers as he went down from Jerusalem to Jericho. They stripped and beat him and went off leaving him half-dead. A priest happened to be going down that road, but when he saw him, he passed by on the opposite side. Likewise a Levite came to the place, and when he saw him, he passed by on the opposite side. But a Samaritan[4] traveler who came upon him was moved with compassion at the sight. He approached the victim, poured oil and wine over his wounds and bandaged them. Then he lifted him up on his own animal, took him to an inn and cared for him. The next day he took out two silver coins and gave them to the innkeeper with the instruction, 'Take care of him. If you spend more than what I have given you, I shall repay you on my way back.' Which of these three, in your opinion, was neighbor to the robbers' victim?"

He answered, "The one who treated him with mercy." Jesus said to him, "Go and do likewise." (Luke 10:29–37)

The sermon on the mount: love your enemies

[Jesus said:] "You have heard that it was said, 'An eye for an eye and a tooth for a tooth.' But I say to you, offer no resistance to one who is evil. When someone strikes you on (your) right cheek, turn the other one to him as well. If anyone wants to go to law with you over your tunic, hand him your cloak as well. Should anyone press you into service for one mile, go with him for two miles. Give to the one who asks of you, and do not turn your back on one who wants to borrow.

"You have heard that it was said, 'You shall love your neighbor and hate your enemy.' But I say to you, love your enemies, and pray for those who persecute you, that you may be children of your heavenly Father, for he makes his sun rise on the bad and the good, and causes rain to fall on the just and the unjust. For if you love those who love you, what recompense will you have? Do not the tax collectors do the same? And if you greet your brothers only, what is unusual about that? Do not the pagans do the same? So be perfect, just as your heavenly Father is perfect." (Matthew 5:38–48)

A new commandment

[Jesus said:] "I give you a new commandment: love one another. As I have loved you, so you also should love one another. This is how all will know that you are my disciples, if you have love for one another." (John 13:34–5)

St Paul's poem about love

If I speak in human and angelic tongues but do not have love, I am a resounding gong or a clashing cymbal. And if I have the gift of prophecy and comprehend all mysteries and all knowledge, or if I have all faith so as to move mountains but do not have love, I am nothing. If I give away everything I own but do not have love, I gain nothing.

Love is patient, love is kind. It is not jealous, it is not pompous, it is not inflated, it is not rude, it does not seek its own interests, it is not quick-tempered, it does not brood over injury, it does not rejoice over wrongdoing but rejoices with the truth. It bears all things, believes all things, hopes all things, endures all things. Love never fails.

So faith, hope, love remain, these three; but the greatest of these is love. (1 Corinthians 13:1–13)

Non-believers can know the moral law

Those who observe the law will be justified. For when the Gentiles who do not have the law by nature observe the prescriptions of the law, they are a law for themselves even though they do not have the law. They show that the demands of the law are written in their hearts. (Romans 2:13–5)

Study questions

1 Formulate the particular commandments that deal with how to treat others. How do these connect with the passage from the prophet Isaiah?
2 Explain the passage about Nathan and David – and its point.
3 How do the beatitudes differ from the ten commandments? Try to express the commandments that you formulated in question 1 as beatitudes.
4 Formulate the golden rule and the two love norms.
5 Explain the good Samaritan parable. What is the point of the parable?
6 Explain the stress on motivation and on love of enemies in the sermon on the mount.
7 What points strike you the most in St Paul's poem about love?

For further study

These excerpts are from the *New American Bible* (New York: Catholic Book Publishing, 1992). For further information, see *The Catholic Study Bible* (New York: Oxford University Press, 1990) or some other biblical commentary. Harry Gensler's *Ethics: A Contemporary Introduction* (London and New York: Routledge, 1998) discusses related views in Chapters 3 and 8.

Related readings in this anthology include Lewis (who sees ethics as based on faith in God); King (who was much influenced by the Bible in his struggles against segregation); Ricoeur (who talks about how to understand the golden rule in its Biblical context); Nagel (who sees ethics as based on concern for others but not as based on belief in God); Hertzler (who discusses love of neighbor and the golden rule); and Nietzsche (who strongly rejects Christian ideas about ethics).

Notes

1 Deuteronomy 5:6–21 also lists the commandments. The division into *ten* commandments came after Exodus and Deuteronomy were written.
2 The "law and the prophets" (the Torah and the prophetic writings) were two major parts of the Jewish Bible. Jesus summed up its moral teachings in the golden rule and in the love norms (see the next section).
3 Parallel passages include Mark 12:35–7 and Luke 20:41–4. The two norms had occurred separately in Deuteronomy 6:5 (love of God) and Leviticus 19:18 (love of neighbor). Scholars debate whether Jesus was original in combining the two.
4 Jews and Samaritans tended to dislike each other.

PART II

FURTHER APPROACHES TO MORALITY: INTUITIONISM, EMOTIVISM, AND PRESCRIPTIVISM

G. E. MOORE
Irreducible Ethical Truths

G. E. Moore, a British philosopher who lived from 1873 to 1958, was a founder of analytic philosophy and a champion of common sense. His work in ethics, which focused on what "good" means and on how we can know that something is good, set the stage for further controversies.

According to Moore, we ought always to do whatever will have the best total consequences. To determine our duty in concrete situations, we need to know, through empirical investigation, the consequences of our actions; and we also need to know, through moral intuition, what kinds of things are good in themselves. The notion of "good," which is central to ethics, is objective but indefinable; it is an error to define "good" in terms like "desired" or "socially approved." Instead, "good" just means "good" – and the basic moral principles about good are self-evident truths.

As you read the selection, ask yourself whether Moore succeeds in showing that "good" is an objective irreducible concept. What are the pros and cons of basing ethics on moral intuitions?

The questions of ethics

I have tried to distinguish two questions which moral philosophers have almost always confused: What kind of things ought to exist for their own sakes? and What kind of actions ought we to perform? I have tried to show what it is that we ask about a thing, when we ask whether it ought to exist for its own sake, is good in itself or has intrinsic value; and what it is that we ask about an action, when we ask whether we ought to do it.

Once we recognize the meaning of the questions, it becomes plain what reasons are relevant to them. For the first question, no evidence can be adduced: from no other truth can they be inferred. We can guard against error only by taking care, that we have before our minds that question, and not some other. As for the second question, any answer to it is capable of evidence and argument; but so many considerations are relevant to its truth as to make certainty impossible. Such evidence must consist of truths about the results of the action – causal truths – plus ethical truths of our first or self-evident class. Any other kind of evidence is irrelevant.

To express that ethical propositions of my first class are incapable of evidence, I have sometimes called them "Intuitions." When I call such propositions "Intuitions," I mean that they are incapable of evidence; I imply nothing as to our cognition of them.

How to define "good"

How "good" is to be defined is the most fundamental question in Ethics. If I am asked "How is good to be defined?" my answer is that it cannot be defined. Disappointing as this answer may appear, it is of great importance. It amounts to this: That propositions about the good are synthetic and never analytic;[1] and that is no trivial matter. And the same thing may be expressed by saying that nobody can foist upon us such an axiom as that "Pleasure is the only good" or that "The good is the desired" on the pretense that this is the very meaning of the word.

"Good" is a simple notion, just as "yellow" is; as you cannot explain to one who does not already know it what yellow is, so you cannot explain what good is. Definitions of the kind that I was asking for, which describe the nature of the object or notion denoted by a word, are only possible when the object or notion is complex. You can give a definition of a horse, because a horse has different properties and qualities. When you have reduced a horse to its simplest terms, then you can no longer define those terms. They are simply which you think of or perceive, and to one who cannot think of or perceive them, you can never, by any definition, make their nature known. Yellow and good are notions of that simple kind, out of which definitions are composed and with which the power of defining ceases.

"Good" is incapable of definition, in the most important sense. The most important sense of "definition" is that in which a definition states what parts invariably compose a certain whole; and in this sense "good" has no definition because it is simple and has no parts. It is one of those innumerable objects of thought which are incapable of definition, because they are the ultimate terms by which whatever is capable of definition must be defined. That there must be such terms is obvious; since we cannot define everything. There is, therefore, no intrinsic difficulty in the contention that "good" denotes a simple and indefinable quality.

Consider yellow. We may try to define it by its physical equivalent; we may state what light-vibrations must stimulate the normal eye, in order that we may perceive it. But those light-vibrations are not what we mean by yellow. Indeed we should never have been able to discover their existence, unless we had first been struck by the difference of quality between different colors. Those vibrations are what corresponds in space to the yellow which we perceive.

The naturalistic fallacy

All things which are good may be also something else, just as all things which are yellow produce a certain kind of light vibration. Ethics aims at discovering those other properties which are good. But many philosophers have thought that when they named these other properties they were defining good; that these properties were entirely the same with goodness. This view I call the "naturalistic fallacy."

Such philosophers do not agree among themselves. One will affirm that good is pleasure, another that good is that which is desired; and each will argue to prove that the other is wrong. But how is that possible? One says that good is nothing but the object of desire, and tries to prove that it is not pleasure. But from his assertion, that good just means the object of desire, one of two things must follow as regards his proof:

1. He may be trying to prove that the object of desire is not pleasure. But then where is his Ethics? The position is merely a psychological one.

2. Or the discussion is verbal. When A says "Good means pleasant" and B says "Good means desired," they may merely wish to assert that most people have used the word for what is pleasant and for what is desired respectively. And this is not a whit more an ethical discussion than the last was. They are anxious to persuade us that what they call good is what we ought to do. "Do act so, because the word 'good' is used to denote such actions": such, on this view, would be their teaching. How perfectly absurd is the reason! "You are to do this, because most people use a certain word to denote such conduct." – My dear sirs, what we want to know from you as ethical teachers, is not how people use a word; what we want to know is what is good. When people say "Pleasure is good," we cannot believe that they merely mean "Pleasure is pleasure."

Pleasure is indefinable. We can describe its relations to other things, but define it we cannot. If anybody tried to define pleasure as any other natural object, for instance, that pleasure means the sensation of red, we should laugh at him. Well, that would be the same fallacy which I have called the naturalistic fallacy. When I say "I am pleased," I do not mean that "I" am the same thing as "having pleasure." And similarly "pleasure is good" does not mean that "pleasure" is the same thing as "good." When a man confuses two natural objects with one another, there is no reason to call the fallacy naturalistic. But if he confuses "good," which is not a natural object, with any natural object, then there is a reason for calling that a naturalistic fallacy. Even if good were a natural object, that would not alter the nature of the fallacy. Only the name which I have called it would not be so appropriate. It does not matter what we call it, provided we recognize it. It is to be met with in almost every book on Ethics. It is a very simple fallacy. When we say that an apple is yellow, that does not bind us to hold that "apple" means nothing else than "yellow." Why, then, should it be different with "good"? There is no sense in saying that pleasure is good, unless good is something different from pleasure.

If "good" does not denotes something simple and indefinable, only two alternatives are possible: either it is a complex; or else it means nothing at all, and there is no such subject as Ethics. Both of these may be dismissed by a simple appeal to facts.

1. Whatever definition be offered, it may always be asked significantly of the complex so defined, whether it is itself good.[2] For instance, one might think that to be good means what we desire to desire. Now it may be true that what we desire to desire is always good; but it is doubtful whether this is the case, and the fact that we understand what is meant by doubting it, shows that we have two different notions before our minds.

2. The same consideration is sufficient to dismiss the hypothesis that "good" has no meaning. It is natural to suppose that "Pleasure is the good" does not assert a connection between two different notions, but involves only one, that of pleasure. But one who asks "Is pleasure good?" is not wondering whether pleasure is pleasure. And if he try this with each suggested definition, he will recognize that good is a unique object and we can ask how it connects with other objects. "Is this good?" is different from "Is this pleasant, or desired?" and has a distinct meaning.

"Good," then, is indefinable.

Our first conclusion as to the subject-matter of Ethics is, then, that there is a simple, indefinable, unanalyzable object of thought by reference to which it must be defined.

Study questions

1 What does Moore see as the two basic questions of Ethics? What is the proper method for arriving at answers to these questions?

2 How can we guard against errors about self-evident moral truths?

3 How is "good" to be defined?

4 Why do there have to be indefinable terms and simple properties? Can our visual term "yellow" be defined in terms of "giving such and such a wavelength of light"?
5 What is the naturalistic fallacy?
6 If naturalism were true, how could we argue from how people use words to how we ought to live?
7 How would Moore criticize the attempt to define "good" as, for example, "what we desire to desire"? Explain his reasoning here.

For further study

This selection has excerpts, sometimes simplified in wording, from George Edward Moore's *Principia Ethica* (Cambridge: Cambridge University Press, 1903), pages vii–x and 1–21. For more on his views, see the rest of this work and his *Ethics* (Oxford: Oxford University Press, 1912), which deals more with his view that our duties consist in trying to maximize good consequences. Harry Gensler's *Ethics: A Contemporary Introduction* (London and New York: Routledge, 1998) discusses Moore's intuitionism in Chapter 4 and his consequentialism in Chapter 10.

Related readings in this anthology include Ross (who defends Moore's intuitionism but criticizes his consequentialism – which our selection does not emphasize); and Ayer and Mackie (who agree that "good" cannot be defined descriptively but see it as expressing emotions instead of something objective).

Notes

1 An "analytic" statement (like "All bachelors are unmarried") is one that is necessarily true because of the meaning of words. Moore claims that statements about the good cannot be analytic.
2 This is Moore's influential "open question argument." Here is another example of how it works. Suppose that someone claims that "good" means "socially approved." We can still significantly ask "Are socially approved things necessarily good?" – and we can consistently answer "no." Hence "socially approved" and "good" do not mean the same thing.

W. D. ROSS
Objective *Prima Facie* Duties

W. D. Ross, a British philosopher who lived from 1877 to 1971, made important contributions to the study of Aristotle and to moral philosophy. In the latter area, he tried to systematize and defend our commonsense beliefs about morality.

Ross defended ethical intuitionism. He argued that there are objective ethical truths, that the basic ones are self-evident, and that skeptical attacks on morality fail. He further argued that our ethical intuitions are best captured neither by a utilitarianism that seeks to maximize good consequences nor by exceptionless principles, but by a set of *prima facie* duties that hold "other things equal."

As you read the selection, think about the duty to keep promises. Suppose that you make a promise to a friend. What, if anything, could justify breaking the promise? Is the duty to keep promises based on objective criteria? How do we know we have such duties?

Utilitarianism

An attractive theory has been put forward by Moore: that what makes actions right is that they produce more *good* than could have been produced by any other action open to the agent.

This theory is the culmination of attempts to base rightness on some result. The first attempt based rightness on the advantage or pleasure of the agent. This theory comes to grief over the fact that a great part of duty consists in observing the rights and interests of others, whatever the cost to ourselves. Plato may be right in holding that a regard for the rights of others never in the long run involves a loss of happiness for the agent. But this, if true, is irrelevant to rightness. As soon as a man does an action *because* he thinks he will promote his own interests, he is acting not from rightness but from self-interest.

Hedonistic utilitarianism supplies a much-needed amendment. It points out correctly that the fact that a pleasure will be enjoyed by the agent is no reason why he *ought* to bring it into being rather than an equal or greater pleasure to be enjoyed by another. But hedonistic utilitarianism needs a correction. Pleasure is not the only thing that we think good in itself; we think of good character, or an intelligent understanding of the world, as good or better. A great advance is made by substituting "productive of the greatest good" for "productive of the greatest pleasure."

But when a plain man fulfills a promise because he thinks he ought to, what makes him think it right is that he promised. That his act will produce the best consequences is not his reason for calling it right. What lends color to the theory we are examining is the exceptional cases in which the consequences of fulfilling a promise would be so disastrous that we judge it right not to do so. If I promised to meet a friend, I think myself justified in breaking my engagement if by doing so I could prevent a serious accident or bring relief to the victims of one. The supporters of the view we are examining hold that my thinking so is due to my thinking that I shall bring more good into existence. A different account may, however, be given. Besides the duty of fulfilling promises, I have a duty of relieving distress, and when I think it right to do the latter at the cost of the former, it is not because I think I shall produce more good but because I think it is more of a duty. If I could bring equal amounts of good into being by fulfilling my promise and by helping someone to whom I had made no promise, the former is my duty. Yet on the view that what is right is what produces the most good, it would not be so.

There are two simple theories that offer a solution for such cases. One is the view of Kant, that there are certain duties, such as those of fulfilling promises and of telling the truth, which admit of no exception. The other is the view that there is only the duty of producing good, and that all "conflicts of duties" should be resolved by asking "by which action will the most good be produced"? But it is more important that our theory fit the facts than that it be simple; the account we have given corresponds better with what we really think, that normally promise-keeping should come before benevolence, but when the good to be produced by benevolence is great and the promise comparatively trivial, the act of benevolence becomes our duty.

The "ideal utilitarianism" of Moore unduly simplifies our relations. It says that the only morally significant relation in which my neighbors stand to me is that of being possible beneficiaries by my action. They do stand in this relation to me, and this is morally significant. But they may also stand to me in the relation of promisee to promiser, of creditor to debtor, of wife to husband, of child to parent, of friend to friend, and of fellow countryman to fellow countryman; and each of these relations is the foundation of a *prima facie* duty, which is more or less incumbent on me according to the circumstances. When I am in a situation in which more than one of these *prima facie* duties is incumbent on me, I have to study the situation as fully as I can until I form the considered opinion that in the circumstances one of them is more incumbent than any other; then I am bound to think that this is my actual duty in the situation.

Our basic duties

I suggest "*prima facie* duty" to refer to the characteristic which an act has, in virtue of being of a morally significant kind (e.g. the keeping of a promise), which would make it an actual duty if it were not at the same time of another morally significant kind. Whether an act is an actual duty depends on *all* its morally significant kinds.

There is nothing arbitrary about these *prima facie* duties. Each rests on a circumstance of moral significance. Of *prima facie* duties I suggest, without claiming completeness, this division.[1]

1. Some duties rest on my previous acts. (a) Some rest on a promise or an implicit promise, such as the implicit promise not to tell lies which seems implied in the act of conversation. These are duties of fidelity. (b) Some rest on a previous wrongful act. These are duties of reparation.
2. Some rest on previous acts of other men, i.e. services done to me. These are duties of gratitude.
3. Some rest on the possibility of a distribution of pleasure or happiness not in accord with the merit of the persons concerned; there arises a duty to upset or prevent such a distribution. These are duties of justice.
4. Some rest on the fact that there are other beings in the world whose condition we can make better in virtue, intelligence, or pleasure. These are duties of beneficence.
5. Some rest on the fact that we can improve our own virtue or intelligence. These are duties of self-improvement.
6. We should distinguish from (4) the duty of not injuring others. Non-maleficence is a distinct duty of a more stringent character. We do not in general consider it justifiable to kill one person to keep another alive, or to steal from one to give alms to another.

Ideal utilitarianism does not do justice to the personal character of duty. If the only duty is to produce the most good, who is to have the good – whether myself, my benefactor, a person to whom I have made a promise, or a stranger – should make no difference. But it does make a difference.

To the objection that this catalogue of duties is unsystematic, it may be replied that it makes no claim to be ultimate. It classifies duties which reflection seems to reveal. If I have not misstated them, the list will be correct as far as it goes though not necessarily complete. If further reflection discovers a better classification, so much the better.

It may be objected that our theory in cases of conflicting *prima facie* duties leaves us with no principle to discern our actual duty. But this objection is not one which the rival theory can bring forward. For when we have to choose between the production of two goods, say knowledge and pleasure, the "ideal utilitarian" theory can only fall back on an opinion that one of the goods is the greater; and this is no better than that one of two duties is the more urgent.

There is no reason to anticipate that every act is a duty for the same reason. What makes me sure that I have a *prima facie* duty may sometimes lie in the fact that I have made a promise; in another case, it may lie in the fact that I have done a wrong. And if on reflection I find that neither of these reasons is reducible to the other, I must not assume that such a reduction is possible.

We may attempt to arrange the duties in a more systematic way. It seems self-evident that if some things are intrinsically good, then it is a *prima facie* duty to bring them into existence as much as possible. There are three main intrinsic goods – virtue, knowledge, and, with limitations, pleasure. Since a virtuous disposition, for instance, is good whether it is in myself or in another, it is my duty to bring it into existence in both cases. Pleasure is difficult; for while we recognize a duty to produce pleasure for others, it is not so clear that we recognize a duty to produce pleasure for ourselves. If there are things that are bad in themselves we ought, *prima facie*, not to bring them upon others; and on this fact rests the duty of non-maleficence.

Duties are compounded together in complex ways. Thus the duty of obeying the laws of one's country arises partly (as Socrates contends in the *Crito*) from the duty of gratitude for the benefits one has received from it; partly from the implicit promise to obey which seems involved in our residence in the country and in invoking its laws for our protection; and partly (if we are fortunate) from the fact that its laws are instruments for the general good.

I need to talk about the relation between *prima facie* and actual duties. If it is sometimes right to break a promise, there must be a difference between *prima facie* and actual duty. When we think ourselves justified in breaking a promise to relieve someone's distress, we continue to recognize a *prima facie* duty to keep our promise, and this leads us to feel, not shame or repentance, but compunction, for behaving as we do; we recognize, further, that it is our duty to make it up somehow to the promisee for the breaking of the promise. Any act contains various elements in virtue of which it falls under various categories. In virtue of being the breaking of a promise, for instance, it tends to be wrong; in virtue of being an instance of relieving distress it tends to be right. Being one's duty belongs to an act in virtue of its whole nature.

The same distinction may be found in natural laws. As subject to gravity, each body tends to move in a particular direction with a particular velocity; but its actual movement depends on *all* the forces to which it is subject. It is only by recognizing this distinction that we can preserve the absoluteness of laws of nature, and only by recognizing a corresponding distinction we can preserve the absoluteness of the principles of morality.

What in ethics is self-evident

That an act, as fulfilling a promise or promoting the good of others, is *prima facie* right, is self-evident; not that it is evident from the beginning of our lives, or as soon as we attend to it for the first time, but in the sense that when we have reached sufficient mental maturity and have given sufficient attention to the proposition it is evident without any need of proof or evidence beyond itself. It is self-evident just as a mathematical axiom, or the validity of a form of inference, is evident. The moral order expressed in these propositions is as much part of the fundamental nature of the universe (and of any possible universe with moral agents) as is the numerical structure expressed in the axioms of arithmetic. Our confidence in these propositions involves the same trust in our reason as does mathematics; and we have no justification for trusting it in the latter and distrusting it in the former. Both cases deal with propositions that cannot be proved but that need no proof.

Judgments about actual, concrete duty have none of this certainty. A statement is certain only when it is either self-evident or a valid conclusion from self-evident premises. Our judgments about particular duties are neither. (1) They are not self-evident. Where an act has two characteristics, in virtue of one of which it is *prima facie* right, and in virtue of the other *prima facie* wrong, we are not certain whether we ought to do it; we are taking a moral risk. Any act will probably in the course of time bring much good or evil for many human beings, and thus have a *prima facie* rightness or wrongness of which we know nothing. (2) Judgments about particular duties are not logical conclusions from self-evident premises. The judgment as to the rightness of a particular act is like the judgment as to the beauty of a work of art. A poem is in respect of certain qualities beautiful and in respect of others not; and our judgment as to the beauty it possesses on the whole is never reached by logical reasoning. In this and the moral case, we have probable opinions which are not logical conclusions from self-evident principles.

There is much truth in the description of the right act as a fortunate act. We cannot be certain that it is right. This does not, however, make the doing of our duty a matter of chance. There is a parallel with personal advantage. We never *know* what act will in the long run be to our advantage. Yet we are more likely to secure our advantage if we estimate to the best of our ability the probable tendencies of our actions, than if we act on caprice. And similarly we are more likely to do our duty if we reflect to the best of our ability on the *prima facie* rightness or wrongness of various possible acts, than if we act without reflection. With this greater likelihood we must be content.

The principles of duty are not self-evident from the beginning of our lives. They come to be self-evident as mathematical axioms do. We find by experience that this couple of matches and that couple make four matches: by reflection on this and similar discoveries we come to see that two and two make four. In a similar way, we see the *prima facie* rightness of a particular act of fulfilling a promise, and then of other such acts, and when we have reached sufficient maturity to think in general terms, we apprehend *prima facie* rightness to belong to any fulfillment of promise. What comes first in time is the apprehension of the *prima facie* rightness of an individual act. From this we come to apprehend the self-evident general principle.

Rightness and the best consequences

"Right" and "optimific"[2] might stand in either of two relations. (1) It might be self-evident that any act that is optimific is right and any act that is right is optimific. Moore thinks that the coextensiveness of "right" and "optimific" is self-evident; he rejects any proof of it. Or (2) we might establish that they are invariably connected by an inductive inquiry.

It might seem as if the constant connection of the two attributes was self-evident. It might seem absurd that it could be right to do what would produce consequences that are less good. Yet this is not absurd. Suppose that one has made a promise. *Prima facie* it is our duty to fulfill the promise. A slight gain in the value of the total consequences will not justify us in doing something else. Suppose that the fulfillment of a promise to A would produce 1,000 units of good[3] for him, but that by doing some other act I could produce 1,001 units of good for B, to whom I have made no promise, the other consequences being of equal value; do we think it self-evident that it is my duty to do the second act? I think not. Only a much greater disparity of value between the total consequences would justify us in violating our *prima facie* duty to A. Promises are not to be treated so lightly as this theory would imply. A promise constitutes a serious moral limitation to our freedom of action.

The coextensiveness of the right and the optimific is, then, not self-evident. There remains the question whether it can be established inductively. Such an inquiry would have to be thorough and extensive. We should have to take a large variety of the acts which we, to the best of our ability, judge to be right. We should have to trace their consequences into an unending future. But no such inductive inquiry has been carried through. Utilitarians have been so persuaded of the self-evident connection of "right" and "optimific" that they have not attempted an inductive inquiry.

Utilitarianism tries to show that the sanctity of promises rests on consequences. When you break a promise you not only fail to confer a certain advantage on your promisee but you diminish confidence in the fulfillment of promises. You thus strike a blow at a very useful practice – and you tend to bring about a state wherein each man, being unable to rely on the keeping of promises by others, will have to do everything for himself, to the impoverishment of human well-being.

Utilitarians say that the case I put never arises – the case in which by fulfilling a promise I shall bring into being 1,000 units of good for my promisee, and by breaking it 1,001 units of good for someone else, the other effects of the being of equal value. The other effects, they say, never are of equal value. By keeping my promise I strengthen the system of mutual confidence; by breaking it I weaken it; and the difference is enough to outweigh the slight superiority in the *immediate* effects of the second act.

But let us suppose the good effects of the second act to be assessed not at 1,001 but at 1,000+x (where x makes up for the deterioration of mutual confidence). Then its good effects are slightly greater than those of the fulfillment of the promise; and the utilitarian has to say that the promise should be broken. Now, is that the way we think about promises? Do we really think that the slightest total advantage, no matter who enjoys it, by the breach of a promise frees us from the obligation? To make a promise is not merely to adapt an ingenious device for promoting well-being; it is to put oneself in a new *prima facie* duty to him, not reducible to the duty of promoting the well-being of society. Also, the effect of a single promise in strengthening or weakening the fabric of mutual confidence is greatly exaggerated. And if we suppose two men dying together alone, do we think that the duty of one to fulfill a promise made to the other would be extinguished if neither act would have any effect on the general confidence? Any one who holds this has not reflected on what a promise is.

So "right" and "optimific" are not identical, and we do not know by intuition or induction that they coincide. However, when we are under no special obligation, such as to a promisee, we ought to do what will produce the most good.

Evidence for ethical principles

In what has preceded, a good deal has been made of "what we really think" about moral questions; a theory has been rejected because it does not agree with what we really think. It might be said that this is wrong; that we should not be content to expound our present moral consciousness but should criticize it in the light of theory. Now our moral consciousness has undergone a good deal of modification at the hands of moral theory. But if we are told that we should give up our view that there is a special obligatoriness to keeping promises, because it is self-evident that the only duty is to produce as much good as possible, we have to ask ourselves whether we really, when we reflect, *are* convinced that this is self-evident, and whether we *can* get rid of our view that promise-keeping has a bindingness independent of producing the maximum good. In my own experience I find that I cannot; and most people will find the same, and that they cannot lose the sense of special obligation. It seems, on reflection, self-evident that a promise, as such, is something that *prima facie* ought to be kept, and it does *not*, on reflection, seem self-evident that production of maximum good is the only thing that makes an act obligatory.

"What we think" about moral questions contains a considerable amount that we know. This forms the standard by which the truth of any moral theory has to be tested, instead of having itself to be tested by reference to a theory.

It would be a mistake to found natural science on what thoughtful and well-educated people think about the subject before they have studied it scientifically. Such opinions are often misinterpretations of sense-experience; and the man of science must appeal to sense-experience itself. In ethics no such appeal is possible. The moral convictions of thoughtful and well-educated people are the data of ethics just as sense-perceptions are the data of natural science. Just as some of the latter have to be rejected as illusory, so have some of the former; but as the latter are rejected only when they conflict with other more accurate sense-perceptions, the former are rejected only when they conflict with other convictions which stand better the test of reflection. The moral convictions of the best people is the cumulative product of the moral reflection of many generations; and this the theorist should treat with the greatest respect. The verdicts of the moral consciousness of the best people are the foundation on which he must build; though he must first compare them with one another and eliminate any contradictions they may contain.

Study questions

1   According to Moore, what makes actions right? What two approaches does his view improve upon and why is it an improvement?

2   Explain the example about a promise to meet a friend. How do the views of Moore and Kant lead to counterintuitive results about one's duty to keep promises?

3   How does utilitarianism oversimplify our moral relationships to others?

4 What is a *prima facie* duty?

5 Ross's first duty in his list could be expressed as the command "Keep your promises." Express his other duties as commands.

6 Are the duty to do good (beneficence) and the duty not to harm (non-maleficence) equally strong?

7 What kinds of things are good in themselves?

8 What does Ross mean by calling a moral principle "self-evident"? Does this mean it is evident from the beginning of our lives, or as soon as we attend to it?

9 How do we come to recognize axioms of mathematics and ethics? Why are both equally worthy of our trust?

10 Consider Ross's example about the amount of good produced by breaking or keeping a promise. Could it be right to do an act that would bring about consequences less good than those of some alternative act?

11 In what two ways could the truth of utilitarianism be evident to us? How do both ways fail?

12 How do some utilitarians object to Ross's criticism of their view based on promise keeping? How does Ross respond?

13 What is our ultimate evidence for ethical principles?

For further study

This selection has excerpts, sometimes simplified in wording, from William David Ross's *The Right and the Good* (Oxford: Clarendon Press, 1930), pages 16–41; for more on his approach, you might consult this book or his later *Foundations of Ethics* (Oxford: Clarendon Press, 1939). For the views that Ross was attacking, see G. E. Moore's *Principia Ethica* (Cambridge: Cambridge University Press, 1903) and *Ethics* (Oxford: Oxford University Press, 1912), and Immanuel Kant's *Groundwork of the Metaphysics of Morals* (New York: Harper & Row, 1964 translation by H. J. Paton, originally published in 1785). Harry Gensler's *Ethics: A Contemporary Introduction* (London and New York: Routledge, 1998) discusses Ross's intuitionism in Chapter 4 and his nonconsequentialism in Chapter 11.

Related readings in this anthology include Moore (who also defends intuitionism and self-evidence); Ayer, Mackie, and Sartre (who attack it); Mill, Singer, and Smart (who defend utilitarianism); Williams, Rawls, and O'Neill (who attack it); and Brandt (who offers a rule utilitarian alternative).

Notes

1 I am *assuming* the correctness of our main convictions on *prima facie*

duties. To me it seems as self-evident as anything could be that to make a promise is to create a moral claim. Many readers will say that they do not know this to be true. If so, I cannot prove it to them; I can only ask them to reflect again, in the hope that they will ultimately agree that they know it to be true. The main moral convictions of the plain man seem to me to be, not opinions for philosophy to prove or disprove, but knowledge from the start; I find little difficulty in distinguishing these essential convictions from other moral convictions which I have, which are merely fallible opinions. [Note from Ross]

2   Ross uses "optimific" to mean "having the best consequences."

3   I am assuming that good is objectively quantitative, but not that we can accurately assign an exact measure to it. Since it is of a definite amount, we can *suppose* that its amount is so and so, though we cannot with any confidence *assert* that it is. [Note from Ross]

A. J. AYER

Ethical Claims Express Feelings

A. J. Ayer, a British philosopher who lived from 1910 to 1989, was an advocate of logical positivism. This movement saw empirical science as our main source of knowledge and was skeptical of traditional philosophy.

Logical positivism proposed that only two types of statements make genuine truth claims (claims that are true or false). First, there are empirical statements (like "It is snowing outside"); these can in principle be shown by our sense experience to be true, or at least highly probable. Second, there are analytic statements (like "All bachelors are single"); these are true because of the meaning of words. Since moral judgments do not fit in either category, they cannot be true or false. Instead of being truth claims, they only express emotions. "This is bad" is much like "Boo on this!"

As you read the selection, ask yourself if you find Ayer's starting point plausible. Are there only two kinds of genuine truth claims? Does this emotion-based interpretation of ethics make sense to you?

Logical positivism

I require of an empirical hypothesis that some possible sense experience be relevant to determine its truth or falsehood. If a putative proposition fails this and is not a tautology, then it is metaphysical and neither true nor false but literally senseless.[1] Much philosophy is metaphysical by this criterion; in particular, it cannot be significantly asserted that there is a non-empirical world of values, that men have immortal souls, or that there is a transcendent God.

To make our position clearer, we may formulate it another way. Let us call a proposition which records an actual or possible observation an experiential proposition. Then it is the mark of a genuine factual proposition that some experiential propositions can be deduced from it with certain other premises without being deducible from those other premises alone.

An objection

There is one objection to be met before we can claim to have justified our view that all synthetic[2] propositions are empirical hypotheses. This objection is based on the supposition that our speculative knowledge is of two kinds – that which relates to empirical fact and that which relates to value. It will be said that "statements of value" are genuine synthetic propositions, but that they cannot be represented as hypotheses used to predict our sensations; and that the existence of ethics and aesthetics as speculative knowledge presents an objection to our radical empiricist thesis. In face of this objection, it is our business to give an account of "judgments of value" which is satisfactory in itself and consistent with our empiricist principles.

The ordinary system of ethics, as elaborated by ethical philosophers, is far from being a homogeneous whole. There are, first of all, definitions of ethical terms, or judgments about the legitimacy of certain definitions. Secondly, there are descriptions of moral experience and its causes. Thirdly, there are exhortations to moral virtue. Lastly, there are actual ethical judgments.

Only the first of our four classes, namely that relating to the definitions of ethical terms, is ethical philosophy. The descriptions of moral experience and its causes must be assigned to psychology or sociology. The exhortations to moral virtue are not propositions at all, but ejaculations or commands designed to provoke the reader to action. Accordingly, they do not belong to philosophy or science. As for the ethical judgments, we have not yet determined how they should be classified. But inasmuch as they are neither definitions, nor comments upon definitions, nor quotations, they do not belong to ethical philosophy. A strictly philosophical treatise on ethics should make no ethical pronouncements. But it should, by giving an analysis of ethical terms, show the category to which such pronouncements belong. And this is what we are now about to do.

Ethical philosophers often discuss whether it is possible to find definitions which would reduce all ethical terms to one or two fundamental terms. But this question is not relevant to our present inquiry. We are not now concerned to discover which term is to be taken as fundamental; whether, for example, "good" can be defined in terms of "right" or "right" in terms of "good," or both in term of "value." What we are interested in is the possibility of reducing the whole sphere of ethical terms to non-ethical terms. We are inquiring whether statements of ethical value can be translated into statements of empirical fact.

That they can be so translated is the contention of ethical philosophers called subjectivists, and of those who are known as utilitarians. The utilitarian defines the rightness of actions, and the goodness of ends, in terms of the pleasure, happiness, or satisfactions to which they give rise; the subjectivist, in terms of the feelings of approval which a certain person, or group, has towards them. Each definition makes moral judgments into a sub-class of psychological or sociological judgments. If either was correct, it would follow that ethical assertions were not generically different from factual assertions; and the account which we have already given of empirical hypotheses would apply to them also.

Nevertheless we shall not adopt either analysis. We reject the subjectivist view that to call an action right, or a thing good, is to say that it is generally approved of, because it is not self-contradictory to assert that some actions which are generally approved of are not right, or that some things which are generally approved of are not good. And we reject the alternative subjectivist view that a man who asserts that a certain action is right, or that a certain thing is good, is saying that he himself approves of it, on the ground that a man who confessed that he sometimes approved of what was bad or wrong would not be contradicting himself. And a similar argument is fatal to utilitarianism. We cannot agree that to call an action is right is say that of all the actions possible in the circumstances it would cause, or be likely to cause, the greatest happiness, or the greatest balance of pleasure over pain, or the greatest balance of satisfied over unsatisfied desire, because we find that it is not self-contradictory to say that it is sometimes wrong to perform the action which would actually or probably cause the greatest happiness, or the greatest balance of pleasure over pain, or of satisfied over unsatisfied desire. And since it is not self-contradictory to say that some pleasant things are not good, or that some bad things are desired, it cannot be that "x is good" is equivalent to "x is pleasant," or "x is desired." And therefore we should conclude that the validity of ethical judgments is not empirically calculable.

We are not denying that it is possible to invent a language in which ethical symbols are definable in non-ethical terms, or that it is desirable to invent such a language; we are denying that the reduction of ethical to non-ethical statements is consistent with the conventions of our actual language.

In admitting that normative ethical concepts are irreducible to empirical concepts, we seem to be leaving the way clear for the "absolutist" view[3] of ethics – that statements of value are controlled only by a mysterious "intellectual intuition." This makes statements of value unverifiable. For what seems intuitively certain to one person may seem doubtful, or even false, to another. Unless it is possible to provide some criterion to decide between conflicting intuitions, a mere appeal to intuition is worthless as a test of validity. In the case of moral judgments, no such criterion can be given. Some moralists claim that they "know" that their own judgments are correct. But such an assertion has not the slightest tendency to prove the validity of any moral judgment. For dissenting moralists may equally well "know" that their views are correct. When such differences arise with an empirical proposition, one may attempt to resolve them by some empirical test. But with ethical statements, there is no empirical test.

Since we claim that a synthetic proposition is significant only if it is empirically verifiable, the acceptance of an "absolutist" theory of ethics would undermine our argument. And as we have already rejected the "naturalistic" theories[4] which are supposed to provide the only alternative to "absolutism," we have reached a difficult position. We shall meet the difficulty by showing that the correct treatment of ethical statements is afforded by a third theory, which is compatible with our radical empiricism.

Ethics is based on emotions

We admit that fundamental ethical concepts are unanalyzable. So far we agree with the absolutists. But, unlike the absolutists, we are able to explain this fact about ethical concepts. We say that the reason they are unanalyzable is that they are pseudo-concepts. The presence of an ethical symbol in a proposition adds nothing to its factual content. Thus if I say to someone, "You acted wrongly in stealing that money," I am not stating anything more than if I had simply said, "You stole that money." In adding that this action is wrong I am not making any further statement. I am simply evincing my moral disapproval. It is as if I had said, "You stole that money," in a tone of horror, or written it with special exclamation marks. The tone or exclamation marks add nothing to the literal meaning. They merely show that the expression of it is attended by certain feelings in the speaker.

If I generalize my statement and say, "Stealing money is wrong," I produce a sentence with no factual meaning – that is, expresses no proposition which can be true or false. It is as if I had written "Stealing money!!" – where the shape of the exclamation marks show, by a convention, that moral disapproval is the feeling expressed. There is nothing said here which can be true or false. Another man may disagree with me about the wrongness of stealing, in the sense that he may not have the same feelings, and he may quarrel with me on account of my moral sentiments. But he cannot, strictly speaking, contradict me. For in saying that a certain type of action is right or wrong, I am not making any factual statement, not even a statement about my own state of mind. I am merely expressing moral sentiments.

What we have been saying about "wrong" applies to all normative ethical symbols. In every case in which one would be said to be making an ethical judgment, the function of the ethical word is purely "emotive." It is used to express feeling about objects, not to make any assertion about them.

Ethical terms do not serve only to express feeling. They are calculated also to arouse feeling, and so to stimulate action. Some of them are used to give commands. "It is your duty to tell the truth" may be regarded both as the expression of an ethical feeling about truthfulness and as the expression of the command "Tell the truth."

We can now see why it is impossible to find a criterion for the validity of ethical judgments. It is not because they have an "absolute" validity mysteriously independent of sense-experience, but because they have no objective validity whatsoever. If a sentence makes no statement, there is no sense in asking whether it is true or false. Moral judgments do not say anything. They are pure expressions of feeling and do not come under the category of truth and falsehood. They are unverifiable for the same reason as a cry of pain or a command is unverifiable – they do not express genuine propositions.

How this differs from subjectivism

Although our theory of ethics might be said to be radically subjectivist, it differs from the orthodox subjectivist theory. For the orthodox subjectivist does not deny, as we do, that the sentences of a moralizer express genuine propositions. His view is that they express propositions about the speaker's feelings. If this were so, ethical judgments would be capable of being true or false. They would be true if the speaker had the relevant feelings, and false if he had not.

Whereas the subjectivist holds that ethical statements assert the existence of certain feelings, we hold that ethical statements are expressions of feeling which do not necessarily involve any assertions.

The main objection to the ordinary subjectivist theory is that the validity of ethical judgments is not determined by the nature of their author's feeling.[5] And this is an objection which our theory escapes. For it does not imply that the existence of any feelings is a necessary and sufficient condition of the validity of an ethical judgment. It implies, on the contrary, that ethical judgments have no validity.

The limits of ethical reasoning

There is, however, an argument against subjectivist theories which our theory does not escape. Moore pointed out that if ethical statements were simply statements about the speaker's feelings, it would be impossible to argue about value. If a man said that thrift was a virtue, and another replied that it was a vice, they would not be disputing with one another. One would be saying that he approved of thrift, and the other that he didn't; and these might both be true. Moore held it to be obvious that we do dispute about value.

The conclusion that it is impossible to dispute value follows from our theory also. This may seem to be a very paradoxical assertion. For we do engage in disputes which are ordinarily regarded as disputes about value. But, in all such cases, the dispute is not really about value, but about fact. When someone disagrees with us about the value of an action, we do resort to argument to win him over to our way of thinking. But we do not attempt to show by our arguments that he has the "wrong" ethical feeling towards a situation whose nature he has correctly apprehended. What we attempt to show is that he is mistaken about the facts. We argue that he has misconceived the agent's motive: or that he has misjudged the effects of the action, or its probable effects in view of the agent's knowledge, or that he has failed to take into account the special circumstances. Or we employ general arguments about the effects which actions of a certain type produce. We hope that we have only to get our opponent to agree with us about the empirical facts for him to adopt the same moral attitude towards them as we do. And as the people with whom we argue generally have had the same moral education, our expectation is usually justified. But if our opponent has undergone different moral "conditioning" from ourselves, so that, even when he acknowledges the facts, he still disagrees with us about the moral value of the actions, then we abandon the attempt to convince him by argument. We say that it is impossible to argue with him because he has a distorted or undeveloped moral sense; which signifies that he employs different values from our own. We feel that our own values are superior, and therefore speak in derogatory terms of his. But we cannot bring forward any arguments. Because argument fails when we come to deal with pure questions of value, as distinct from questions of fact, we finally resort to mere abuse.

Argument is possible on moral questions only if some system of values is presupposed. If our opponent concurs with us in expressing moral disapproval of all actions of a given type t, then we may get him to condemn a particular action A, by bringing forward arguments to show that A is of type t. For whether A does or does not belong to that type is a plain question of fact. Given that a man has certain moral principles, we argue that he must, in order to be consistent, react morally to certain things in a certain way. What we do not and cannot argue about is the validity of these moral principles.

If anyone doubts the accuracy of this account of moral disputes, let him try to construct even an imaginary argument on value which does not reduce itself to an argument about logic or empirical fact. He will not succeed in producing a single example. He must then allow that the impossibility of purely ethical arguments is not a ground of objection to our theory, but rather a point in favor of it.

Ethical philosophy consists simply in saying that ethical concepts are pseudo-concepts and therefore unanalyzable. The further task of describing the different feelings that ethical terms express, and the different reactions that they provoke, is a task for the psychologist. There cannot be an ethical science, if by ethical science one means the elaboration of a "true" system of morals. As ethical judgments are mere expressions of feeling, there can be no way of determining the validity of any ethical system and no sense in asking whether any such system is true.

Study questions

1 Explain the logical positivism principle and how it leads Ayer to reject claims about values, God, and the afterlife.
2 What objection to logical positivism is based on ethics?
3 What four parts does a typical "system of ethics" have? State which of the parts are philosophical and which are not, and explain why.
4 Why does Ayer reject the idea that "good" is definable in empirical terms?
5 Why does Ayer reject the idea that moral judgments can be known by intuition as self-evident truths?
6 How does Ayer analyze moral judgments? What does "Stealing is wrong" mean? Are such judgments true or false?
7 Besides expressing feelings, what do moral judgments do?
8 What is the proper criterion for determining the validity of a moral judgment?
9 On Ayer's view, does "Stealing is wrong" mean "I disapprove of stealing" or "I dislike stealing"?
10 To what extent are ethical disagreements resolvable by rational means?

For further study

This selection has excerpts, sometimes simplified in wording, from Alfred Jules Ayer's *Language, Truth, and Logic* (New York: Dover, 1946), pages 31, 38-9, 102-12. Other defenses of emotivism include C. L. Stevenson's *Facts and Values* (New Haven: Yale University Press, 1963); William Frankena's last chapter of his *Ethics* (Englewood Cliffs, NJ: Prentice-Hall, 1973); Alan Gibbard's *Wise Choices, Apt Feelings* (Cambridge, MA: Harvard University Press, 1990); and Simon Blackburn's *Essays in Quasi-Realism* (Oxford: Oxford University Press, 1993). For more about logical positivism, see Ayer's book. Also helpful are John Passmore's "Logical positivism" and R. W. Ashby's "Verifiability principle" – both in the *Encyclopedia of Philosophy* (London and New York: Macmillan and the Free Press, 1967), edited by Paul Edwards. Harry Gensler's *Ethics: A Contemporary Introduction* (London and New York: Routledge, 1998) discusses emotivism in Chapter 5.

Related readings in this anthology include Hume and Mackie (who give somewhat analogous views); Lewis, Moore, Nagel, and Ross (who present contrasting objective views of ethics); and Hare (who tries to give rational ways of reasoning about values without assuming that there are ethical truths or ethical facts).

Notes

1   Ayer here asserts the logical positivist view that every genuine truth claim has to be either empirical (testable by sense experience) or analytic (true by definition). Whatever fails this test is "metaphysical" (by which he means "nonsensical"). He uses "tautology" as another term for "analytic."

2   Ayer uses "synthetic statement" to mean, roughly, "statement that is not true-by-definition." And he uses "proposition" to mean "truth claim" ("claim that is true or false"). So, his "All synthetic propositions are empirical" expresses his central logical positivist thesis: that all genuine truth claims are either empirical or analytic.

3   What Ayer calls the "absolutist view" is the "intuitionist" or "nonnaturalist" view held by Moore and Ross.

4   Ayer calls "naturalistic" any view that defines evaluative terms like "good" using ideas from sense experience (like "socially approved" or "productive of pleasure").

5   Here is another way to express Ayer's objection. Subjectivism says that "X is good" means "I like X." From subjectivism, the absurdity follows that if I began to like to torture people then "Torturing people is good" would become true.

J. L. MACKIE
Values Are Subjective

J. L. Mackie, an Australian philosopher who lived from 1917 to 1981, was skeptical about ethics. While admitting that ethical judgments claim to assert independent ethical truths or facts, he argued that there are no such objective ethical truths or facts.

Mackie was not a conventional subjectivist or emotivist. According to Mackie, "X is good" is not intended to describe or express our feelings; so it is not equivalent in meaning to "I like X" or "Hurrah for X!" Instead, "X is good" is intended to make a claim about an objective realm of values. But the problem, according to Mackie's "error theory," is that there is no such objective realm of values. So moral judgments, taken literally, are all false; they only succeed in expressing feelings.

As you read the selection, ask yourself whether moral judgments typically do claim objectivity and whether Mackie shows that this objectivity is an illusion.

Moral skepticism

There are no objective values. The statement is liable to provoke one of three reactions. Some will think it not merely false but pernicious; they will see it as a threat to morality and everything else worthwhile. Others will regard it as a trivial truth, too obvious to be worth mentioning. Others will say that it is meaningless or empty, that no real issue is raised by whether values are part of the fabric of the world.

The view I am adopting may be called moral skepticism. Another name is "subjectivism." But this has more than one meaning. What is often called moral subjectivism is the doctrine that "This action is right" means "I approve of this action." But the view I am now discussing is to be distinguished in two respects from any such doctrine. First, what I have called moral skepticism is a negative doctrine, not a positive one: it says what there isn't, not what there is. It says that there do not exist entities or relations of a certain kind, objective values or requirements, which many people have believed to exist. Secondly, what I have called moral skepticism is an ontological thesis, not a linguistic or conceptual one. It is not a view about the meanings of moral statements. The denial that there are objective values does not commit one to any particular view about what moral statements mean.

Is objectivity a real issue?

R. M. Hare has said that he does not understand what is meant by "the objectivity of values." We know how to recognize the activity called "thinking that some act is wrong," and it is to this that the subjectivist and the objectivist are both alluding, though one calls it "an attitude of disapproval" and the other "a moral intuition": but these are different names for the same thing. He sums up his case thus: "Think of one world into whose fabric values are objectively built, and another in which those values have been annihilated. In both worlds the people go on being concerned about the same things – there is no difference in the 'subjective' concern which people have for things, only in their 'objective' value. Now what is the difference between these two worlds? Can any answer be given except 'None whatever'?"

Subjective concern, the activity of valuing or of thinking things wrong, may go on in the same way whether there are objective values or not. But there is a difference between the two worlds. In the one there is something that backs up and validates some of the subjective concern which people have, in the other there is not. Further differences come to light if we consider how subjective concern is acquired or changed. If the fabric of the world validated certain kinds of concern, then it would be possible to acquire these merely by finding something out, by letting one's thinking be controlled by how things were. But in the world in which objective values have been annihilated, the acquiring of new subjective concern means the development of something on the emotive side by the person who acquires it.

The main tradition of European moral philosophy from Plato onwards has combined the view that moral values are objective with the recognition that moral judgments are prescriptive.[1] In Plato's theory the Forms, and in particular the form of the Good, are eternal, extramental, realities. They are a central structural element in the fabric of the world. Just knowing or "seeing" them will not merely tell men what to do but will ensure that they do it, overruling any contrary inclinations. Similarly, Kant believes that pure reason can by itself be practical, though he does not explain how it can be so.

Perhaps when Hare says that he does not understand what is meant by "the objectivity of values" he means that he cannot understand how values could be objective, he cannot frame for himself any clear, detailed, picture of what it would be like for values to be part of the fabric of the world. Even Kant hints at a similar difficulty. The difficulty of seeing how values could be objective is a strong reason for thinking that they are not so, but it is not a good reason for saying that this is not a real issue.

I believe that as well as being a real issue it is an important one. It matters for general philosophy. It would make a difference to our metaphysics if we had to find room for objective values – perhaps something like Plato's Forms – in our picture of the world. It would make a difference to our epistemology if it had to explain how such objective values can be known, and to our philosophical psychology if we allow such knowledge to direct choices and actions. Less obviously this issue will affect certain kinds of moral argument. Sidgwick considers a discussion between an egoist and a utilitarian, and points out that if the egoist claims that his happiness is objectively desirable or good, the utilitarian can argue that the egoist's happiness "cannot be more objectively desirable or more a good than the similar happiness of any other person." In other words, if ethics is built on objective goodness, then egoism as a first order system of ethics can be refuted.

Hypothetical and categorical imperatives

We may make this issue clearer by referring to Kant's distinction between hypothetical and categorical imperatives. "If you want X, then you ought to do Y" will be a hypothetical imperative if it is based on the supposed fact that Y is the only available means to X. The reason for doing Y lies in its causal connection with the desired end, X; the oughtness is contingent upon the desire. "You ought to do Y" will be a categorical imperative if you ought to do Y irrespective of any desire for any end to which Y would contribute, if the oughtness is not contingent upon any desire.

A categorical imperative would express a reason for acting which was unconditional in the sense of not being contingent upon being a means to fulfill some desire of the agent. Kant held that moral judgments are categorical imperatives and it can plausibly be maintained that many moral judgments contain a categorically imperative element. My thesis that there are no objective values is specifically the denial that any categorically imperative element is objectively valid. The objective values I deny would be action directing absolutely, not contingently upon the agent's desires and inclinations.

The claim to objectivity

My thesis may seem trivially true. Of course, some will say, valuing, preferring, and condemning are human activities, and there is no need to look for values prior to such activities. But this should not be conceded so easily. The main tradition of European moral philosophy includes the contrary claim, that there are objective values of the sort I have denied.

This objectivism is not only a feature of the philosophical tradition. It has also a firm basis in ordinary thought and the meanings of moral terms. The ordinary user of moral language means to say something that involves a call for action that is absolute, not contingent on any desire. Someone in a state of moral perplexity wants to arrive at some judgment. The question is not whether he wants to do the action, whether it will satisfy him, whether he will have a pro-attitude towards it, or even whether he can recommend such actions in relevantly similar cases. He wants to know whether this action would be wrong in itself.

The prevalence of this tendency to objectify values is confirmed by a pattern of thinking that we find in existentialists. The denial of objective values can carry with it an extreme emotional reaction, a feeling that nothing matters, that life has lost its purpose. Of course this does not follow; the lack of objective values is not a good reason for abandoning subjective concern or for ceasing to want anything. But the abandonment of a belief in objective values can cause, at least temporarily, a decay of subjective concern and sense of purpose. That it does so is evidence that the people in whom this reaction occurs have objectified their concerns and purposes, have been giving them a fictitious external authority.

This view, that conceptual analysis would reveal a claim to objectivity, is sometimes confirmed by philosophers officially on the other side. Bertrand Russell, for example, says that "ethical propositions should be expressed in the optative mood, not in the indicative"; he defends himself effectively against the charge of inconsistency in both holding ultimate ethical valuations to be subjective and expressing emphatic opinions on ethical questions. Yet at the end he admits:

> Certainly there seems to be something more. Suppose that some one were to advocate the introduction of bullfighting in this coun-
> try. In opposing the proposal, I should feel, not only that I was
> expressing my desires, but that my desires in the matter are right,
> whatever that may mean. I am not satisfied.

He concludes: "While my own opinions as to ethics do not satisfy me, those of other people satisfy me still less."

So moral judgments claim objectivity, that there are objective values. This is incorporated in the meanings of moral terms. Any analysis which omits this claim to objective, intrinsic, prescriptivity is incomplete.

If second order ethics[2] were confined to conceptual analysis, it ought to conclude that moral values are objective: that they are so is part of what our moral statements mean: the moral concepts of the ordinary man as well as of the main line of western philosophers are concepts of objective value. But conceptual analysis is not enough. The claim to objectivity, however ingrained in our language and thought, is not self-validating. It can and should be questioned. The denial of objective values will be put forward as an "error theory," a theory that although most people in making moral judgments implicitly claim to be pointing to something objectively prescriptive, these claims are all false. It is this that makes the name "moral skepticism" appropriate.

Since this goes against assumptions ingrained in our thought and built into the ways in which language is used, and since it conflicts with common sense, it needs solid support. It is not something we can accept casually. If we adopt this view, we must argue explicitly for it. Traditionally it has been supported by arguments of two main kinds, which I call the argument from relativity and the argument from queerness, but these can be supplemented in several ways.

The argument from relativity

The argument from relativity has as its premises the well-known variation in moral codes from one society to another, from one period to another, and between groups within a community. Such variation doesn't entail first or second order ethical views. Yet it may indirectly support second order subjectivism: radical differences between first order moral judgments make it difficult to treat those judgments as apprehensions of objective truths.

It is not mere disagreement that tells against the objectivity of values. Disagreement on history or biology does not show that there are no objective issues in these fields. But scientific disagreement results from inadequate evidence, and it is implausible to interpret moral disagreement the same way. Disagreement about moral codes seems to reflect different ways of life. People mainly approve of monogamy because they participate in monogamy. Of course, the standards may be an idealization of the way of life: the practice may be less rigid than the norms. And moral judgments are not purely conventional. There are moral heretics and moral reformers, people who have turned against the established rules of their communities. But this can usually be understood as the extension, in ways which seemed to be required for consistency, of rules arising out of an existing way of life. In short, the argument from relativity has some force because the variations in the moral codes are more readily explained by the hypothesis that they reflect ways of life than by the hypothesis that they express perceptions, most of them inadequate and badly distorted, of objective values.

The counter to this argument is to say that the items for which objective validity is to be claimed are not specific moral rules but rather very basic principles which are recognized at least implicitly in all societies: the principle of universalizability, perhaps; or some utilitarian principle of promoting the general happiness. Such principles, with differing concrete circumstances, will beget different moral rules.

The argument from relativity can be only partly countered in this way. One would have to say that it is only in these principles that the objective moral character attaches immediately: other moral judgments are objectively true, but only derivatively and contingently – if things had been otherwise, different sorts of actions would have been right. And despite the recent prominence of universalization, utilitarian principles, and the like, these are far from the whole of what is affirmed as basic in ordinary thought. Much of this is concerned rather with what Hare calls "ideals." People judge that some things are good or right, not because they exemplify some general principle, but because they arouse certain immediate responses. "Moral sense" or "intuition" is an initially more plausible description of what supplies many of our basic moral judgments than "reason." With regard to all these starting points of moral thinking the argument from relativity remains in full force.

The argument from queerness

Even more important is the argument from queerness. This has two parts, one metaphysical, the other epistemological. If there were objective values, then they would be entities or qualities of a strange sort, utterly different from anything else in the universe. If we were aware of them, it would have to be by some special faculty of moral perception or intuition, utterly different from ordinary ways of knowing. These points were recognized by Moore when he spoke of non-natural qualities, and by the intuitionists in their talk about a "faculty of moral intuition." Intuitionism has long been out of favor, and it is easy to point out its implausibilities. The suggestion that moral judgments are made by sitting down and having an ethical intuition is a travesty of moral thinking. But, however complex the real process, it will require some input of this distinctive sort. When we ask the awkward question, how we can be aware of this authoritative prescriptivity, of the truth of these ethical premises, none of our ordinary accounts of sensory perception or introspection or the confirming of hypotheses or inference or conceptual analysis will provide a satisfactory answer; "a special intuition" is a lame answer, but one to which the clearheaded objectivist is compelled to resort.

The best move for the objectivist is to look for companions in guilt. Richard Price argues that it is not moral knowledge alone that such an empiricism as that of Locke and Hume is unable to account for, but also our knowledge of number, identity, substance, the necessary existence and infinite extension of time and space, necessity and possibility in general, power, and causation. If the understanding, which Price defines as the faculty that discerns truth, is a source of simple ideas of so many other sorts, may it not also be a power of immediately perceiving right and wrong, which yet are real characters of actions?

This is an important counter to the argument from queerness. The only adequate reply would be to show how, on empiricist foundations, we can construct an account of the knowledge that we have of all these matters. I cannot even begin to do that here, though I have undertaken some parts of the task elsewhere. I can only state my belief that satisfactory accounts of most of these can be given in empirical terms.

How much simpler and more comprehensible would the approach to ethics be if the supposedly objective moral quality were replaced by some sort of subjective emotional response.

Patterns of objectification

Considerations of these kinds suggest that it is less paradoxical to reject the common-sense belief in the objectivity of moral values, provided that we can explain how this belief, if it is false, has become established and is so resistant to criticisms.

On a subjectivist view, we can understand the supposed objectivity of moral qualities as arising from the projection or objectification of moral attitudes. This would be analogous to the "pathetic fallacy," the tendency to read our feelings into objects. If a fungus fills us with disgust, we may ascribe to the fungus a quality of foulness. But there is more than this at work. Moral attitudes are partly social in origin: socially established patterns of behavior put pressure on individuals, and each individual tends to internalize these pressures and to join in requiring these patterns of behavior of himself and of others. Moreover, there are motives that support objectification. We need morality to control the ways in which people behave towards one another, often in opposition to contrary inclinations. We therefore want our moral judgments to be authoritative for other agents as well as for ourselves: objective validity would give them the authority required.

Another way of explaining the objectification is to say that ethics is a system of law from which the legislator has been removed. Some features of modern European moral concepts are traceable to the theological ethics of Christianity. The stress on quasi-imperative notions, on what ought to be done or on what is wrong in a sense close to "forbidden," are relics of divine commands. Admittedly, the central ethical concepts for Plato and Aristotle also are prescriptive or intrinsically action guiding, but in concentrating rather on "good" than on "ought" they show that their moral thought is an objectification of the desired and satisfying rather than of the commanded.

Elizabeth Anscombe has argued that modern, non-Aristotelian concepts of moral "ought" are survivals outside the framework of thought that made them intelligible, namely the belief in divine law.

There is much to be said for this view. But it would be a mistake to see the problem of objective prescriptivity as merely a post-operative complication of a society from which a dominant system of theistic belief has been excised. Many who admit divine commands believe moral values to have an independent authority. Responding to Plato's Euthyphro dilemma, they believe that God commands a thing because it is in itself good, not that it is good because he commands it.[3] The apparent objectivity of moral value is a widespread phenomenon which has more than one source: the persistence of a belief in something like divine law when the belief in the divine legislator has faded is only one factor. There are several different patterns of objectification, all of which have left characteristic traces in our actual moral concepts and moral language.

Study questions

1   Why is Mackie not a conventional subjectivist or emotivist?
2   What is Hare's view about the objectivity of values? Why does Mackie reject Hare's view?
3   What is the difference between a hypothetical imperative and a categorical imperative?
4   Do moral judgments claim to be objective?
5   Using the idea of a categorical imperative, explain why Mackie calls his theory "moral skepticism." About what is he skeptical?
6   Mackie sees Plato's theory of the Forms as a prime example of the views he opposes. Explain why.
7   Does Mackie think that the mere fact of moral disagreement shows that there are no moral truths? Why does he think disagreement in science is different from disagreement over moral claims?
8   Explain the argument from queerness. What is it meant to show?
9   What misleads people into thinking that moral values are objective?

For further study

This selection has excerpts, sometimes simplified in wording, from John Leslie Mackie's *Ethics: Inventing Right and Wrong* (London: Penguin, 1977), pages 15–46; for more on his view, consult this book. For views that Mackie criticizes, see Plato's *Republic* (Indianapolis: Hackett Publishing Company, 1974, translation by G. M. A. Grube); Immanuel Kant's *Groundwork for the Metaphys-*

ics of Morals (New York: Harper & Row, 1964, translation by H. J. Paton, originally published in 1785); and Elizabeth Anscombe's "Modern Moral Philosophy," in Philosophy 33 (1958): 24–42. For more on the debate about objective values, see Essays on Moral Realism (London and Ithaca, NY: Cornell University Press, 1988), edited by Geoffrey Sayre-McCord. Harry Gensler's Ethics: A Contemporary Introduction (London and New York: Routledge, 1998) discusses related issues in Chapters 2, 5, and 6.

Related readings in this anthology include Ayer, Hare, Hume, and Sartre (who oppose objective values); and Kant, Moore, Nagel, and Ross (who defend objective values).

Notes

1 See Swindal and Spurgin's sketch of the history of ethics on pages 25–40.
2 Mackie calls metaethics "second order ethics" and normative ethics "first order ethics." The introduction to this anthology explains the distinction.
3 For more on Mackie's point, see Plato's Euthyphro or Chapter 3 of Harry Gensler's Ethics: A Contemporary Introduction (London and New York: Routledge, 1998).

R. M. HARE

Universal Prescriptions

R. M. Hare, a British philosopher born who lived from 1919 to 2002, proposed a highly original "universal prescriptivism" approach to ethics.

According to Hare, moral judgments *prescribe* (express desires) *universally* (about *all* similar cases). To have a moral belief is thus to desire that a kind of act be done in the present case and in all similar cases – including cases where we imagine ourselves in another person's place. This leads to a golden-rule consistency condition. Suppose that I believe that I ought to enslave you. To be consistent, I must desire that I would be enslaved if I were in your place. If I cannot desire this, then I cannot consistently believe that I ought to enslave you.

As you read the selection, ask yourself whether moral judgments are universal prescriptions instead of truth claims. Does Hare's method of moral reasoning make sense? Does Hare succeed in making ethics rational, or are there too many escape routes?

Freedom and reason

The function of moral philosophy – or at any rate the hope with which I study it – is that of helping us to think better about moral questions by exposing the logical structure of the language in which this thought is expressed.

I ask the reader to suppose that someone (himself perhaps) is faced with a serious moral problem – one that calls forth all the powers of thought, imagination, and feeling. I wish to draw attention to two features which any such serious moral problem will have. The first is that a man who is faced with such a problem knows that it is his problem, and that nobody can answer it for him. One of the most important constituents of our freedom, as moral agents, is the freedom to form our opinions about moral questions.

Against this conviction, we have another which seems to contradict it. This is, that the answering of moral questions is, or ought to be, a rational activity. We feel that it matters what answer we give, and that finding an answer should engage our rational powers to the limit. This is why, when people grow to understand that in moral questions they are free to form their opinions, they feel this freedom not as an emancipation but as a burden.

This antinomy [paradox] is the source of nearly all the central controversies of moral philosophy. Most moral philosophers have taken their stand on one side or the other, and this left them denying important truths. It is the task of moral philosophy to look for a way of resolving the antinomy between freedom and reason. The key to the problem is the study of the concepts which brought us into perplexity.

Moral judgments are prescriptive and universalizable. Because moral judgments are universalizable, we can speak of moral thought as rational; and their prescriptivity is connected with our freedom to form our moral opinions. I shall use prescriptivity and universalizability to expound a theory of moral reasoning. I shall end with a discussion of moral questions concerning race relations, on which the views which I put forward have some bearing.

Moral reasoning

And as you would that men should do to you,
do you also to them likewise. (Luke 6:31)

The rules of moral reasoning correspond to the two features of moral judgments. When we try to decide what we ought to do, we look for an action to which we can commit ourselves (prescriptivity) and also prescribe for others in like circumstances (universalizability).

I will now try to exhibit the bare bones of the theory of moral reasoning by considering a simple example adapted from a parable (Matthew 18:23). A owes money to B, and B owes money to C, and it is the law that creditors may put their debtors into prison. B asks himself, "Can I say that I ought to take this measure against A?" He wants to do it. But when he seeks to say, "I ought to put A into prison because he will not pay me what he owes," he reflects that this involves accepting "Anyone who is in my position ought to put his debtor into prison if he does not pay." But C is in the same position of unpaid creditor with regard to himself (B), and the cases are otherwise identical; if anyone in this position ought to put his debtors into prison, then so ought C to put him (B) into prison. To accept the moral prescription "C ought to put me into prison" would commit him to accepting "Let C put me into prison"; and this he is not ready to accept. But then neither can he accept the judgment that he (B) ought to put A into prison for debt.

A provisional moral principle has been rejected because its consequences proved unacceptable. Any rational activity has its discipline, and this is the discipline of moral thought: to test the moral principles that suggest themselves to us by following out their consequences and seeing whether we can accept them.

We must ask what we have to have for such moral arguments to work. The first requisite is that the facts of the case should be given. Secondly we have the logical framework provided by the meaning of the word "ought" (i.e. prescriptivity and universalizability). Because moral judgments have to be universalizable, B cannot say that he ought to put A into prison for debt without committing himself to the view that C, who is in the same position vis-à-vis himself, ought to put him into prison; and because moral judgments are prescriptive, this would be, in effect, prescribing to C to put him into prison; and this he is unwilling to do, since he has a strong inclination not to go to prison. This inclination gives us the third ingredient: if B did not mind what happened to himself or to anybody else, the argument would not touch him. The three necessary ingredients, then, are (1) facts; (2) logic; (3) inclinations. These enable us, not to arrive at an evaluative conclusion, but to reject an evaluative proposition.

The example was made simpler by supposing that B actually stood to some other person in exactly the same relation as A does to him. This is not necessary for the argument; it is sufficient that he should consider hypothetically such a case. That hypothetical cases will do as well as actual ones enables us to guard against a possible misinterpretation. It might be thought that what moves B is the *fear* that C will actually do to him as he does to A. But this fear is not only irrelevant to the moral argument; it does not even provide a strong nonmoral motive unless the circumstances are exceptional. C may, after all, not find out what B has done to A.

In most cases a power of imagination and readiness to use it is a fourth ingredient in moral arguments, alongside logic, facts, and inclinations. The absence of one ingredient may render the rest ineffective. For example, impartiality by itself is not enough. If, in becoming impartial, B became completely apathetic, then there would be nothing to make him accept or reject one moral principle rather than another. That is why those who advocate "Ideal Observer Theories" of ethics[1] sometimes postulate as their imaginary ideal observer an impartially sympathetic spectator. To take another example, if the person had no imagination, then the fact that someone can do the same thing to him may pass him by. If, again, he lacks the readiness to universalize, then the vivid imagination of the sufferings which he is inflicting on others may only spur him on to intensify them, to increase his own vindictive enjoyment. And if he is ignorant of the facts (for example about what is likely to happen to a person if one takes out a writ against him), then there is nothing to tie the argument to particular choices.

Escape routes

The best way of testing the argument is to consider ways in which B might escape from it. There are a number of such ways; and all of them may be successful, at a price. We may classify these maneuvers into two kinds. There are first the moves which depend on using the moral words in a different way. Secondly, there are moves which can be made by B, even though he is using the moral words in the same way as we are.

Two people using the word "ought" in the same way may disagree about what ought to be done in a certain situation, either because they differ about the facts, or because one of them lacks imagination, or because their different inclinations make one reject some prescription which the other can accept. For all that, ethics (i.e. the logic of moral language) is a powerful engine for producing moral agreement, for if two people are willing to use the moral word "ought," and to use it in the way that I have been describing, the other sources of disagreement are eliminable. People's inclinations about most important matters tend to be the same (few people, for example, like being starved or run over by motor-cars). The facts are often, given patience, ascertainable. Imagination can be cultivated. If these three factors are looked after, agreement on the use of "ought" is the only other necessary condition for producing moral agreement in typical cases. And this agreement in use is normally already there; all that is needed is to think clearly.

[Hare then analyzes cases where the opponent either uses "ought" in some non-standard way or else refuses to make moral judgments. In these cases, the opponent is not entering the moral arena and so cannot be defeated by moral argument. The opponent also might say, "Yes, I desire that I would be imprisoned in this case"; this desire would be unusual, especially since imprisonment will not help to get the money back.]

The remaining maneuver consists in asserting that there are morally relevant differences between his case and that of others. In our example, we have ruled this out by assuming that the case of B and C is exactly similar to that of A and B; from this it follows that there are no morally relevant differences. Since the B/C case may be a hypothetical one, this condition of exact similarity can always be fulfilled, and this maneuver is based on a misconception.

Suppose that B alleges that the fact that A has black skin entitles him, B, to put him in prison, but that C ought not to do the same thing to him, B, because his skin is white. The answer to this is implicit in what has been said about hypothetical cases. The fact that no two actual cases are identical has no bearing on the problem. We only have to imagine an identical case in which the roles are reversed. What does B say about a hypothetical case in which he has a black skin, and A and C are white-skinned? This forces him to count as morally relevant only those properties which he allows to be relevant even when other people have them. And this rules out special pleading.

Our argument does not involve any deduction of a moral judgment from a factual statement about people's inclinations. We are not saying "You are averse to this being done to you in a hypothetical case; and from this it follows logically that you ought not to do it to another." This would be a breach of Hume's Law ("No 'ought' from an 'is'"), to which I have declared my adherence.[2] The point is, rather, that his inclinations being what they are, he cannot assent sincerely to a certain singular prescription, and if he cannot do this, he cannot assent to a universal prescription which entails it, when conjoined with factual statements about circumstances whose truth he admits. If he assented to the factual statements and the universal prescription, but refused to assent to the singular prescription, he would be guilty of a logical inconsistency.

If, on the other hand, a man says "I want to be put in prison, if ever I am in that situation," we can accuse him of having eccentric desires. But it is not an incorrect use of words to want eccentric things. Logic does not prevent me from wanting to be put in a gas chamber if a Jew. It is in the logical possibility of wanting anything that the "freedom" in my title consists. And that lets by the "fanatic."

It is possible for a man to hold an ideal which requires that he should be sent to a gas chamber if a Jew. For reason to have a place in morals it is not necessary to close this escape by means of a logical barrier; it is sufficient that, men and the world being what they are, hardly anybody is going to take it with his eyes open. When we are arguing with the vast majority who are not going to take it, the reply that somebody else *might* take it does not help his case.

Race relations

What is needed to consolidate the theoretical suggestions is to apply them to an important moral problem.[3] The best problem is that which arises when there is conflict between races. Allusion has already been made to this problem; but it deserves a more extended treatment. By "more extended," I do not mean a comprehensive treatment; for that would take us into history, sociology, psychology, and politics. Any treatment which does not include these other fields is truncated and superficial; for we need to know why (historically and psychologically) people give way to racial bitterness, and what changes in social conditions would remove it. And we discover that there are many people who are unable to adopt the philosophical approach which looks for rational arguments and is prepared to test their cogency. It is no use hoping by philosophy alone to make them change; a deep understanding of psychology is required. Moreover, it would be necessary to consider the scientific basis, if there is one, of the classification of people into races, and of the grading of these races in intelligence and other qualities (if such is possible, which seems doubtful). But there is a philosophical problem involved, whose neglect will also make any account superficial. We need to determine what is right and wrong about the way people behave; and to this end we must examine how it is possible to reason cogently about moral questions.

[Hare then analyzes various arguments about racism.] Having dealt with a number of arguments which are unsatisfactory, and with others which are incomplete, in that they appeal to antecedent moral principles, we come now to the constructive part of this chapter. It is based on the account of moral language and moral reasoning given in the preceding chapters.

Let us ask, first, why factual arguments are relevant to moral questions. What need is supplied by the bogus claim that Germans have some special element in their heredity which distinguishes them from other men? Or why does it make a difference that a certain policy would have a certain result? It looks as if facts are held to be relevant to moral arguments. But why is this?

Facts are relevant to moral arguments because they make a difference between cases which would otherwise be similar. Let us consider why the Nazis set so much store by the claim that there is something in the blood of Germans which differentiates them from other races. The explanation is that they were proposing to treat other races in a different way from Germans, and wanted a reason why they ought to do this. It is part of the meanings of the moral words that we are logically prohibited from making different moral judgments about two cases when we cannot adduce any difference which is the ground for the difference in moral judgments. This is one way of stating universalizability. Since the Nazi cannot justify his different treatment of Germans and Jews without adducing some difference between their cases, he invents a difference. What is important to the would-be discriminator is that there should be some qualitative difference between the class of people whom he wishes to oppress, exploit, or persecute and those whom he does not.

Now these examples of spurious moral reasoning are parodies. How do we distinguish the parody from its original? If we do not think that it is an adequate justification for discriminating against a person that his skin is black, how would we distinguish those features which justify different treatment from those which do not?

There are those who try to answer this question in the following way. They look at the differences that people call morally relevant; they list them, reduce them to a system, and then say that we mean by "morally relevant difference" just these differences, and mean by "morality" just that system of evaluations which takes these, and no other, differences into account. There are many objections to this procedure; I will here mention just two. First, how do we know that we could not get a different list if we did the investigation in South Africa, or Soviet Russia, or ancient Sparta? Secondly, to make such a list does not explain anything; we want to know what leads to things getting put on the list or left off it. The proponents of this view have not gone far enough in their search for an explanation.

Let us suppose that we are having an argument with a man who maintains that a black skin, by itself, is a sufficient ground for discrimination. We tell him, and he believes, the following story. The Soviet Institute of Race Relations (a more enterprising body than its Western counterparts) has just succeeded in breeding a new kind of bacillus, which Soviet agents are at this very moment broadcasting in areas of racial conflict throughout the world. This bacillus is very catching, and the symptom of the disease which it induces is that, if the patient's skin was white, it turns permanently black, and vice versa. Now when the person with whom we are arguing has absorbed this story, we ask him whether he still thinks that skin-color by itself is a sufficient ground for moral discrimination. It is unlikely that he will go on saying that it is; for then he will have to say that if he catches the disease the former blacks will have acquired the right to oppress *him*, and all his formerly white friends.

There are two stages in the process of universalization. The first is when we have found a universal principle, not containing proper names or other singular terms,[4] from which the moral judgment which we want to make follows, given the facts. This stage is easy to pass, even for proponents of scandalous moral views. It is passed, for example, by the principle that it is all right for black people to be oppressed by white people. But the next stage is more difficult. It is necessary, not merely that this principle should be produced, but that the person actually hold it. It is necessary not merely to *quote* a maxim, but (in Kantian language) to *will* it to be a universal law. Here prescriptivity, the second logical feature of moral judgments, makes its appearance. For willing it to be a universal law involves willing it to apply even when the roles played by the parties are reversed. And this test will be failed by all maxims or principles which look attractive to oppressors on the first test. If we apply these two tests, both founded on the logical, formal features of moral terms, we shall be able to sort out, in the field of race relations, the grounds of discrimination which we are prepared to count as morally relevant from those which we are not.

However there is an escape for the sufficiently determined racialist. Let us suppose that there is a racialist the mainspring of whose racialism is a horror of miscegenation; the source of this horror is not any belief about the consequences of miscegenation. So he is not moved by alleged facts about the weakening of the human stock by mating between people of different colors, or about the unsatisfactory life lived by people of mixed descent. If these were his grounds, we could argue with him in a scientific way, trying to show that the offspring of mixed marriages are just as likely to be vigorous and intelligent; or that the bad social effects of miscegenation would be removed if he and people like him abandoned their attempts to enforce a color bar. Rather, his grounds are simply a horror of the idea of a black man mating with a white woman. This cannot be touched by any scientific or factual argument. It may be that, if miscegenation is to be prevented, it is necessary to have a rigid color bar and other repressive measures. Then it will be hard for us to argue with this man. He detests miscegenation so much that he is prepared to live in a police state to avoid it.

And he must be prepared for more than this. He must, if he is going to universalize his moral judgments, be prepared that he should not merely live in a police state, but live in it in the same conditions as he is now prepared to make the blacks live in. He must be prepared that he should be subject to arbitrary arrest and maltreatment on grounds of skin color, and to butchery if he tries to protest.

Now it may be that there are people that fanatical; but there are very few. The repression happens because these few people have on their side a multitude of other people who are not prepared to suffer thus, but who have not thought through the argument. They think, perhaps, that all will be well without too much repression; or that blacks do not mind being treated like this; or that there is a scientific basis for belief in racial superiority. All these beliefs can perhaps be refuted by scientists and others without any help from the philosopher; but they are apt, collectively, to form an amalgam in the minds of racialists which makes into allies of the fanatic many people who are not, in themselves, in the least fanatical. The contribution of the philosopher is to take this amalgam apart, deposit such beliefs as are open to scientific refutation in the in-trays of the scientists, and, when the scientists have dealt with them, exhibit the prescriptive remainder of racialism for what it is – something that fanatics may hold but which the bulk of a people – even a people as hard-pressed as the white South Africans – never will.

Study questions

1 Explain the antinomy between freedom and reason. How does Hare's view try to resolve the antinomy?
2 Explain universalizability and prescriptivity. To what rules of reasoning do these lead?
3 Making use of the two-debtor example, explain how golden-rule reasoning works in ethics.
4 What four elements are needed for golden-rule reasoning to work?
5 How is Hare's approach like that of the ideal observer and divine command theories?

6   How can an opponent escape from Hare's golden-rule reasoning?
7   What are some non-philosophical aspects of racialism? Is everyone open to rational argument on such matters as racialism?
8   What are some general questions of fact allegedly relevant to controversies about race relations?
9   Sketch Hare's argument against racialism.

For further study

This selection has excerpts, sometimes simplified in wording, from Richard Mervyn Hare's *Freedom and Reason* (Oxford: Clarendon Press, 1963), pages v, 1–6, 86–111, 203–4, and 213–21. Hare's *The Language of Morals* (Oxford: Clarendon Press, 1952) gave an earlier form of the view and focused more on moral language. Hare's later *Moral Thinking* (Oxford: Clarendon Press, 1981) used the same general approach to defend utilitarianism. Harry Gensler's *Ethics: A Contemporary Introduction* (London and New York: Routledge, 1998) discusses Hare's view in Chapter 6; his *Formal Ethics* (London and New York: Routledge, 1998) has technical criticisms of Hare's approach in Section 6.5.

Related readings in this anthology include Ayer (who also sees moral judgments as not making truth claims); Mackie (who discusses Hare's view on moral objectivity); Kant, Nagel, O'Neill, and Sartre (whose approaches have some similarities to that of Hare); Hertzler and Ricoeur (who also discuss the golden rule); Singer and Smart (utilitarians who assume something like Hare's analysis of ethical terms); and Benedict, Gensler and Tokmenko, and King (who also discuss racial segregation).

Notes

1   There are affinities, though also differences, between this type of theory and my own. Since for many Christians God occupies the role of "ideal observer," the moral judgments which they make may be expected to coincide with those arrived at by the method which I am advocating. [Note from Hare]
2   Hume's Law claims that one cannot validly deduce a moral conclusion from descriptive premises alone. For example, "People ought not to kill" does not follow from "Killing is disapproved by society."
3   Hare published this in 1963, when Dr Martin Luther King and President John F. Kennedy were opposing segregation in the United States.
4   Hare requires that basic moral principles not use proper names (like "Hare") or pointer terms (like "me"). So "Everyone ought to serve Hare" and "Everyone ought to serve me" cannot be basic moral principles.

JEAN-PAUL SARTRE
An Existentialist Ethics

Jean-Paul Sartre, a French philosopher who lived from 1905 to 1980, was a staunch defender of existentialism. Though Kierkegaard, Nietzsche, and Heidegger had already laid the groundwork for existentialism, Sartre was responsible for much of its philosophical formulation. He also popularized it through his plays, novels, and literary essays.

Existentialism is primarily an ontological theory, and thus about the nature of being. Sartre sees the ontology of the *human* being as unique because its existence precedes its essence. Since Sartre thinks a God would necessarily pre-determine our essence before our existence, Sartre finds the very idea of God dehumanizing.

Though not itself an ethical theory, existentialism has ethical implications. Existentialism stresses freedom and personal responsibility; if we turn from these, then we are guilty of "bad faith." Sartre also demands that a kind of universality guide our actions: in choosing for ourselves we must choose "for all." Thus we are responsible for others.

This selection was written shortly after World War II, during which some of the French had collaborated with the Nazis. Sartre was critical of the collaborators, whom he saw as abnegating their responsibilities. Do Sartre's existentialist views give good grounds for such criticisms?

Existentialism

What is meant by the term *existentialism*? Most people who use the word would be rather embarrassed if they had to explain it. Yet it can be defined easily. What complicates matters is that there are two kinds of existentialist; first, those who are Christian, among whom I would include Jaspers and Gabriel Marcel, both Catholic; and on the other hand the atheistic existentialists, among whom I class Heidegger, and then the French existentialists and myself.[1] What they have in common is that they think that existence precedes essence, or, if you prefer, that subjectivity must be the starting point.

Just what does that mean? Let us consider some object that is manufactured, for example, a paper-cutter: here is an object which has been made by an artisan whose inspiration came from a concept. Thus, the paper-cutter is at once an object produced in a certain way and one having a specific use; and one can not postulate a man who produces a paper-cutter but does not know what it is used for. For the paper-cutter, essence – that is, the ensemble of both the production routines and the properties which enable it to be both produced and defined – precedes existence.

When we conceive God as the Creator, He is generally thought of as a superior sort of artisan. When God creates He knows exactly what He is creating. Thus, the concept of man in the mind of God is comparable to the concept of paper-cutter in the mind of the manufacturer. Thus, the individual man is the realization of a certain concept in the divine intelligence.

In the eighteenth century, the atheism of the *philosophes* discarded the idea of God, but not the notion that essence precedes existence. Man has a human nature; this human nature, which is the concept of the human, is found in all men, which means that each man is a particular example of a universal concept, man. Thus, here too the essence of man precedes the historical existence that we find in nature.

Atheistic existentialism, which I represent, is more coherent. It states that if God does not exist, there is at least one being in whom existence precedes essence, a being who exists before he can be defined by any concept, and that this being is man. What is meant here by saying that existence precedes essence? It means that, first of all, man exists, turns up, appears on the scene, and, only afterwards, defines himself. If man, as the existentialist conceives him, is indefinable, it is because at first he is nothing. Only afterward will he be something, and he himself will have made what he will be. Thus, there is no human nature, since there is no God to conceive it.

Man is nothing else but what he makes of himself. Such is the first principle of existentialism. It is also what is called subjectivity, the name we are labeled with when charges are brought against us. But what do we mean by this, if not that man has a greater dignity than a stone or table? For we mean that man first exists, that is, that man first of all is the being who hurls himself toward a future and who is conscious of imagining himself as being in the future. Man is at the start a plan which is aware of itself. Thus, existentialism's first move is to make every man aware of what he is and to make the full responsibility of his existence rest on him. And when we say that a man is responsible for himself, we do not only mean that he is responsible for his own individuality, but that he is responsible for all men.

Universality

When we say that man chooses his own self, we mean that every one of us does likewise; but we also mean that in making this choice he also chooses all men. In fact, in creating the man that we want to be, there is not a single one of our acts which does not at the same time create an image of man as we think he ought to be. To choose is to affirm at the same time the value of what we choose, because we can never choose evil. We always choose the good, and nothing can be good for us without being good for all.

Thus, our responsibility is much greater than we might have supposed, because it involves all mankind. If I am a workingman and choose to join a Christian trade-union rather than be a communist, and if by being a member I want to show that the best thing for man is resignation, that the kingdom of man is not of this world, I am not only involving my own case – I want to be resigned for everyone. As a result, my action has involved all humanity. To take a more individual matter, if I want to marry, to have children; even if this marriage depends solely on my own circumstances or passion or wish, I am involving all humanity in monogamy and not merely myself. Therefore, I am responsible for myself and for everyone else. I am creating a certain image of man of my own choosing. In choosing myself, I choose man.

Anguish

This helps us understand what the content is of such rather grandiloquent words as anguish, forlornness, despair. As you will see, it's all quite simple.

The existentialists say that man is anguish. What that means is this: the man who involves himself and who realizes that he is not only the person he chooses to be, but also a lawmaker who is, at the same time, choosing all mankind as well as himself, can not help escape the feeling of his total and deep responsibility. Of course, there are many people who are not anxious; but we claim that they are hiding their anxiety, that they are fleeing from it. Certainly, many people believe that when they do something, they themselves are the only ones involved, and when someone says to them, "What if everyone acted that way?" they shrug their shoulders and answer, "Everyone doesn't act that way." But really, one should always ask himself, "What would happen if everybody looked at things that way?" There is no escaping this disturbing thought except by a kind of double-dealing. A man who lies and makes excuses for himself by saying "not everybody does that," is someone with an uneasy conscience, because the act of lying implies that a universal value is conferred upon the lie.

For every man, everything happens as if all mankind had its eyes fixed on him and were guiding itself by what he does. And every man ought to say to himself, "Am I really the kind of man who has the right to act in such a way that humanity might guide itself by my actions?" And if he does not say that to himself, he is masking his anguish.

There is no question here of the kind of anguish which would lead to quietism,[2] to inaction. It is a matter of a simple sort of anguish that anybody who has had responsibilities is familiar with. For example, when a military officer takes the responsibility for an attack and sends a certain number of men to death, he chooses to do so, and in the main he alone makes the choice. Doubtless, orders come from above, but they are too broad; he interprets them, and on this interpretation depend the lives of ten or fourteen or twenty men. In making a decision he can not help having a certain anguish. All leaders know this anguish. That doesn't keep them from acting; on the contrary, it is the very condition of their action. For it implies that they envisage a number of possibilities, and when they choose one, they realize that it has value only because it is chosen.

When we speak of forlornness, we mean only that God does not exist and that we have to face all the consequences of this. The existentialist is strongly opposed to a certain kind of secular ethics which would like to abolish God with the least possible expense. About 1880, some French teachers tried to set up a secular ethics which went something like this: God is a useless and costly hypothesis; we are discarding it; but, meanwhile, in order for there to be an ethics, a society, a civilization, it is essential that certain values be taken seriously and that they be considered as having an a priori[3] existence. It must be obligatory, a priori, to be honest, not to lie, not to beat your wife, to have children, etc. So we're going to try a little device which will make it possible to show that values exist all the same, inscribed in a heaven of ideas, though God does not exist.

The existentialist, on the contrary, thinks it very distressing that God does not exist, because all possibility of finding values in a heaven of ideas disappears along with Him; there can no longer be an a priori Good, since there is no infinite and perfect consciousness to think it. Nowhere is it written that the Good exists, that we must be honest, that we must not lie; because we are on a plane where there are only men. Dostoievsky said, "If God did not exist, everything would be possible." That is the very starting point of existentialism. Indeed, everything is permissible if God does not exist, and as a result man is forlorn, because neither within him nor without does he find anything to cling to. He cannot start making excuses for himself.

If existence really does precede essence, there is no explaining things away by reference to a fixed and given human nature. In other words, there is no determinism, man is free, man is freedom. On the other hand, if God does not exist, we find no values or commands to turn to which legitimize our conduct. So, in the bright realm of values, we have no excuse behind us, nor justification before us. We are alone, with no excuses.

That is the idea I shall try to convey when I say that man is condemned to be free. Condemned, because he did not create himself, yet, in other respects is free; because, once thrown into the world, he is responsible for everything he does.

No omens

The existentialist does not think that man is going to help himself by finding in the world some omen by which to orient himself. Because he thinks that man will interpret the omen to suit himself. Therefore, he thinks that man, with no support and no aid, is condemned every moment to invent man.

To give an example which will enable you to understand forlornness better, I shall cite the case of one of my students who came to see me: his older brother had been killed in the German offensive of 1940, and the young man, with immature but generous feelings, wanted to avenge him. His mother lived alone with him; the boy was her only consolation.

The boy was faced with the choice of leaving for England and joining the Free French Forces – leaving his mother behind – or remaining with his mother and helping her to carry on. He was fully aware that the woman lived only for him and that his going off – and perhaps his death – would plunge her into despair. He was also aware that every act that he did for his mother's sake was a sure thing, in that it was helping her to carry on, whereas every effort he made toward going off and fighting was an uncertain move which might run aground and prove completely useless; for example, on his way to England he might, while passing through Spain, be detained indefinitely in a Spanish camp. As a result, he was faced with two very different kinds of action: one, concrete, immediate, but concerning only one individual; the other concerned an incomparably vaster group, a national collectivity, but for that very reason was dubious. And, at the same time, he was wavering between two kinds of ethics. On the one hand, an ethics of sympathy, of personal devotion; on the other, a broader ethics, but one whose efficacy was more dubious. He had to choose between the two.

Who could help him choose? Christian doctrine? No. Christian doctrine says, "Be charitable, love your neighbor, take the more rugged path, etc." But which is the more rugged path? Whom should he love as a brother? The fighting man or his mother? Which does the greater good, the vague act of fighting in a group, or the concrete one of helping a particular human being to go on living? Who can decide a priori? Nobody. No book of ethics can tell him. The Kantian ethics says, "Never treat any person as a means, but as an end." Very well, if I stay with my mother, I'll treat her as an end and not as a means; but by virtue of this very fact, I'm running the risk of treating the people around me who are fighting, as means; and, conversely, if I go to join those who are fighting, I'll be treating them as an end, and, by doing that, I run the risk of treating my mother as a means.

If values are vague, and if they are always too broad for the concrete and specific case that we are considering, the only thing left for us is to trust our instincts. That's what this young man tried to do; and when I saw him, he said, "In the end, feeling is what counts. I ought to choose whichever pushes me in one direction. If I feel that I love my mother enough to sacrifice everything else for her – my desire for vengeance, for action, for adventure – then I'll stay with her. If, on the contrary, I feel that my love for my mother isn't enough, I'll leave."

But how is the value of a feeling determined? What gives his feeling for his mother value? Precisely the fact that he remained with her. I may say that I like so-and-so well enough to sacrifice a certain amount of money for him, but I may say so only if I've done it. I may say "I love my mother well enough to remain with her" if I have remained with her. The only way to determine the value of this affection is, precisely, to perform an act which confirms and defines it. But, since I require this affection to justify my act, I find myself caught in a vicious circle.

The feeling is formed by the acts one performs; so, I can not refer to it in order to act upon it. Which means that I can neither seek within myself the true condition which will impel me to act, nor apply to a system of ethics for concepts which will permit me to act. You will say, "At least, he did go to a teacher for advice." But if you seek advice from a priest, for example, you have chosen this priest; you already knew, more or less, just about what advice he was going to give you. In other words, choosing your adviser is involving yourself. If the young man chooses a priest who is resisting or collaborating, he has already decided on the kind of advice he's going to get. Therefore, in coming to see me he knew the answer I was going to give him, and I had only one answer to give: "You're free, choose, that is, invent." No general ethics can show you what is to be done; there are no omens in the world. The Catholics will reply, "But there are." Granted – but, in any case, I myself choose the meaning they have.

Further charges

We have answered a number of the charges concerning existentialism. You see that it can not be taken for a philosophy of quietism, since it defines man in terms of action; nor for a pessimistic description of man – there is no doctrine more optimistic, since man's destiny is within himself; nor for an attempt to discourage man from acting, since it tells him that the only hope is in his acting and that action is the only thing that enables a man to live. Consequently, we are dealing here with an ethics of action and involvement.

Nevertheless, we are charged with immuring man in his private subjectivity. We are told, "So you're able to do anything, no matter what!" In one sense choice is possible, but what is not possible is not to choose. I can always choose, but I ought to know that if I do not choose I am still choosing.

What art and ethics have in common is that we have creation and invention in both cases. We can not decide a priori what there is to be done. I pointed that out quite sufficiently when I mentioned the case of the student who came to see me, and who might have applied to all the ethical systems, Kantian or otherwise, without getting any sort of guidance. He was obliged to devise his law himself. Never let it be said by us that this man – who, taking affection, individual action, and kind-hearted-ness toward a specific person as his ethical first principle, chooses to remain with his mother, or who, preferring to make a sacrifice, chooses to go to England – has made an arbitrary choice. Man makes himself. He isn't ready made at the start. In choosing his ethics, he makes himself, and force of circumstances is such that he can not abstain from choosing one. We define man only in relationship to involvement. It is therefore absurd to charge us with arbitrariness of choice.

In the second place, it is said that we are unable to pass judgment on others. In a way this is true, and in another way, false. It is true in this sense, that, whenever a man sanely and sincerely involves himself and chooses his configuration, it is impossible for him to prefer another configuration. But, nevertheless, one can still pass judgment. First, one can judge (and this is perhaps not a judgment of value, but a logical judgment) that certain choices are based on error and others on truth. If we have defined man's situation as a free choice, with no excuses, every man who takes refuge behind the excuse of his passions, every man who sets up a determinism, is a dishonest man.

The objection may be raised, "But why mayn't he choose himself dishonestly?" I reply that I am not obliged to pass moral judgment on him, but that I do define his dishonesty as an error. One can not help considering the truth of the matter. Dishonesty is obviously a falsehood because it belies the complete freedom of involvement. On the same grounds, I maintain that there is also dishonesty if I choose to state that certain values exist prior to me. Suppose someone says to me, "What if I want to be dishonest?" I'll answer, "There's no reason for you not to be, but I'm saying that the strictly coherent attitude is that of honesty."

Besides, I can bring moral judgment to bear. When I declare that freedom in every concrete circumstance can have no other aim than to want itself, if man has once become aware that in his forlornness he imposes values, he can no longer want but one thing, and that is freedom, as the basis of all values. That doesn't mean that he wants it in the abstract. A man who belongs to a communist or revolutionary union wants concrete goals; these goals imply an abstract desire for freedom; but this freedom is wanted in something concrete. We want freedom for freedom's sake and in every particular circumstance. And in wanting freedom we discover that it depends entirely on the freedom of others, and that the freedom of others depends on ours. I can take freedom as my goal only if I take that of others as a goal as well. Consequently, when, in all honesty, I've recognized that man is a being in whom existence precedes essence, that he is a free being who, in various circumstances, can want only his freedom, I have at the same time recognized that I can want only the freedom of others.

Therefore though the content of ethics is variable, a certain form of it is universal. Kant says that freedom desires both itself and the freedom of others. Granted. But he believes that the formal and the universal are enough to constitute an ethics. We, on the other hand, think that principles which are too abstract run aground in trying to decide action. Once again, take the case of the student. In the name of what, in the name of what great moral maxim do you think he could have decided, in perfect peace of mind, to abandon his mother or to stay with her? There is no way of judging. The content is always concrete and thereby unforeseeable; there is always the element of invention. The one thing that counts is knowing whether the inventing that has been done, has been done in the name of freedom.

The third objection is the following: "Fundamentally, values aren't serious, since you choose them." My answer to this is that I'm quite vexed that that's the way it is; but if I've discarded God the Father, there has to be someone to invent values. You've got to take things as they are. Moreover, to say that we invent values means nothing else but this: life has no meaning a priori. Before you come alive, life is nothing; it's up to you to give it a meaning, and value is nothing else but the meaning that you choose.

From these few reflections it is evident that nothing is more unjust than the objections that have been raised against us. Existentialism is nothing else than an attempt to draw all the consequences of a coherent atheistic position. It isn't trying to plunge man into despair at all. But if one calls every attitude of unbelief despair, like the Christians, then the word is not being used in its original sense. Existentialism isn't so atheistic that it wears itself out showing that God doesn't exist. Rather, it declares that even if God did exist, that would change nothing. There you've got our point of view. Not that we believe that God exists, but we think that the problem of His existence is not the issue. In this sense existentialism is optimistic, a doctrine of action, and it is plain dishonesty for Christians to make no distinction between their own despair and ours and then to call us despairing.

Study questions

1　According to Sartre, what is existentialism's "first move"?
2　How does he use the example of a paper cutter to illustrate the distinction between essence and existence?
3　Sartre claims that each of our acts creates "an image of man as we think he ought to be." How could one criticize this claim?

4 What are the ramifications of his claim "we can never choose evil"? Does Sartre mean this literally?

5 What causes our anguish, according to Sartre?

6 On his terms, why must an existentialist be an atheist?

7 What does he mean by his famous phrase that man is "condemned to be free"?

8 Sartre says that no ethical system or advisor can tell the student in his example what decision to make. Is he correct about this? If he is, then can there be any such thing as an ethical theory?

9 Why can Sartre claim that his existentialism is optimistic?

10 If you adopted his version of existentialism, would you act differently from how you act now? If yes, in what ways would you act differently? If no, then why would you not act differently?

For further study

This selection has excerpts, sometimes simplified in wording, from a lecture Sartre gave in 1946, translated by B. Frechtman in *Existentialism and Human Emotions* (New York: Philosophical Library, 1957), pages 12–51. It was originally published in *L'Existentialisme est un Humanisme* (Paris: Nagel, 1946). For more on Sartre's ethics, see his "Freedom and Responsibility" in *Existentialism and Human Emotion*, pages 52–9; his play *No Exit* (New York: Alfred A. Knopf, 1949); and his "Freedom and Responsibility" and "Ethical Implications," in *Being and Nothingness* (Secaucus, NJ: The Citadel Press, 1977), pages 529–35, 543–6.

Other examples of existentialist ethical writings include Kierkegaard's "Truth Is Subjectivity," in *Concluding Unscientific Postscript* (Princeton: Princeton University Press, 1968); Heidegger's Introduction to *Being and Time* (New York: Harper, 1962); Gabriel Marcel's "What is a Free Man," in *Man Against Mass Society* (Chicago: Gateway, 1962); Karl Jaspers's "Freedom," in *Philosophy II* (Chicago: University of Chicago Press, 1969); Albert Camus's novels *The Stranger* (New York: Alfred A. Knopf, 1946), *The Myth of Sisyphus* (New York: Alfred A. Knopf, 1955), and *The Fall* (New York: Alfred A. Knopf, 1956); Maurice Merleau-Ponty's "Freedom" in *The Phenomenology of Perception* (New York: Humanities Press, 1962); Simon de Beauvoir's *The Second Sex* (New York: Alfred Knopf, 1952); Martin Buber's *I and Thou* (New York: Charles Scribner, 1970); and Paul Tillich's *The Courage to Be* (New Haven: Yale University Press, 1952).

Related readings in this volume include Ayer, Hume, and Mackie (who also have subjective approaches to ethics); Habermas, Hare, Kant, and Nagel (who also endorse universalization); Moore and Ross (who defend objective values on a non-religious basis – an approach that Sartre criticizes); and C. S. Lewis (who bases ethics on religion).

Notes

1   Sartre here refers to Karl Jaspers (1883–1969), a German who analyzed decision making in the context of struggle, guilt, and death; Gabriel Marcel (1889–1973), a Frenchman who used existentialism to illuminate Catholic philosophical concerns, such as the existence of God, the analogy of being, and a spirituality of transcendence; and Martin Heidegger (1889–1976), an influential German who analyzed human existence phenomenologically in respect to its temporal and historical character.

2   Sartre uses "quietism" to refer to an attitude of inaction in the face of individual and social problems. Historically, the term referred to a form of Christian mysticism that enjoined contemplation and the beatific annihilation of the will.

3   Sartre uses "a priori" to refer to knowledge not based on sense experience.

PART III

ETHICAL METHODOLOGY: JUSTIFYING MORAL CLAIMS, THE GOLDEN RULE, AND TWO APPLICATIONS

WILLIAM K. FRANKENA
Moral Justification

William K. Frankena, an American philosopher who lived from 1912 to 1994, was known for his broad interests in moral philosophy and for his moderate and sensible philosophical views.

Frankena proposes that you arrive at moral beliefs by imagining what you would favor from a certain perspective, which he calls the "moral point of view." You try to be rational (informed, clearheaded, and so forth) and concerned about everyone's good; then you see what you favor from this perspective. Your moral belief is "rational" or "justified" if you would favor it from this perspective; your belief is "true" if everyone who was ideally rational and took this perspective would agree.

As you read the selection, ask yourself if you find Frankena's method plausible. Are there other elements that you would like to add? Do you find his defense of the moral life convincing?

A theory of justification

What makes some normative judgments moral, some aesthetic, and some prudential is the fact that different points of view are taken in the three cases, and that the point of view taken is indicated by the kinds of reasons that are given. Consider three judgments: (a) I say that you ought to do X and give as the reason the fact that X will help you succeed in business; (b) I say you should do Y and cite as the reason the fact that Y will produce a striking contrast of colors; and (c) I say you should do Z and give as the reason the fact that Z will keep a promise or help someone. Here the reason I give reveals the point of view I am taking and the kind of judgment I am making.

Now let us take up the justification of nonmoral normative judgments. We are interested primarily in judgments of intrinsic value such as were discussed in the previous chapter,[1] for such judgments are relevant to ethics because, through the principle of beneficence,[2] the question of what is good or bad comes to bear on the question of what is right or wrong. We cannot *prove* basic judgments of intrinsic value in any strict sense of proof, but this fact does not mean that we cannot justify them or reasonably claim them to be justified. But how can we do this? By taking what I shall call the evaluative point of view as such, unqualified by any such adjective as "aesthetic," "moral," or "prudential," and then trying to see what judgment we are led to make when we do so, considering the thing in question wholly on the basis of its intrinsic character, not its consequences or conditions.

What is it to take the nonmorally evaluative point of view? It is to be free, informed, clear-headed, impartial, willing to universalize; in general, it is to be "calm" and "cool" in one's consideration of such items as pleasure, knowledge, and love, for the question is simply what it is rational to choose. If one considers an item in this reflective way and comes out in favor of it, one is rationally justified in judging it to be intrinsically good, even if one cannot prove one's judgment. In doing so, one claims that everyone else who does likewise will concur; and one's judgment is really justified if this claim is correct, which, of course, one can never know for certain. If others who also claim to be calm and cool do not concur, one must reconsider to see if both sides are really taking the evaluative point of view, considering only intrinsic features, clearly understanding one another, and so on. More one cannot do and, if disagreement persists, one may still claim to be right (i.e., that others will concur eventually if ...); but one must be open-minded and tolerant.

What about the justification of moral judgments? First, we must take the moral point of view, as Hume indicated, not that of self-love or aesthetic judgment, nor the more general point of view involved in judgments of intrinsic value. We must also be free, impartial, willing to universalize, conceptually clear, and informed about all possibly relevant facts. Then we are justified in judging that a certain act or kind of action is right, wrong, or obligatory, and in claiming that our judgment is objectively valid, at least as long as no one who is doing likewise disagrees. Our judgment or principle is really justified if it holds up under sustained scrutiny of this sort from the moral point of view on the part of everyone. Suppose we encounter someone who claims to be doing this but comes to a different conclusion. Then we must do our best, through reconsideration and discussion, to see if one of us is failing to meet the conditions in some way. If we can detect no failing on either side and still disagree, we may and I think still must each claim to be correct, for the conditions never are perfectly fulfilled by both of us and one of us may turn out to be mistaken after all. If what was said about relativism is true, we cannot both be correct. But both of us must be open-minded and tolerant if we are to go on living within the moral institution of life and not resort to force or other immoral or nonmoral devices.

If this line of thought is acceptable, then we may say that a basic moral judgment, principle, or code is justified or "true" if it is or will be agreed to by everyone who takes the moral point of view and is clearheaded and logical and knows all that is relevant about himself, mankind, and the universe.

The fact that moral judgments claim a consensus on the part of others does not mean that the individual thinker must bow to the judgment of the majority in his society. He is not claiming an *actual* consensus, he is claiming that in the end – which never comes or comes only on the Day of Judgment – his position will be concurred in by those who freely and clear-headedly review the relevant facts from the moral point of view. In other words, he is claiming an *ideal* consensus that transcends majorities and actual societies. One's society and its code and institutions may be wrong. Here enters the autonomy of the moral agent – he must take the moral point of view and must claim an eventual consensus with others who do so, but he must judge for himself.

The moral point of view

What is the moral point of view? According to one theory, one is taking the moral point of view if and only if one is willing to universalize one's maxims. Kant would probably accept this if he were alive. But I pointed out that one may be willing to universalize from a prudential point of view; and also that what one is willing to universalize is not necessarily a moral rule. A more plausible characterization to my mind, however, is that of Kurt Baier. He holds that one is taking the moral point of view if one is not being egoistic, one is doing things on principle, one is willing to universalize one's principles, and in doing so one considers the good of everyone alike.

Hume thought that the moral point of view was that of sympathy, and it seems to me he was on the right wavelength. I have already argued that the point of view involved in a judgment can be identified by the kind of reason that is given for the judgment when it is made or if it is challenged. Then the moral point of view can be identified by determining what sorts of facts are reasons for moral judgments or moral reasons. Roughly following Hume, I now want to suggest that moral reasons consist of facts about what actions, dispositions, and persons do to the lives of sentient beings, including beings other than the agent in question, and that the moral point of view is that which is concerned about such facts.

My own position, then, is that one is taking the moral point of view if and only if (a) one is making normative judgments about actions, desires, dispositions, intentions, motives, persons, or traits of character; (b) one is willing to universalize one's judgments; (c) one's reasons for one's judgments consist of facts about what the things judged do to the lives of sentient beings in terms of promoting or distributing nonmoral good and evil; and (d) when the judgment is about oneself or one's own actions, one's reasons include such facts about what one's own actions and dispositions do to the lives of other sentient beings as such, if others are affected. One has a morality or moral action-guide only if and insofar as one makes normative judgments from this point of view and is guided by them.

Why be moral?

Why should we take part in the moral institution of life? Why should we adopt the moral point of view?

We have already seen that the question, "Why should ... ?" is ambiguous, and may be a request either for motivation or for justification. Here, then, one may be asking for (1) the motives for doing what is morally right, (2) a justification for doing what is morally right, (3) motivation for adopting the moral point of view and otherwise subscribing to the moral institution of life, or (4) a justification of morality and the moral point of view. It is easy to see the form an answer to a request for (1) and (3) must take; it will consist in pointing out the various prudential and non-prudential motives for doing what is right or for participating in the moral institution of life. Most of these are familiar or readily thought of and need not be detailed here. A request for (2) might be taken as a request for a *moral* justification for doing what is right. Then, the answer is that doing what is morally right does not need a justification, since the justification has already been given in showing that it is right. On this interpretation, a request for (2) is like asking, "Why morally ought I to do what is morally right?" A request for (2) may also, however, be meant as a demand for a nonmoral justification of doing what is morally right; then, the answer to it will be like the answer to a request for (4). For a request for (4), being a request for reasons for subscribing to the moral way of thinking, judging, and living, must be a request for a nonmoral justification of morality. What will this be like?

There seem to be two questions here. First, why should *society* adopt such an institution as morality? Why should it foster such a system for the guidance of conduct in addition to convention, law, and prudence? To this the answer seems clear. The conditions of a satisfactory human life for people living in groups could hardly obtain otherwise. The alternatives would seem to be either a state of nature in which all or most of us would be worse off than we are, even if Hobbes[3] is wrong in thinking that life in such a state would be "solitary, poor, nasty, brutish, and short"; or a leviathan civil state more totalitarian than any yet dreamed of, one in which the laws would cover all aspects of life and every possible deviation by the individual would be closed off by an effective threat of force.

The other question has to do with the nonmoral reasons (not just motives) there are for an *individual's* adopting the moral way of thinking and living. To some extent, the answer has just been given, but only to some extent. For on reading the last paragraph an individual might say, "Yes. This shows that society requires morality and even that it is to my advantage to have others adopt the moral way of life. But it does not show that I should adopt it, and certainly not that I should *always* act according to it. And it is no use arguing on moral grounds that I should. I want a nonmoral justification for thinking I should." Now, if this means that he wants to be shown that it is always to his advantage – that is, that his life will invariably be better or, at least, not worse in the prudential sense of better and worse – if he thoroughly adopts the moral way of life, then I doubt that his demand can always be met. Through the use of various familiar arguments, one can show that the moral way of life is likely to be to his advantage, but it must be admitted in all honesty that one who takes the moral road may be called upon to make a sacrifice and, hence, may not have as good a life in the nonmoral sense as he would otherwise have had.

Nonmoral justification is not necessarily egoistic or prudential. If A asks B why he, A, should be moral, B may reply by asking A to try to decide in a rational way what kind of a life he wishes to live or what kind of a person he wishes to be. That is, B may ask A what way of life A would choose if he were to choose rationally, or in other words, freely, impartially, and in full knowledge of what it is like to live the various alternative ways of life, including the moral one. B may then be able to convince A, when he is calm and cool in this way, that the way of life he prefers, all things considered, includes the moral way of life. If so, then he has justified the moral way of life to A. A may even, when he considers matters in such a way, prefer a life that includes self-sacrifice on his part.

Of course, A may refuse to be rational, calm, and cool. He may retort, "But why should I be rational?" However, if this was his posture in originally asking for justification, he had no business asking for it. For one can only ask for justification if one is willing to be rational. One cannot consistently ask for reasons unless one is ready to accept reasons of some sort. Even in asking, "Why should I be rational?" one is implicitly committing oneself to rationality, for such a commitment is part of the connotation of the word "should."

What kind of a life A would choose if he were fully rational and knew all about himself and the world will, of course, depend on what sort of a person he is (and people are different), but if psychological egoism is not true of any of us, it may always be that A would then choose a way of life that would be moral. As Bertrand Russell once wrote:

> We have wishes which are not purely personal ... The sort of life that most of us admire is one which is guided by large, impersonal desires ... Our desires are, in fact, more general and less purely selfish than many moralists imagine ...[4]

Perhaps A has yet one more question: "Is society justified in demanding that I adopt the moral way of life, and in blaming and censuring me if I do not?" If A is asking whether society is morally justified in requiring of him at least a certain minimal subscription to the moral institution of life, then the answer surely is that society sometimes is justified in this, as Socrates argued in the *Crito*. But society must be careful here. For it is itself morally required to respect the individual's autonomy and liberty, and in general to treat him justly; and it must remember that morality is made to minister to the good lives of individuals and not to interfere with them any more than is necessary. Morality is made for man, not man for morality.

Study questions

1 What distinguishes *moral* normative judgments from normative judgments that are *aesthetic* or *prudential*?
2 What is the "nonmorally evaluative point of view" and how can we use it to justify nonmoral judgments of intrinsic value?
3 What is the "moral point of view" and how can we use it to justify moral judgments? Under what conditions can we call a moral judgment "true"?
4 Why should society foster morality?
5 Are thinking and living morally always in one's self-interest?
6 What is it to "choose rationally"? Would we choose to live the moral life if we were to choose rationally?

For further study

This selection has excerpts from William K. Frankena's *Ethics* (Englewood Cliffs, NJ: Prentice-Hall, 1972), pages 110–16. For a collection of Frankena's essays, see *Perspectives on Morality*, edited by K. E. Goodpaster (Notre Dame, IN: University of Notre Dame Press, 1976). For a related view, see Kurt Baier's *The Moral Point of View* (New York: Random House, 1965), especially Chapter 5. For Thomas Hobbes's view, see his *Leviathan* (Oxford: Basil Blackwell, 1947, first published in 1651); Richard Brandt gave a more recent version of this view in his "Rationality, egoism, and morality," in the *Journal of Philosophy* 69 (1972): 681–97. Harry Gensler's *Ethics: A Contemporary Introduction* (London and New York: Routledge, 1998) discusses how to justify moral judgments in Chapter 9.

Related readings in this anthology include Habermas, Hare, Hume, Kant, and Rawls – all of whom talk about justifying ethical judgments from a rational perspective.

Notes

1 Frankena earlier argued that various things – not just pleasure and the avoidance of pain – are intrinsically good. Judgments about intrinsically

good relate equally to moral judgments (which are concerned with every-one's good) and to prudential judgments about self-interest (which are concerned with one's individual good).

2   Frankena's principle of beneficence directs us to do good and avoid harm. More precisely, it includes these four duties, in increasing order of strength: to promote good, to remove harm (what is bad), to prevent harm, and not to inflict harm.

3   Frankena refers to Thomas Hobbes (1588–1679), who saw people as enlightened egoists who agree to social rules to protect their own inter-ests. In an imagined "state of nature" prior to society, people out of self-interest would frequently lie, steal, and kill; this would make life miserable for everyone. To avoid these problems, enlightened egoists would agree to have an absolute monarch enforce social rules; the chief among these rules would be the golden rule: "Treat others as you want to be treated." Contemporary followers of Hobbes (like Richard Brandt) replace this "absolute monarch" with various kinds of sanctions. People who violate the social rules are made to suffer external sanctions like disapproval, alienation, and legal penalties, and internal sanctions like guilt, anxiety, and the loss of self-respect. People who follow the social rules are praised and made to feel their self-worth.

4   *Religion and Science* (New York: Henry Holt and Co., 1935), pp. 252–4. [Note from Frankena]

JÜRGEN HABERMAS
Discourse Ethics

Jürgen Habermas, a German philosopher born in 1929, is a member of the Frankfurt School and a proponent of critical theory. Started by a group of German sociologists, political scientists, and philosophers between the world wars, critical theory is an interdisciplinary analysis of social, economic, and cultural phenomena. The founders of critical theory borrowed heavily from Marx and Freud, and rejected all forms of irrationality.

Habermas develops a theory of rationality that is particularly sensitive to social and ethical issues. He criticizes theories that reject moral truths; he sees such theories as not sufficiently protecting us from social domination and repression. By modifying some ideas from Kant and G. H. Mead, Habermas develops an approach based on the conditions of rational discussion and intersubjective agreement.

As you read the selection, ask yourself how well Habermas characterizes the conditions for rational discussion. How plausible it is to justify moral norms on the basis of argument and agreement alone?

Universalization

In what follows, I presuppose that a theory of [moral] argumentation must take the form of an "informal logic," because it is impossible to *force* agreement on theoretical and moral-practical issues either by means of deduction or on the basis of empirical evidence.

In theoretical discourse the gap between particular observations and general hypotheses is bridged by some canon or other of induction. An analogous bridging principle is needed for practical discourse. Accordingly, all studies of the logic of moral argumentation end up having to introduce a moral principle as a rule of argumentation that has a function equivalent to the principle of induction in the discourse of the empirical sciences.

Interestingly enough, in trying to identify such a moral principle, philosophers of diverse backgrounds always come up with principles whose basic idea is the same. *All* variants of cognitivist ethics[1] take their bearings from the basic intuition contained in Kant's categorical imperative. What I am concerned with here is not the diversity of Kantian formulations but their underlying idea, which is designed to take into account the impersonal or general character of valid universal commands. The moral principle is so conceived as to exclude as invalid any norm that could not meet with the qualified assent of all who are or might he affected by it. This bridging principle, which makes consensus possible, ensures that only those norms are accepted as valid that express a *general will*. As Kant noted time and again, moral norms must be suitable for expression as "universal laws." He focuses on "that inner contradiction which promptly arises for an agent's maxim when his behavior can lead to its desired goal only upon the condition that it is not universally followed."

The principle of universalization is by no means exhausted by the requirement that moral norms must take the *form* of unconditionally universal "ought" statements. The *grammatical form* of normative statements alone, which does not permit such sentences to refer to or be addressed to particular groups or individuals, is not a sufficient condition for valid moral commands, for we could give such universal form to commands that are plainly immoral. What is more, in some respects the requirement of formal universality may well be too restrictive; it may make sense to submit nonmoral norms of action (whose range of jurisdiction is socially and spatiotemporally limited) to a practical discourse (restricted in this case to those affected and hence relative), and to test them for generalizability.

Other philosophers subscribe to a less formalistic view of the consistency required by the principle of universality. Their aim is to avoid the contradictions that occur when equal cases are treated unequally and unequal ones equally. R. M. Hare has given this requirement the form of a semantic postulate. As we do when we attribute descriptive predicates ("is red"), so we should attribute normative predicates ("is of value," "is good," "is right") in *conformity with a rule,* using the same linguistic expression in all cases that are the same in the respects relevant to the particular case. Applied to moral norms, Hare's consistency postulate comes to this: every individual, before making a particular norm the basis for his moral judgment, should test whether he can advocate or "will" the adoption of this norm by every other individual in a comparable situation. This or another similar postulate is suitable to serve as a moral principle only if it is conceived as a warrant of impartiality in the process of judging. But one can hardly derive the meaning of impartiality from the notion of consistent language use.

Kurt Baier and Bernard Gert come closer to this meaning of the principle of universalization when they argue that valid moral norms must be generally teachable and publicly defendable. The same is true of Marcus Singer when he proposes the requirement that norms are valid only if they ensure equality of treatment. The intuition expressed in the idea of the generalizability of maxims intends something more than this, namely, that valid norms must *deserve* recognition by *all* concerned. True impartiality pertains only to that standpoint from which one can generalize precisely those norms that can count on universal assent because they perceptibly embody an interest common to all affected. It is these norms that deserve intersubjective recognition. Thus the impartiality of judgment is expressed in a principle that constrains *all* affected to adopt the perspectives of *all others* in the balancing of interests. The principle of universalization is intended to compel the *universal exchange of roles* that G. H. Mead called "ideal role taking" or "universal discourse." Thus every valid norm has to fulfill the following condition:

> (U) *All* affected can accept the consequences and the side effects its *general* observance can be anticipated to have for the satisfaction of *everyone's* interests (and these consequences are preferred to those of known alternative possibilities for regulation).

Discourse ethics

We should not mistake this principle of universalization (U) for the following principle, which already contains the distinctive idea of an ethics of discourse.

> (D) Only those norms can claim to be valid that meet (or could meet) with the approval of all affected in their capacity *as participants in a practical discourse.*

This principle of discourse ethics (D), to which I will return after offering my justification for (U), already *presupposes* that we *can* justify our choice of a norm. At this point in my argument, that presupposition is what is at issue. I have introduced (U) as a rule of argumentation that makes agreement in practical discourses possible whenever matters of concern to all are open to regulation in the equal interest of everyone. Once this bridging principle has been justified, we will be able to make the transition to discourse ethics. I have formulated (U) in a way that precludes a monological application of the principle. First, (U) regulates only argumentation among a plurality of participants; second, it suggests the perspective of real-life argumentation, in which all affected are admitted as participants. In this respect my universalization principle differs from the one John Rawls proposes.

Rawls wants to ensure impartial consideration of all affected interests by putting the moral judge into a fictitious "original position," where differences of power are eliminated, equal freedoms for all are guaranteed, and the individual is left in a condition of ignorance with regard to the position he might occupy in a future social order. Like Kant, Rawls operationalizes the standpoint of impartiality in such a way that every individual can undertake to justify basic norms on his own. The same holds for the moral philosopher himself. It is only logical, therefore, that Rawls views the substantive parts of his study, not as the *contribution* of a participant in argumentation to a process of discursive will formation regarding the basic institutions of late capitalist society, but as the outcome of a "theory of justice," which he as an expert is qualified to construct.

If we keep in mind the action-coordinating function that normative validity claims play in the communicative practice of everyday life, we see why the problems to be resolved in moral argumentation cannot be handled monologically but require a cooperative effort. By entering into a process of moral argumentation, the participants continue their communicative action in a reflexive attitude with the aim of restoring a consensus that has been disrupted. Moral argumentation thus serves to settle conflicts of action by consensual means. Conflicts in the domain of norm-guided interactions can be traced directly to some disruption of a normative consensus. Repairing a disrupted consensus can mean one of two things: restoring intersubjective recognition of a validity claim after it has become controversial or assuring intersubjective recognition for a new validity claim that is a substitute for the old one. Agreement of this kind expresses a *common will*. If moral argumentation is to produce this kind of agreement, however, it is not enough for the individual to reflect on whether he can assent to a norm. It is not even enough for each individual to reflect in this way and then to register his vote. What is needed is a "real" process of argumentation in which the individuals concerned cooperate. Only an intersubjective process of reaching understanding can produce an agreement that is reflexive in nature; only it can give the participants the knowledge that they have collectively become convinced of something.

From this viewpoint, the categorical imperative needs to be reformulated as follows: "Rather than ascribing as valid to all others any maxim that I can will to be a universal law, I must submit my maxim to all others for purposes of discursively testing its claim to universality. The emphasis shifts from what each can will without contradiction to be a general law, to what all can will in agreement to be a universal norm." This version of the universality principle does in fact entail the idea of a cooperative process of argumentation. For one thing, nothing better prevents others from perspectively distorting one's own interests than actual participation. It is in this pragmatic sense that the individual is the last court of appeal for judging what is in his best interest. On the other hand, the descriptive terms in which each individual perceives his interests must be open to criticism by others. Needs and wants are interpreted in the light of cultural values. Since cultural values are always components of intersubjectively shared traditions, the revision of the values used to interpret needs and wants cannot be a matter for individuals to handle monologically.

The rules behind an ideal-guided moral discourse

We must return to the justification of the principle of universalization. We are now in a position to specify the role that the transcendental-pragmatic argument can play in this process. Its function is to help to show that the principle of universalization, which acts as a rule of argumentation, is implied by the presuppositions of argumentation in general. This requirement is met if the following can be shown:

> Every person who accepts the universal and necessary communicative presuppositions of argumentative speech and who knows what it means to justify a norm of action implicitly presupposes as valid the principle of universalization, whether in the form I gave it above or in an equivalent form.

It makes sense to distinguish three levels of presuppositions of argumentation along the lines suggested by Aristotle: those *at* the logical level of products, those at the dialectical level of procedures and those at the rhetorical level of processes. First, reasoning or argumentation is designed to *produce* intrinsically cogent arguments with which we can redeem or repudiate claims to validity. This is the level at which I would situate the rules of a minimal logic currently being discussed by Popperians, for example, and the consistency requirements proposed by Hare and others. For simplicity I will follow the catalog of presuppositions of argumentation drawn up by R. Alexy. For the logical-semantic level, the following rules can serve as *examples*:

(1.1) No speaker may contradict himself.
(1.2) Every speaker who applies predicate F to object A must be prepared to apply F to all other objects resembling A in all relevant aspects.
(1.3) Different speakers may not use the same expression with different meanings.

The presuppositions of argumentation at this level are logical and semantic rules that have no ethical content. They are not a suitable point of departure for a transcendental-pragmatic argument.

In *procedural* terms, arguments are processes of reaching understanding that are ordered in such a way that proponents and opponents, having assumed a hypothetical attitude and being relieved of the pressures of action and experience, can test validity claims that have become problematic. At this level are located the pragmatic presuppositions of a special form of interaction, namely everything necessary for a search for truth organized in the form of a competition. Examples include recognition of the accountability and truthfulness of all participants in the search. At this level I also situate general rules of Jurisdiction and relevance that regulate themes for discussion, Contributions to the argument, etc. Again I cite a few examples from Alexy's catalog of rules:

(2.1) Every speaker may assert only what he really believes.
(2.2) A person who disputes a proposition or norm not under discussion must provide a reason for wanting to do so.

Some of these rules obviously have an ethical import. At this level what comes to the fore are presuppositions common both to discourses and to action oriented to reaching understanding as such, e.g., presuppositions about relations of mutual recognition.

But to fall back here directly on the basis of argumentation in action theory would be to put the cart before the horse. Yet the presuppositions of an unrestrained competition for better arguments are relevant to our purpose in that they are irreconcilable with traditional ethical philosophies that have to protect a dogmatic core of fundamental convictions from all criticism.

Finally, in *process* terms, argumentative speech is a process of communication that, in light of its goal of reaching a rationally motivated agreement, must satisfy improbable conditions. In argumentative speech we see the structures of a speech situation immune to repression and inequality in a particular way: it presents itself as a form of communication that adequately approximates ideal conditions. This is why I tried at one time to describe the presuppositions of argumentation as the defining characteristics of an ideal speech situation. I cannot here undertake the elaboration, revision, and clarification that my earlier analysis requires, and accordingly, the present essay is rightly characterized as a sketch or a proposal. The intention of my earlier analysis still seems correct to me, namely the reconstruction of the general symmetry conditions that every competent speaker who believes he is engaging in an argumentation must presuppose as adequately fulfilled. The presupposition of something like an "unrestricted communication community," an idea that Apel developed following Peirce and Mead, can be demonstrated through systematic analysis of performative contradictions. Participants in argumentation cannot avoid the presupposition that, owing to certain characteristics that require formal description, the structure of their communication rules out all external or internal coercion other than the force of the better argument and thereby also neutralizes all motives other than that of the cooperative search for truth.

Following my analysis, R. Alexy has suggested the following rules of discourse for this level:

(3.1) Every subject with the competence to speak and act is allowed to take part in a discourse.

(3.2) a. Everyone is allowed to question any assertion whatever.

   b. Everyone is allowed to introduce any assertion whatever into the discourse.

   c. Everyone is allowed to express his attitudes, desires, and needs.

(3.3) No speaker may be prevented, by internal or external coercion, from exercising his rights as laid down in (3.1) and (3.2).

A few explanations are in order here. Rule (3.1) defines the set of potential participants. It includes all subjects without exception who have the capacity to take part in argumentation. Rule (3.2) guarantees all participants equal opportunity to contribute to the argumentation and to put forth their own arguments. Rule (3.3) sets down conditions under which the rights to universal access and to equal participation can be enjoyed equally by all, that is, without the possibility of repression, be it ever so subtle or covert.

If these considerations are to amount to more than a definition favoring an ideal form of communication and thus prejudging everything else, we must show that these rules of discourse are not mere *conventions;* rather, they are inescapable presuppositions. The presuppositions themselves are identified by convincing a person who contests the hypothetical reconstructions offered that he is caught up in performative contradictions.

Study questions

1   How does Habermas define a "bridging principle"? Why are such principles needed? What is Habermas's bridging principle for ethics?

2   What is cognitivist ethics? How does Habermas argue that Kantian ethics is the ground for all cognitivist ethics?

3   Explain Habermas's principles (U) and (D). How does (U) bring in consequences?

4   For Habermas, what is the significance of "recognition" for ethics? How does recognition impact the formulation of (U)?

5   Why does Habermas avoid what he calls "monological application" of (U)? Whom would he accuse of monological application?

6   In what ways are the approaches of Habermas and Rawls similar? How does Habermas criticize Rawls's approach?

7   What is Habermas's "unrestricted communication community"? How do participants in argumentation discover it?

8   How does Habermas guarantee that the rules for discourse are not merely arbitrary conventions?

For further study

This selection has excerpts, sometimes simplified in wording, from Jürgen Habermas's "Discourse ethics: Notes on a program of philosophical justification," in *Moral Consciousness and Communicative Action* (Cambridge, MA: MIT Press, 1990), translated by C. Lenhardt and S. Weber Nicholsen. For other ethical writings, see his *Legitimation Crisis* (Boston: Beacon Press, 1975), translated by T. McCarthy – especially Part III; *Justification and Application: Remarks on Discourse Ethics* (Cambridge, MA: MIT Press, 1994), translated by C. Cronin – especially Chapters 1 and 2, which respond to criticisms; and *Between Facts and Norms*, (Cambridge, MA: MIT Press, 1996), translated by W. Rehg – especially Chapter 3. For analysis and criticism of Habermas's discourse ethics, see James Swindal's *Reflection Revisited: Jürgen Habermas's Emancipative Theory of Truth* (New York: Fordham University Press, 1999), Chapters 4 and 5; William Rehg's *Insight and Solidarity* (Berkeley: University of California Press, 1994); Seyla Benhabib's *Critique Norm and Utopia* (New York: Columbia University Press, 1986); Benhabib's edited collection of articles on discourse ethics in *The Communicative Ethics Controversy* (Cambridge, MA: MIT Press, 1990); Nancy Fraser's "What's critical about critical theory?: The case of Habermas and gender," in *Unruly Practices* (Minneapolis: University of Minnesota Press, 1989); and Joseph Heath's "The Problem of Foundationalism in Habermas's Discourse Ethics," *Philosophy and Social Criticism* 21 (1995): 77–100.

Related readings in this volume include Hare, Kant, Nagel, O'Neill, and Sartre (who also develop principles of universalization); Frankena and Rawls (who provide somewhat related views about the method to be used in arriving at moral beliefs); and Ayer and Mackie (whose noncognitivism Habermas would oppose).

Note

1   Habermas's term "cognitivist ethics" refers to any approach that recognizes moral truths and moral knowledge.

IMMANUEL KANT
Ethics Is Based on Reason

Immanuel Kant, a German philosopher who lived from 1724 to 1804, has had a great influence on contemporary ethics. For this reason, we thought it helpful to include some short excerpts from his writings.

Kant believed in an objective right and wrong based on reason. We should do the right thing just *because* it is right – and not because it promotes our desires or self-interest. We know what is right, not by relying on moral intuitions or facts about the world, but by reasoning about what we can consistently will. To test a moral maxim, we ask ourselves whether we can consistently will that everyone follow it (and thus act that way toward us); we must reject the maxim if we cannot will this.

As you read the selection, ask yourself whether Kant's ideal of moral motivation is plausible. Do moral duties command categorically? Does Kant's way to test moral principles work?

Good will

In order that an action should be morally good, it is not enough that it conform to the moral law; it must also be done for the sake of the law.

Nothing can possibly be conceived which can be called good, without qualification, except a good will. Intelligence, wit, judgment, and the other talents of the mind, or courage, resolution, perseverance, as qualities of temperament, are undoubtedly good and desirable in many respects; but these may become extremely bad if the will which uses them is not good.[1] It is the same with the gifts of fortune. Power, riches, honor, health, and contentment inspire pride, and often presumption, if there is not a good will to correct the influence of these on the mind.

A good will is good, not because of its attainment of some proposed end, but simply by virtue of the volition; that is, it is good in itself. The preeminent good which we call *moral* can consist in nothing else than the conception of law itself, insofar as this determines the will.

How to test a maxim

What sort of law can that be, the conception of which must determine the will, even without regard to the effect expected from it? As I have deprived the will of every impulse which could arise to it from obedience to any law, there remains nothing but the universal conformity of its actions to law in general, i.e., I am never to act otherwise than that I could also will that my maxim should become a universal law. It is the simple conformity to law in general that serves the will as its principle. The common reason of men in its practical judgments perfectly coincides with this and always has in view the principle here suggested.

Let the question be, for example: May I when in distress make a promise with the intention not to keep it? I readily distinguish two significations the question may have: Whether it is prudent, or whether it is right, to make a false promise? Now it is a wholly different thing to be truthful from duty and to be so from apprehension of injurious consequences. In the first case, the very notion of the action already implies a law for me; in the second case, I must first look about elsewhere to see what results may affect myself. For to deviate from the principle of duty is beyond all doubt wicked; but to be unfaithful to my maxim of prudence may often be advantageous to me, although to abide by it is certainly safer.

The shortest way to discover whether a lying promise is consistent with duty is to ask myself, "Should I be content that my maxim (to extricate myself from difficulty by a false promise) should hold good as a universal law, for myself as well as for others?" and should I be able to say to myself, "Every one may make a deceitful promise when he finds himself in a difficulty from which he cannot otherwise extricate himself"? While I can will the lie, I cannot will that lying should be a universal law. For with such a law there would be no promises, since it would be vain to allege my intention in regard to my future actions to those who would not believe this allegation, or if they did so would pay me back in my own coin. Hence my maxim, as soon as it be made a universal law, would necessarily destroy itself.[2]

I do not need far-reaching penetration to discern what to do in order that my will may be morally good. Inexperienced in the course of the world, incapable of being prepared for all its contingencies, I only ask myself: Can you will that your maxim should be a universal law? If not, then it must be rejected, and that not because of a disadvantage from it to myself or to others, but because it cannot enter as a principle into a possible universal legislation, and reason extorts from me immediate respect for such legislation. Acting from pure respect for the practical law is what constitutes duty, to which every other motive must give place, because it is the condition of a will being good in itself, and the worth of such a will is above everything else.

Categorical and hypothetical imperatives

An objective principle, in so far as it is obligatory, is called a *command* (of reason), and the formula of the command is called an *imperative*.

All imperatives are expressed by the word *ought*, and indicate the relation of an objective law of reason to a will which is not necessarily determined by it. They say that something would be good to do, but they say it to a will which does not always do a thing because it is conceived to be good.

Now all imperatives command either hypothetically or categorically. The former represent the practical necessity of a possible action as means to something else that is willed (or which one might will). The categorical imperative represents an action as necessary of itself without reference to another end, i.e., as objectively necessary.[3]

A categorical imperative commands a certain conduct immediately, without having as its condition any other purpose to be attained by it. This imperative may be called that of morality. There is but one [basic] categorical imperative: Act only on that maxim whereby you can at the same time will that it should become a universal law.

Treat people with respect – do not just use them

Man, and generally any rational being, exists as an end in himself, not merely as a means to be arbitrarily used by this or that will. Nonrational beings have only a relative value as means, and are therefore called *things*; rational beings, on the contrary, are called *persons*, because their very nature points them out as ends in themselves.

If then there is a categorical imperative, it must be drawn from that which is necessarily an end for everyone because it is an end in itself. The foundation is: rational nature exists as an end in itself. I necessarily conceive my own existence as being so; so this is a subjective principle of action. But every other rational being regards its existence similarly, so it is at the same time an objective principle. Accordingly the practical imperative will be as follows: So act as to treat humanity, whether in your own person or in that of any other, in every case as an end in itself, never only as means.

Study questions

1 Why is a good will the only thing good without qualification? Give an example showing why other things are not good without qualification.

2 Under what conditions is a will good? Is it good just if it produces good results – or just if it accords with our duty?

3 What is Kant's test of a moral maxim? Apply the test to making a dishonest promise. Can you see problems with his test?

4 Explain the difference between hypothetical and categorical imperatives. Give an example of each.

5 How should our treatment of persons differ from our treatment of things?

For further study

This selection has excerpts, sometimes simplified in wording, from T. K. Abbott's translation of Immanuel Kant's 1789 *Fundamental Principles of the Metaphysics of Morals* (London: Longmans, Green, and Company, 1934). This work (often called *"The Groundwork of the Metaphysics of Morals"*) is also available in other translations; the one by H. J. Paton (New York: Harper & Row, 1964) has a helpful commentary. You might also consult Kant's 1788 *Critique of Practical Reason* (New York: Library of Liberal Arts, 1956), translated by L. W. Beck. To see Kant apply his framework, see his *Lectures on Ethics* (Cambridge: Cambridge University Press, 1997), translated by P. Heath and J. B. Schneewind, especially parts I to III. For Kant's life and general thought, see *Kant: A Biography*, by Manfred Kuehn (Cambridge: Cambridge University Press, 2001).

Related readings in this anthology include those from Habermas, Hare, Kohlberg, Nagel, O'Neill, Rawls, and Sartre (all of whom are inspired in some way by Kant's approach and accept some analogue of Kant's test of moral maxims); Hume and Mill (who support historically important opposing views); and Mackie (who expresses his rejection of objective values in terms of a rejection of Kantian categorical imperatives).

Notes

1 To appreciate Kant's point, consider a serial killer who is more effective at his chosen task because he is extremely intelligent.

2 Kant's followers disagree on how best to apply the "universal law" test. Hare's creative approach (see his reading in this anthology) suggests that we test a proposed moral maxim by (1) understanding the consequences of following it on affected individuals, (2) imagining ourselves in the place of these individuals, and (3) asking whether we desire that the maxim be followed regardless of where we imagine ourselves in the situation.

3 These are *hypothetical imperatives*: "If you want to relieve your headache, then you ought to take aspirin" and "If you want people to be honest to you, then you ought to be honest to them." In contrast, a *categorical (or moral) imperative* commands an action directly (not as a means to some further end) – as in "You ought to be honest to others."

JOYCE HERTZLER
The Golden Rule and Society

Joyce Hertzler, an American social scientist who lived from 1895 to 1975, made important contributions in various areas, especially sociology of language and the relationships between society and values.

Hertzler discusses the golden rule from historical, sociological, and philosophical perspectives. Hertzler points out that the golden rule is found in almost all cultures of the world and tries to explain why the principle is so popular.

As you read the selection, keep in mind some areas of social conflict that seem important to you. Can the golden rule give a useful perspective in dealing with such conflicts?

The social need for moral principles

Ever since man has lived in groups larger and more complex than the simple reproductive unit, he has been seeking simple formulas covering his relationships with his fellows. The principles had to be readily remembered and transmitted. They also had to incorporate rules readily comprehensible to and applicable by the individual members of the group.

Among the finest and most frequently used of such formulas are the so-called "Golden Rule" and the "Law of Love," both of which were given their classical statements in Western civilization by Jesus of Nazareth. The first he stated in the words, "All things whatsoever ye would that men should do to you, do ye even so to them." The second he stated simply: "Thou shalt love thy neighbor as thyself." These two ideas are very closely allied: in fact, their inherent implications are essentially the same. Both rest basically on self-love, and require behavior toward others that is in conformity with what is opined by the individual to be good or desirable for him.

Both of these social formulas have appeared in slightly modified form among people widely separated in time and space. Their efficacy, or at least their advocacy, seems to be more or less universal. The purpose of this paper is first to note the time, place, and form of some of the more significant statements as they are presented by the history of social thought, and, secondly, to analyze them, particularly the Golden Rule, from the sociological point of view in an effort to determine some of the reasons for their frequency and persistence.

The wide popularity of the Golden Rule

A study of the proverbs of primitive peoples presents an occasional thought that comes very close to the Golden Rule in its implications. Thus the Yorubas of West Africa say, "He who injures another injures himself." While this proverb expresses social interdependence, some connotations of a golden rule nature are also evident. The Moroccan tribesmen have several: "He who has done something will have it done to him"; "He who sows good will reap peace"; and the strikingly significant statement "What you desire for yourself you should desire for others." The Ba-Congo expressed the thought of the Golden Rule in two of their proverbs. "If you see a jackal in your neighbor's garden drive it out, one may get into yours one day, and you would like the same done for you." "O man, what you do not like, do not to your fellows."

In the *Upanishads* of Indian Brahmanism, going back to the period 800–600 BC, is found this striking passage:

> Let no man to do another that which would be repugnant to himself; this is the sum of righteousness. A man obtains the proper rule by regarding another's case as like his own.

While Zoroaster (660–583 BC) did not state the Law of Love or the Golden Rule, neither idea is foreign to his general social philosophy. In the Zoroastrian literature that came after him there are several significant passages. One reads, "When men love and help one another to the best of their power, they derive the greatest pleasure from loving their fellow men"; another, "That nature alone is good which shall not do unto another whatever is not good for its own self."

Gautama (560–480 BC), the founder of Buddhism, has the idea, but does not give precise expression to it. He says in one passage,

> All men tremble at the rod, all men fear death:
> Putting oneself in the place of others, kill not nor cause to kill.
> All men tremble at the rod, unto all men life is dear;
> Doing as one would be done by, kill not nor cause to kill.

Elsewhere he stated, "One should seek for others the happiness one desires for oneself."

Confucius (551–479 BC) gives us the first specific statement of the rule in its negative form, sometimes referred to as the "Silver Rule." In the *Analects*, he expressed it in the words: "What I do not wish men to do to me, I also wish not to do to men." In the *Doctrine of the Mean*, he puts the same thought thus: "Do not unto others what you would not they should do unto you." In the *Great Learning*, he further elaborates,

> What a man dislikes in those who are over him, let him not display toward those who are under him; what he dislikes in those who are under him, let him not display toward those who are over him! This is called the standard, by which, as a measuring square, to regulate one's conduct.

Tsze-kung is said to have asked the master if there was one word which might serve as a rule of practice for all one's life, and Confucius answered, "Is not Reciprocity such a word?" In another utterance Confucius showed that he understood it in its positive and most comprehensive force.

> There are four things in the moral life of man, not one of which I have been able to carry out in my life. To serve my father as I would expect my son to serve me: that I have not been able to do. To serve my sovereign as I would expect a minister under me to serve me: that I have not been able to do. To act towards my elder brother, as I would expect my younger brother to act towards me: that I have not been able to do. To be the first to behave toward friends as I would expect them to behave towards me: that I have not been able to do.

In Exodus, which takes us back to at least 750 BC in the history of the Hebrews, we have a rule admonishing helpfulness to enemies, and in Leviticus, written during the Babylonian Exile (586–538 BC), we have the first statement of the Law of Love, "Thou shalt love thy neighbor as thyself."

The idea is also found among the ancient Greeks. Plato (428–347 BC) several times in the *Republic* lays down rules of essentially the same purport. In the *Laws* (Book XI, p. 913, Jowett translation) he states "... do to others as I would that they should do to me." Isocrates, a contemporary of Plato, stated: "Do not do to others that at which you would be angry if you suffered it from others." According to Diogenes Laertius when the question was put to Aristotle (384–322 BC) as to how we ought to behave to our friends, the answer he gave was, "Exactly as we would wish our friends to behave to us." In the famous passage in the *Nicomachean Ethics* in which he discusses "self-love" and the "good man," without specifically stating the Golden Rule, Aristotle nevertheless gives a pointed exposition of it.

The Judaistic sources of the period just preceding the Christian era also provide examples. They show that the Golden Rule had been authoritatively proclaimed in Israel long before Jesus' time. In the Talmud (Palestinian), in the instructions given by Tobit to his son Tobias, after admonishing him to love his brethren, the father says: "What is displeasing to thyself, that do not unto any other." Hillel, the great doctor of Hebrew law at Jerusalem during the time of King Herod, is responsible for the following occurrence. When a heathen who wished to become a Jew asked him for a short summary of the Law regarding the relation of a man to his neighbor, he said: "Whatsoever thou wouldest that men should not do to thee, do not do that to them. This is the whole Law; the rest is mere commentary." Hillel, incidentally, was the grandfather of Gamaliel, the instructor of Paul of Tarsus.

The recorded statements of the Golden Rule next in historical order are those of Jesus (5 BC–28 AD). The one given in Matthew 7:12, and stated at the beginning of this paper, is the best known and the one cited almost to the exclusion of all others. It is the first positive phrasing of the rule. Luke gives a slightly different version: "As ye would that men should do unto you, do ye also to them likewise." The Law of Love – "Thou shalt love thy neighbor as thyself" – is given in three different places in the Gospels. Paul (1–67 AD), the apostle and interpreter of Jesus, had several statements of the Law of Love, but none of the Golden Rule. In two well-known passages he points out that he who observes the rule "Thou shall love thy neighbor as thyself" fulfills the Law. The Latin fathers make frequent reference to the Golden Rule using the version "Whatsoever *good things* ye would that men should do unto you, even so do ye also unto him." Augustine is said to be responsible for the saying that "Do as thou wouldst be done by" is a sentence which all nations under heaven are agreed upon.

Several of the Roman thinkers of the first and second centuries AD state the Golden Rule in one form or another. There is every reason for believing that their statements were independent of any Christian influence. Seneca, the Stoic (3–65 AD), states the principle several times. In the forty-seventh *Epistle to Lucilius* we find it thus: "This is then, the sum and substance of my advice: Treat your inferior as you would be treated by your superiors." In *On Anger* he says, "Let us put ourselves in the place of him with whom we are angry: at present an over-weaning conceit of our own fortune makes us prone to anger and we are quite willing to do to others what we cannot endure should be done to ourselves." Epictetus, another Roman stoic, active around 90 AD, in his *Fragments* writes, "What you avoid suffering, do not attempt to make others suffer. You avoid slavery: take care that others are not your slaves."

The thought also appears in the seventeenth century. Thomas Hobbes (1588–1657) mentions it in several of his works. He declares that moral regulations, which he calls "immutable and eternal laws of nature," may all be summarized in the simple formula, "Do not that to another which thou wouldst not have done to thyself." Again, "When any one questions whether what he plans to do to another will be done in accordance with the law of nature or not, let him imagine himself in the other man's place." Samuel Pufendorf (1632–94) comments on the latter rule: "For in this way, when self-love and passions, which strongly bow down one scale of the balance, are transformed to the other scale, it will be easy to see which way the balance turns." Pufendorf also mentions that the Inca, Manco Capoc, the founder of the empire of Peru, laid down this rule for his citizens: "Do not to another what you would not yourself experience."

More recently we have the famous categorical imperative of Immanuel Kant, "Act as if the maxim of thy action were to become by thy will a universal law," and the related statement, "So act as to treat humanity, whether in thine own person or in that of another, in every case as an end withal, never as a means only," both closely allied to the Golden Rule. John Stuart Mill also has the significant statement, "To do as you would be done by, and to love your neighbor as yourself, constitute the ideal perfection of utilitarian morality."

These later European statements may all have been suggested by the statements in the New Testament attributed to Jesus. The significant thing about them is that various philosophers found the principle indispensable.

Why the Golden Rule is so popular

One of sociology's major concerns is social order. No society or group can exist if social order is not established and maintained. Without it there is discord, disruptive conflict, and chaos; without it there can be none of that individual freedom, self-determination, and self-realization that most men crave. Such order, however, rests upon the formation of effective social control devices of various kinds.

As one examines the rules of social behavior among the various cultures, one is struck by their diversity. The age, the environment, the cultural level, and the historical experience of the given people seem to dictate specific forms. What is required or accepted here may be wrong there; and what is right now may be wrong tomorrow. That this viewpoint is correct in most phases of human behavior goes without saying. But a similar cultural study shows also occasional uniformities in the principles of social order. We find certain supposed fundamentals quite generally adhered to by peoples removed from each other in space, time, and cultural level – universals which persist and which the changing scene does not invalidate.

Significant among such more or less universal social rules is the Golden Rule. Sociology's interest in it rests primarily upon its efficacy as an agent in social control, and upon the sociological and social psychological principles involved in its operation. The Golden Rule has grown out of the experience of diverse groups. It, like other precepts or maxims, is a product of generations and centuries of careful observation and analysis of the relations of the individual and the group. Its widespread advocacy in different eras and among various peoples points to inherent elements that have given it considerable success as a social rule, elements that rest not only upon certain uniformities of human nature, but also of the individual–group relation.

The first feature of the Golden Rule is that, unlike the great mass of social control devices, it is not a dictatorial social influence intimidating, coercing, or subtly shaping behavior from without, as do the mores, law, public opinion, or other institutionalized pressures. The Golden Rule operates from within the individual, and results in the voluntary limitation of behavior. It is control that is subjective, self-initiatory, and self-coercive, but which redounds to social benefit, due to the uniqueness of its psychology.

The second aspect of the Golden Rule is that it does not require any great individual intelligence. It uses the clever psychological principle of starting with the individual actor, who, on the basis of his own experience and reflection, or with the aid of imagination, has fairly definite feelings about what is good nor not for him as he contemplates the possible behavior of other people. Jesus very definitely in the Rule of Love makes self-love the basis and this is implicit in his statement of the Golden Rule. This famous rule then starts from the individual's own desires regarding his welfare.

Thirdly, again on the basis of his own experience, the individual accepts the other fellow as one more or less like himself, and transfers, or perhaps expands, in his imagination, his own motives or desires to this other fellow. Thus the guide of the individual's action toward another is not his supposition of what his fellow's desire may be, but his own desire transferred in imagination to him. You do the same good for another that you might reasonably desire for yourself if you were in his place, or you refrain from committing an act to the other fellow that, if perpetrated upon you, would be hateful or unpleasant to you. The rule thus also rests on the fact that man can, in terms of his own experience, visualize and appreciate his neighbor's predicament, and that he can act or refrain from acting to him as he would have his neighbor act or refrain from acting toward him.

In the fourth place, there is a difference in the sociological implications of the negative and positive statements of the rule. The negative statement, as for example that of Confucius, or Hillel, or Epictetus, is not likely to lead to beneficent attitudes. It merely establishes order. It assumes that the possible actor has been injured by others in the past, or has been the victim of aggression. He then merely transfers the "don't-hurt-me" attitude to the other fellow. Spooner summarizes the matter well when he states,

> It would appear then, that the maxim (speaking of the negative statement) obtained a wide acceptance among the best and most enlightened intellects of the ancient world; but it was for them a

restraining principle, a guide of what they ought not do rather than of what they ought.

There is no implication, however, in the Golden Rule that is retaliation. There can be no retaliation until there has been action. The *lex talionis*,[1] another ancient but faulty maxim, is addressed to the sufferer of an action. The application of the Golden Rule precedes the act. It is rather an admonition to engage in conduct that is good for the other fellow, as you see it, or the avoidance of behavior that will be bad for him.

The positive statement, as for example, that of Jesus, "All things whatsoever ye would that men should do to you, do ye even so to them," is broader and more inclusive in its scope, and social or even altruistic in its tendencies. The positive rule puts the social behavior of the individual on a conscious and rational plane. It takes him beyond his own immediate selfish good, and commits him to an eminently satisfactory general social policy. I desire health, and knowing that this depends upon healthful conditions of living, I do all in my power to make such conditions available for others. I want safety on the highways; I drive carefully and sanely, and become an active exponent of road safety. In brief, the positive statement tends to the shaping of an ever improving social order. The negative statement leads to a functional equilibrium and maintains existing social control.

The positively stated Golden Rule conforms perfectly with that great and widely accepted criterion of social value, namely, that the objective of social life is the fullest possible life for the individual. If the individual is striving for facility of thought, opportunity for the free exercise of workmanship, the emancipation of creative intelligence, the freedom of aesthetic expression, and the opportunities for the expansion of spirit for himself, he will provide these facilities for others in the corporate life of man. Furthermore, the positive Golden Rule stimulates those inner forces and capacities that must be cultivated if there is to be a high type of culture.

The positively stated Golden Rule presents greater difficulties of realization than the negative. It demands more of the individual and requires the play of the higher elements of human nature to carry it out. The negative statements, to be placed in successful operation, need only "won't power" which is a common attribute of people.

The Golden Rule, in the fifth place, is not particularistic, nor does it apply only in a common interest group. It is universal in its application. We human beings tend to be only fair and just to "our own kind of folks." But if we act in accord with the positive Golden Rule we unavoidably have to consider *every* fellow with whom contact is made or likely to be made. Any principle or condition of inequality, status, or class alignment is inconsistent with it.

It has sometimes been contended that the Golden Rule is an "under dog" philosophy.[2] Even the most superficial analysis, however, shows this to be erroneous. Primitives have it among their tribal maxims, and class lines are less closely drawn among them than among civilized peoples. Among historical advocates, Amen-em-apt was an Egyptian nobleman; Gautama was a prince; Lao-tze was a scholar; Confucius was an officer of state and a philosopher-teacher; Hillel was a great churchman and scholar; Jesus, to be sure, was of lowly origin; Seneca was the tutor and adviser of Nero, and probably the second wealthiest man of Rome; Marcus Aurelius was a Roman emperor; and Alfred was an English king. All of these presented the Golden Rule, not from the view of any class, but as a universal behavior policy.

From the general operative point of view, the Golden Rule has the advantage of controlling the individual without stirring up his antagonism and opposition through too much outer restraint. Its compulsion comes from within the individual. It is one of the highest types of control, because it grows out of self-control. It promotes justice and order rather than attempting by coercion to prevent or repress injustice and disorder. It is perhaps the best single rule for social behavior that has ever been enunciated.

Study questions

1 What are Jesus's formulations of the law of love and the golden rule? Give cases where these principles were endorsed outside of Christianity.
2 How does Hertzler see the role of moral principles in society?
3 What five features does the golden rule have? Pick one of the features and explain it in greater detail.
4 Can you think of other positive features of the golden rule? Can you see any problems with the rule?
5 Explain what Hertzler means by saying "the golden rule has the advantage of controlling the individual without stirring up his antagonism and opposition through too much outer restraint."

For further study

This selection has excerpts, sometimes simplified in wording, from Joyce Oramel Hertzler's "On Golden Rules," in the *International Journal of Ethics* 44 (1934): 418–36. Hertzler's most influential work was *A Sociology of Language* (New York: Random House, 1965). Jeffrey Wattles's *The Golden Rule* (New York: Oxford University Press, 1996) has a longer discussion of the historical and religious aspects of the rule. Harry Gensler's *Ethics: A Contemporary Introduction* (London and New York: Routledge, 1998) discusses the golden rule in Chapter 7.

Several other readings in this anthology deal with the golden rule (the Bible, Gensler and Tokmenko, Hare, Nagel, and Ricoeur) or related ideals like love, sympathy, or beneficence (Frankena, Habermas, Hume, King, and Nietzsche). You may want to compare what Hertzler says about cultural universals with what is said by the other two social scientists in this anthology (Benedict and Kohlberg).

Notes

1   The "*lex talionis*" that Hertzler refers to is the "an eye for an eye, and a tooth for a tooth" law of retaliation: if someone hurts you in some way, then you are to hurt the other person in the same way. In contrast, the golden rule requires that you treat X, not as X has actually treated you, but rather in accord with how you are willing that you be treated in X's place.
2   Hertzler may have been thinking of Nietzsche, who thought "love thy neighbor" was part of "slave morality" and thus unworthy of aristocrats. See Nietzsche's reading in this anthology.

PAUL RICOEUR
The Golden Rule and Religion

Paul Ricoeur, a French philosopher born in 1913, works in the area of phenomenological hermeneutics. "Hermeneutics" is an approach to interpreting texts. Ricoeur often analyses biblical texts, looking at them in light of narrative, symbolism, and metaphor. He is heavily influenced by the phenomenological method of continental thinkers (like Edmund Husserl, Karl Jaspers, Gabriel Marcel, and Jean-Paul Sartre) who emphasize an attentiveness to experienced phenomena.

In this selection, Ricoeur interprets biblical passages about ethical conduct. He finds, surprisingly, that passages on the golden rule and on the love of enemies seem to be inconsistent. He appeals to a "rhetoric of paradox" to help relieve the tension. This leads him to re-interpret the golden rule, or at least the motivation behind it.

As you read the selection, ask yourself whether Ricoeur succeeds in making compatible these two seemingly contrary biblical norms.

The problem

If one assumes that the Golden Rule constitutes the basic moral rule about which the wisest may agree, what happens to this rule when it is put within a religious perspective, more precisely, within the perspective of the Jewish-Christian scriptures?

That the Golden Rule expresses our common morality seems to be confirmed by the place it holds in the *Sermon on the Mount* in Mt 7:12 – "So whatever you wish that men would do to you, do so to them; for this is the law and the prophets" – where the Golden Rule seems to be taken for granted as a common good of the Jewish culture; just as in the *Sermon on the Plain* in Lk 6:31 – "And as you wish that men would do to you, do so to them" – the Golden Rule seems to be acknowledged as the common good of Hellenistic culture.

However, it is not the mere citation of the Golden Rule which raises a problem of interpretation, but the impact on it of a context which seems to deny or disavow it. This context is governed by the commandment to love one's enemies. Now, it is this commandment, and not the Golden Rule, that seems to provide expression, at the ethical level, of what we may call the *economy of gift,* at the religious level.

Do we not have to oppose the logic of superabundance,[1] which seems to flow directly from the religious economy of gift, to the logic of equivalence, which finds its perfect expression in the Golden Rule?

Two kinds of arguments support the contention that the Golden Rule is overcome by the new commandment to love one's enemies.

The first argument against the ethical primacy of the Golden Rule is an exegetical one. After having quoted the Golden Rule (Lk 6:31), Jesus, we are told, added the following harsh words which seem to deny what he has just quoted:

> If you love those who love you, what credit is that to you? For even sinners love those who love them. And if you do good to those who do good to you, what credit is that to you? For even sinners do the same.

Jesus continues: "But love your enemies, and do good, and lend, expecting nothing in return." Is this not a denial of the Golden Rule?

The second argument relies on the conceptual kinship which connects the Golden Rule with the rule of retaliation which once governed the penal sphere: "an eye for an eye, and a tooth for a tooth." The common component between retaliation and the Golden Rule is the principle of *equivalence.* The *jus talionis* [rule of retaliation] already constitutes a moral improvement by comparison with sheer vengeance. Vengeance is limitless; retaliation has an element of *measure* provided by the very principle of equivalence. This equivalence, however, still concerns the contents themselves: eye and tooth. With the Golden Rule a new improvement obtains: the reciprocity is anticipated instead of being merely reactive. Furthermore, the rule is addressed to intentions, dispositions, feelings: what you would hate being done to you. However, in spite of this improvement, the Golden Rule remains within the same logic of equivalence, this very logic that the commandment to love one's enemies shatters: nothing is expected in return, no equivalence. The enemy becomes the touchstone of the new ethics; love is boundless, in the same way as vengeance, at the opposite end of the trajectory, was limitless!

The solution

What the previous arguments have underestimated is the breadth of the margin of interpretation that any rule and any text may allow. The Golden Rule, instead of being *denied,* is rather *reinterpreted,* not only according to its potential intent, but according to the new scope which the logic of superabundance conveys to it.

Interpreted literally, the Golden Rule is a refinement of the law of retaliation, of the *jus talionis* ultimately. Its formula would be: I give *in order that* you give. The doer takes the initiative, but for the sake of receiving a reward in return.[2] The expectation of reciprocity keeps the Golden Rule within the iron circle of retaliation. This is what Lk 6:32 means to say: "If you love those who love you, what credit is that to you? For even sinners love those who love them." What perverts the reciprocity implied in the Golden Rule is its diversion for the sake of *self-interest*.

It is at this point that the economy of gift and its logic of superabundance makes the difference between the two readings of the same Golden Rule. I see the logic of superabundance rescuing true reciprocity from its caricature as denounced in Lk 6:32–5. This logic works in the following way. The economy of gift is construed around a *because: because* it has been given to you, go and do alike. Then the rule of reciprocity and even the principle of equivalence may be redeemed from their initial disgrace thanks to the substitution of the new motive of generosity for the ancient motive of self-interest.

Why should this positive interpretation be preferred? For exegetical reasons, first, but also for conceptual and systematic reasons. I shall not insist on the exegetical reasons, because it is not my own area of competence. I only observe that the *Sermon on the Mount* in Matthew is a highly structured discourse and that the Golden Rule occupies a central place in this subtle architecture: "So whatever you wish that men would do to you, do so to them; for this is the law and the prophets." The Golden Rule is not merely quoted here; it is integrated into a new ethics. This would be unthinkable if it could not be reinterpreted according to the new logic of superabundance sealed by the love of enemies. As to the citation of the Golden Rule in Lk 6:31, it is more economical in terms of composition and rhetoric to read the following verses (Lk 6:32–5) as the dismantling of a wrong interpretation.

But I prefer to insist on the conceptual and systematic argument; namely, that of reinterpreting the principle of morality in the light of the symbols which structure the religious experience of Jews and Christians. This reinterpretation is made possible thanks to the *analogy* displayed by the *because:* because it has been given to you, go and do alike. This *like* in turn generates the *imitatio Dei* [imitation of God], that we read of in the Jewish context of the *Sermon on the Mount* – "You, therefore, must be perfect, as your heavenly Father is perfect" (Mt 5:48) – and in the more Hellenistic context of the *Sermon on the Plain* – "Be merciful, even as your Father is merciful" (Lk 6:36). The response is governed by this rule of analogy which brings the rule of morality within the religious perspective. This analogical link is what makes possible the reinterpretation of the Golden Rule in terms of the economy of gift.

The conclusion: a rhetoric of paradox

I do not claim that love for enemies, held as the touchstone of the logic of superabundance, and the Golden Rule, held as the highest expression of the logic of equivalence, coincide. The one is unilateral. The other is bilateral. The one expects nothing in return. The other legitimates a certain kind of reciprocity. My contention – indeed, my main point – is that the tension between them is essential and central to genuine Christian ethics. We must take into account the *rhetoric of paradox*. As all genuine paradoxes, the new commandment reorients by disorienting. I already said how it can be done, by submitting the *in order that* to the *because* implied in the primacy of gift. The antecedent generosity of the *because* preserves the Golden Rule from the perversion latent in the prospective *in order that*. This salvific motivation constitutes the *reason of the heart* par excellence.

Now why is this reorientation so important? Because a disorientation without a reorientation would amount to an ethical void. No penal law, no justice in general could be derived from the naked commandment of the love for enemies. Which economic fairness could derive from the commandment, "Lend, expecting nothing in return"?

In this sense the commandment of love for enemies is not ethical but su-pra-ethical. In order that the supra-ethical does not turn to the a-moral, it must reinterpret the principle of morality summarized in the Golden Rule. By so doing, the new commandment elevates the principle of morality above itself.

Such, to my mind, is the basic reason why the new commandment could not eliminate the Golden Rule and should not be substituted for it. The so-called Christian ethics – or, I should prefer to say, the common ethics in a religious perspective – relies to my mind on this *tension* between unilateral love and bilateral justice. The practical consequences of this common ethics are innumerable and perfectly feasible. The incorporation of a motive of compassion and generosity in all our codes, penal codes and codes of social justice, constitutes a reasonable task, although difficult and endless. The Golden Rule is put in this concrete way in the midst of a basic conflict between self-interest and self-sacrifice. The same rule may be invoked by the exponents of both motivations.

Let me close by quoting a wonderful verse from the *Sermon on the Plain* which conflates, so to say, the lack of measure proper to love and the sense of measure characteristic of justice: "give, and it will be given to you; good measure, pressed down, shaken together, running over, will be put into your lap. For the measure you give will be the measure you get back." (Lk 6:38) The lack of measure is the good measure. Such is the poetic transposition of the rhetoric of paradox: superabundance becomes the hidden truth of equivalence. The Golden Rule is repeated. But repetition means transfiguration.

Study questions

1   How does the command to love one's enemies (which expresses the "economy of the gift") seem to conflict with the golden rule? Construct an example that illustrates the conflict.

2   Explain the "exegetical" and the "conceptual kinship" arguments.

3   How does Ricoeur reinterpret the golden rule in light of the "logic of superabundance"? How does he justify this reinterpretation?

4   How does the "rhetoric of paradox" deal with the tension that Ricoeur claims remains between the golden rule and the command to love one's enemies?

5   What does he mean by his claim that the command to love one's enemies is "supra-ethical"? How would we actually go about applying a supra-ethical principle to our everyday ethical decisions?

For further study

This selection has excerpts, sometimes simplified in wording, from Paul Ricoeur's "The Golden Rule," in *New Testament Studies* 36 (1990): 392–7. For a detailed description of Ricoeur's phenomenological hermeneutics, see his three volume *Time and Narrative* (Chicago: University of Chicago Press, 1984–8), translated by K. McLaughlin and D. Pellauer. For his ethical writings, see his *Oneself As Another* (Chicago: University of Chicago Press, 1992), translated by K. Blamey – especially studies 7–9; *Freedom and Nature: The Voluntary and the Involuntary* (Evanston, IL: Northwestern University Press, 1966), translated by E. Kohak; and *The Symbolism of Evil* (Boston: Beacon Press, 1969), translated by E. Buchanan. Other sources include *The Narrative Path: The Later Works of Paul Ricoeur* (Cambridge, MA: MIT Press, 1989), edited by P. Kemp and D. Rasmussen; *On Paul Ricoeur: Narrative and Interpretation* (New York: Routledge, 1991), edited by D. Wood; and Charles Reagan's *Paul Ricoeur: His Life and Works* (Chicago: University of Chicago Press, 1996). Harry Gensler's *Ethics: A Contemporary Introduction* (London and New York: Routledge, 1998) discusses the golden rule in Chapter 7.

Several other readings in this anthology deal with the golden rule (the Bible, Gensler and Tokmenko, Hare, Hertzler, and Nagel) or related ideas like love, sympathy, or beneficence (Frankena, Habermas, Hume, King, and Nietzsche). Lewis also gives a theological account of ethics. Sartre gives a notion of absolute freedom that Ricoeur rejects.

Notes

1 Ricoeur's "logic of superabundance" is the idea that we should treat others with overflowing generosity – as God has treated us – not just as we *consent* to being treated or are (minimally) *willing* to be treated ourselves.

2 The self-interest interpretation of the golden rule to which Ricoeur refers was common in ancient Greece: we ought to treat others well (as we want to be treated) because then others will treat us well. Ricoeur argues for a transformation of the rule: because God has first loved us abundantly, we are inspired to love others (to treat them as we want to be treated) in a selfless manner.

FRIEDRICH NIETZSCHE
Master and Slave Morality

Friedrich Nietzsche, a German philosopher and philologist who lived from 1844 to 1900, wrote voluminously on socio-cultural issues. He is widely recognized as an astute critic of many of the main currents of nineteenth-century thinking. Using trenchant prose and powerful wit, he savagely attacked ideals of piety, progress, compassion, and scientific rigor. His criticisms have had a profound impact on continental thinkers, such as Heidegger, Adorno, Foucault, and Derrida.

Nietzsche claims that Christianity gave rise to a bourgeois civilization that inculcated unquestioning conformism and resentment against the powerful. Inspired by Darwinian theories of evolution, he argues that nature endows us – as it does animals – with a will to power that, if un-impeded by repression, drives us to individualist displays of strength and even cruelty. He urges the development of a noble morality that allows such urges to assert themselves as we regain our authentic lives.

As you read the selection, ask yourself whether Nietzsche is merely giving an interesting – and possibly ironic – criticism of some of the cultural norms of his society, or whether he is in fact proposing a normative view of how all humans ought to act.

The will to power

[257] Every elevation of the type "man" has been the work of an aristocratic society – a society believing in gradations of rank and differences of worth among human beings, and requiring slavery in some form. Let us acknowledge how every higher civilization has originated! Men with a natural nature, barbarians in every terrible sense of the word, still in possession of unbroken strength of will and desire for power, threw themselves upon weaker, more moral, more peaceful races. The noble caste was always the barbarian caste: their superiority did not consist first of all in their physical, but in their psychical power – they were more *complete* men (which implies "more complete beasts").

[259] To refrain mutually from injury, from violence, from exploitation, and put one's will on a par with that of others: this may result in good

conduct among individuals when the necessary conditions are given (namely, the actual similarity of the individuals in amount of force and degree of worth, and their co-relation within one organization). As soon, however, as one wished to take this principle more generally, and even as *the fundamental principle of society,* it would immediately disclose what it really is – namely, a Will to the *denial* of life, a principle of dissolution and decay. Here one must think profoundly and resist all sentimental weakness: life itself is *essentially* injury, conquest of the weak, and exploitation. Life *is* precisely Will to Power.

People rave everywhere about coming conditions of society in which "the exploiting character" is to be absent: that sounds to my ears as if they promised a mode of life which should refrain from all organic functions. "Exploitation" does not belong to a depraved, or imperfect and primitive society: it belongs to the *nature* of the living being as a primary organic function; it is a consequence of the intrinsic Will to Power, which is precisely the Will to Life. As a theory this is a novelty – as a reality it is the *fundamental fact* of all history: let us be honest towards ourselves!

Master morality

[260] There is *master-morality and slave-morality.* The distinctions of moral values have either originated in a ruling caste, or among the ruled class.

In the first case, when it is the rulers who determine the conception "good," it is the exalted, proud disposition which determines the order of rank. The noble type of man separates from himself the beings in whom the opposite of this exalted disposition displays itself: he despises them. In this first kind of morality, the antithesis "good" and "bad" means practically the same as "noble" and "despicable"; the antithesis "good" and *"evil"* is of a different origin. The cowardly, the timid, the insignificant, and those thinking merely of narrow utility are despised.

The noble type of man regards *himself* as a determiner of values; he does not require to be approved of; he passes the judgment: "What is injurious to me is injurious in itself"; he knows that it is he himself only who confers honor on things; he is a *creator of values.* He honors whatever he recognizes in himself: such morality is self-glorification. There is the feeling of plenitude, of power, which seeks to overflow, the happiness of high tension, the consciousness of a wealth which would give and bestow: the noble man also helps the unfortunate, but not out of pity, but rather from an impulse generated by the super-abundance of power.

The noble and brave who think thus are the furthest removed from the morality which sees in sympathy, or in acting for the good of others, the characteristic of the moral.

A morality of the ruling class is especially foreign to present-day taste in its principle that one has duties only to one's equals; that one may act towards beings of a lower rank just as seems good to one, or "as the heart desires," and in any case "beyond good and evil."

Slave morality

It is otherwise with the second type of morality, *slave-morality*. Supposing that the oppressed, the suffering, the weary, should moralize, what will be the common element in their moral estimates? Probably a pessimistic suspicion with regard to the situation of man will find expression. The slave has an unfavorable eye for the virtues of the powerful. On the other hand, *those* qualities which serve to alleviate the existence of sufferers are brought into prominence; it is here that sympathy, the helping hand, the warm heart, patience, diligence, humility, and friendliness attain to honor for here these are the most useful qualities, and almost the only means of supporting the burden of existence.

Slave-morality is the morality of utility. Here is the seat of the origin of the famous antithesis "good" and "evil": power and dangerousness are assumed to reside in the evil. According to slave-morality, the "evil" man arouses fear; according to master-morality, it is precisely the "good" man who arouses fear. According to the servile mode of thought, the good man must be the *safe* man: he is good-natured, easily deceived, perhaps a little stupid.

[262] The mediocre alone have a prospect of continuing and propagating themselves – they will be the men of the future, the sole survivors; "be like them! Become mediocre!" is now the only morality which has still a significance, which still obtains a hearing. But it is difficult to preach this morality of mediocrity! It can never avow what it is and what it desires! – it will have difficulty *in concealing its irony!*

The noble Superman

[265] Egoism belongs to the essence of a noble soul, I mean the unalterable belief that to a being such as "we," other beings must naturally be in subjection, and have to sacrifice themselves. The noble soul accepts the fact of his egoism without question, as something that may have its basis in the primary law of things: he would say: "It is justice itself." He acknowledges that there are other equally privileged ones; as soon as he has settled this question of rank, he moves among those equals and equally privileged ones with the same assurance, as regards modesty and delicate respect, which he enjoys in intercourse with himself. It is an *additional* instance of his egoism, this

artfulness and self-limitation in intercourse with his equals; he honors *himself* in them, and in the rights which he concedes to them.

[270] Profound suffering makes noble: it separates. One of the most refined forms of disguise is Epicurism,[1] which takes suffering lightly, and puts itself on the defensive against all that is sorrowful and profound.

[293] There is nowadays a sickly irritability and sensitiveness towards pain, and also a repulsive complaining, an effeminising, which, with the aid of religion and philosophical nonsense, seeks to deck itself out as something superior – there is a regular cult of suffering. The *unmanliness* of that which is called "sympathy" by such groups of visionaries, is always the first thing that strikes the eye.

[3] For today have the petty people become master: they all preach submission and humility and diligence and consideration and the long *et cetera* of petty virtues. Whatever is of the effeminate type, whatever originates from the servile type: *that* wishes now to be master of all human destiny – O disgust! Disgust! Disgust!

These masters of today – surpass them, O my brethren – these petty people: *they* are the Superman's greatest danger! Surpass, you higher men, the petty virtues, the pitiable comfortableness, the "happiness of the greatest number"!

[5] "Man is evil" – so said to me for consolation. Ah, if only it be still true today! For the evil is man's best force. "Man must become better and eviler" – so do *I* teach. The evilest is necessary for the Superman's best. I rejoice in great sin as my great *consolation*.

[24] Once did people say God, when they looked out upon distant seas; now, however, have I taught you to say, Superman. God is a conjecture. Could you *create* a God? Then, I pray you, be silent about all gods! But you could well create the Superman. Not perhaps you yourselves, my brethren! But into fathers and forefathers of the Superman could you transform yourselves: and let that be your best creating!

Study questions

1 Describe the process by which Nietzsche claims that human achievements have an aristocratic origin.

2 How does he make the rather counter-intuitive link between refraining from injury and denying life?

3 How does he justify exploitation?

4 Describe the contrast between master and slave morality. Which does Nietzsche seem to prefer? Why?

5 Nietzsche says "Slave morality is essentially morality of utility" [260]. Why are slaves so interested in the good of all?

6   Can there be more than one superman? If so, how would they interact with each other?
7   What features of religion does Nietzsche highlight? What features does he ignore?

For further study

This selection has excerpts, often simplified in their wording, from two of Friedrich Nietzsche's works: *Beyond Good and Evil*, sections 257–93, and *Thus Spake Zarathustra*, sections 3–24. Both are found in *The Philosophy of Nietzsche* (New York: Modern Library, 1954), translated by H. Zimmern and T. Common. Though most of Nietzsche's works deal with ethical themes, those most relevant to ethics include *On the Genealogy of Morals* (Oxford: Oxford University Press, 1996), translated by D. Smith; *Human, All Too Human* (Stanford: Stanford University Press, 1995), translated by G. Handwerk; *Untimely Meditations* (Cambridge: Cambridge University Press, 1997), translated by D. Breazeale; *The Birth of Tragedy* (New York: Cambridge University Press, 1999), translated by R. Speirs; and *Will to Power* (New York: Random House, 1967), translated by W. Kaufmann and R. J. Hollingdale. For secondary sources, see Walter Kaufmann's *Nietzsche, Philosopher, Psychologist, Antichrist* (Princeton, NJ: Princeton University Press, 1974); Arthur Danto's *Nietzsche as Philosopher* (New York: Columbia University Press, 1980); Karl Löwith's *Nietzsche's Philosophy of the Eternal Recurrence of the Same* (Berkeley: University of California Press, 1997); Alexander Nehemas's *Nietzsche: Life as Literature* (Cambridge, MA: Harvard University Press, 1985).

  Most of the readings in this anthology support some sort of equality or concern for others, and thus would contrast with Nietzsche; see especially Brandt, Mill, Singer, and Smart (who defend various forms of utilitarianism); Hume (who sees sympathy as playing a large role in morality); Ross (who defends duties against injury); King (who criticizes segregation on the basis of love-thy-neighbor); and Hertzler (who stresses that the golden rule was historically supported by people from all classes of society, including the aristocratic class). Also, see Lewis and Ricoeur, both of whom write about the connection between ethics and religion, and the Bible selections, which give the orientation that Nietzsche is criticizing.

Note

1   Nietzsche here rejects ancient Greek Epicureanism, which saw pleasure and the avoidance of pain as the goal of life.

MARTIN LUTHER KING
Racial Segregation

Martin Luther King, an American clergyman and activist who lived from 1929 to 1968, was one of the moral heroes of the twentieth century. He led the struggle against racial segregation in the United States in the 1950s and 1960s.

This selection is from a letter that Dr King wrote on 16 April 1963, while in jail in Alabama for an illegal civil rights march. He defended his actions to fellow Christian ministers who accused him of being a law-breaker and an extremist. Dr King explained that he was protesting against immoral laws; segregation laws were wrong because they violated a higher moral law about how people ought to be treated. Thus his civil disobedience was a dramatic appeal to the conscience of the community.

As you read the selection, ask yourself what views about morality underlie Dr King's thinking about segregation. How would his thinking have been different had he been a cultural relativist or a subjectivist?

Defending his actions

While confined here in the Birmingham City Jail, I came across your recent statement calling our present activities "unwise and untimely." Since I feel that you are men of genuine goodwill and your criticisms are sincerely set forth, I would like to answer your statement in what I hope will be patient and reasonable terms.

I am in Birmingham because injustice is here. Birmingham is probably the most thoroughly segregated city in the United States. Its ugly record of police brutality is known in every section of this country. Its unjust treatment of Negroes in the courts is a notorious reality. There have been more unsolved bombings of Negro homes and churches in Birmingham than any other city in this nation. On the basis of these conditions, Negro leaders sought to negotiate with the city fathers. But the political leaders consistently refused to engage in good faith negotiation.

So we had no alternative except that of preparing for direct action, whereby we would present our very bodies as a means of laying our case before the conscience of the local and national community. We were not unmindful of the difficulties involved. So we decided to go through a process of self-purification. We started having workshops on nonviolence and repeatedly asked ourselves the questions: "Are you able to accept blows without retaliating?" "Are you able to endure the ordeals of jail?"

You may well ask: "Why direct action? Why sit-ins, marches, etc.? Isn't negotiation a better path?" You are exactly right in your call for negotiation. Indeed, this is the purpose of direct action. It seeks so to dramatize the issue that it can no longer be ignored. Just as Socrates felt that it was necessary to create a tension in the mind so that individuals could rise from the bondage of half-truths to the unfettered realm of objective appraisal, we must see the need of having nonviolent gadflies to create the tension in society that will help men to rise from the dark depths of racism to the majestic heights of brotherhood. So the purpose of the direct action is to create a situation so crisis-packed that it will inevitably open the door to negotiation.

We know through painful experience that freedom is never voluntarily given by the oppressor; it must be demanded by the oppressed. For years now I have heard the word "Wait!" This "Wait" has almost always meant "Never." We must come to see that "justice too long delayed is justice denied."

We have waited for more than three hundred and forty years for our constitutional and God-given rights. The nations of Asia and Africa are moving with jet-like speed toward the goal of political independence, and we still creep at horse and buggy pace toward the gaining of a cup of coffee at a lunch counter. It is easy for those who have never felt the stinging darts of segregation to say, "Wait." But when you have seen vicious mobs lynch your mothers and fathers at will and drown your sisters and brothers at whim; when you have seen hate filled policemen curse, kick, brutalize and even kill your black brothers and sisters with impunity; when you see the vast majority of your twenty million Negro brothers smothering in an airtight cage of poverty in the midst of an affluent society; when you suddenly find your speech stammering as you seek to explain to your six-year-old daughter why she can't go to the public amusement park that has just been advertised on television but is closed to colored children; when you have to concoct an answer for a five-year-old son asking in agonizing pathos: "Daddy, why do white people treat colored people so mean?"; when you take a cross-country drive and find it necessary to sleep night after night in the uncomfortable corners of your automobile because no motel will accept you; when you are humiliated day in and day out by nagging signs reading "white" and "colored"; when your first name becomes "nigger," your middle name becomes "boy" (however old you are), and your wife and mother and never given the respected title "Mrs"; when you are harried by day and haunted by night by the fact that you are a Negro, and plagued with inner fears and outer resentments; when you are forever fighting a degenerating sense of "nobodiness"; then you will understand why we find it difficult to wait. I hope, sirs, you can understand our legitimate and unavoidable impatience.

Just and unjust laws

You express a great deal of anxiety over our willingness to break laws. This is certainly a legitimate concern. Since we so diligently urge people to obey the Supreme Court's decision of 1954[1] outlawing segregation in the public schools, it is rather strange and paradoxical to find us consciously breaking laws. One may well ask: "How can you advocate breaking some laws and obeying others?" The answer is found in the fact that there are two types of laws: There are *just* and there are *unjust* laws.

Now, what is the difference between the two? A just law is a man-made code that squares with the moral law or the law of God. An unjust law is a code that is out of harmony with the moral law. To put it in the terms of Saint Thomas Aquinas, an unjust law is a human law that is not rooted in eternal and natural law. Any law that uplifts human personality is just. Any law that degrades human personality is unjust. All segregation statutes are unjust because segregation distorts the soul and damages the personality. It gives the segregator a false sense of superiority, and the segregated a false sense of inferiority. To use the words of Martin Buber, the Jewish philosopher, segregation substitutes and "I-it" relationship for an "I-thou" relationship, and ends up relegating persons to the status of things. So segregation is morally wrong and sinful. So I can urge men to disobey segregation ordinances because they are morally wrong.

Let us turn to a more concrete example of just and unjust laws. An unjust law is a code that a majority inflicts on a minority that is not binding on itself. This is difference made legal. On the other hand a just law is a code that a majority compels a minority to follow that it is willing to follow itself. This is sameness made legal.

Let me give another explanation. An unjust law is a code inflicted upon a minority which that minority had no part in enacting or creating because they did not have the unhampered right to vote. Who can say that the legislature of Alabama which set up the segregation laws was democratically elected? Throughout the state of Alabama all types of conniving methods are used to prevent Negroes from becoming registered voters and there are some counties without a single Negro registered to vote despite the fact that the Negro constitutes a majority of the population. Can any law set up in such a state be considered democratically structured?

These are just a few examples of unjust and just laws. There are some instances when a law is just on its face and unjust in its application. I was arrested Friday on a charge of parading without a permit. Now there is nothing wrong with an ordinance which requires a permit for a parade; but when the ordinance is used to preserve segregation and to deny citizens the First-Amendment privilege of peaceful assembly and peaceful protest, then it becomes unjust.

Conscientious civil disobedience

I hope you can see the distinction I am trying to point out. In no sense do I advocate evading or defying the law as the rabid segregationist would do. This would lead to anarchy. One who breaks an unjust law must do it *openly, lovingly,* and with a willingness to accept the penalty. I submit that an individual who breaks a law that conscience tells him is unjust, and willingly accepts the penalty by staying in jail to arouse the conscience of the community over its injustice, is in reality expressing the very highest respect for law.

Of course, there is nothing new about this kind of civil disobedience. It was practiced superbly by the early Christians who were willing to face hungry lions before submitting to certain unjust laws of the Roman empire. To a degree academic freedom is a reality today because Socrates practiced civil disobedience.

We can never forget that everything Hitler did in Germany was "legal" and everything the Hungarian freedom fighters did in Hungary[2] was "illegal." It was "illegal" to aid and comfort a Jew in Hitler's Germany. But I am sure that if I had lived in Germany during that time I would have aided and comforted my Jewish brothers even though it was illegal.

The charge of extremism

You spoke of our activity in Birmingham as extreme. I stand in the middle of two opposing forces in the Negro community. One is a force of complacency made up of Negroes who, as a result of long years of oppression, have been so completely drained of self-respect and a sense of "somebodiness" that they have adjusted to segregation. The other force is one of bitterness, and hatred comes perilously close to advocating violence; it is expressed in the various black nationalist groups that are springing up over the nation. I have tried to stand between these two forces saying that we need not follow the "do-nothingism" of the complacent or the hatred and despair of the black nationalist. There is the more excellent way of love and nonviolent protest. I'm grateful to God that, through the Negro church, the dimension of nonviolence entered our struggle. If this philosophy had not emerged, I am convinced that by now many streets of the South would be flowing with floods of blood.

As I continued to think about the matter I gradually gained a bit of satisfaction from being considered an extremist. Was not Jesus an extremist for love – "Love your enemies, bless them that curse you, pray for them that despitefully use you." Was not Amos an extremist for justice – "Let justice roll down like waters and righteousness like a mighty stream." Was not Abraham Lincoln an extremist – "This nation cannot survive half slave and half free." Was not Thomas Jefferson an extremist – "We hold these truths to be self-evident, that all men are created equal." So the question is not whether we will be extremist but what kind of extremist will we be. Will we be extremists for hate or will we be extremists for love? Will we be extremists for the preservation of injustice – or will we be extremists for justice?

The church

I have been so greatly disappointed with the white church and its leadership. Of course, there are some notable exceptions. I am not unmindful of the fact that each of you has taken some significant stands on this issue. I commend you, Rev Stallings, for your Christian stand on this past Sunday, in welcoming Negroes to your worship service on a non-segregated basis. I commend the Catholic leaders of this state for integrating Spring Hill College several years ago.

But despite these notable exceptions I must honestly reiterate that I have been disappointed with the church. I do not say that as one of those negative critics who can always find something wrong with the church. I say it as a minister of the gospel, who loves the church; who was nurtured in its bosom; who has been sustained by its spiritual blessings and who will remain true to it.

But again I am thankful to God that some noble souls from the ranks of organized religion have broken loose from the paralyzing chains of conformity and joined us as active partners in the struggle for freedom. They have left their secure congregations and walked the streets of Albany, Georgia, with us. They have gone through the highways of the South on tortuous rides for freedom. Yes, they have gone to jail with us. Some have been kicked out of their churches, and lost support of their bishops and fellow ministers. But they have gone with the faith that right defeated is stronger than evil triumphant.

Over the last few years I have consistently preached that nonviolence demands that the means we use must be as pure as the ends we seek. So I have tried to make it clear that it is wrong to use immoral means to attain moral ends.

Never before have I written a letter this long. I can assure you that it would have been much shorter if I had been writing from a comfortable desk, but what else is there to do when you are alone for days in the dull monotony of a narrow jail cell other than write long letters, think strange thoughts, and pray long prayers?

If I have said anything in this letter that is an overstatement of the truth and is indicative of an unreasonable impatience, I beg you to forgive me. If I have said anything that is an understatement of the truth and is indicative of my having a patience that makes me patient with anything less than brotherhood, I beg God to forgive me.

I hope this letter finds you strong in the faith. I also hope that circumstances will soon make it possible for me to meet each of you, not as an integrationist or a civil rights leader, but as a fellow clergyman and a Christian brother. Let us all hope that the dark clouds of racial prejudice will soon pass away and the deep fog of misunderstanding will be lifted from our fear-drenched communities and in some not too distant tomorrow the radiant stars of love and brotherhood will shine over our great nation.

An historical note

Dr King's appeal to America's conscience was effective. Eight weeks after King's letter, President John F. Kennedy proposed a comprehensive new civil rights law. The following are excerpts from a speech that Kennedy gave on 11 June 1963, on the occasion of the first enrollment of black students at the University of Alabama.

I hope that every American, regardless of where he lives, will stop and examine his conscience. This nation was founded by men of many nations and backgrounds. It was founded on the principle that all men are created equal, and that the rights of every man are diminished when the rights of one man are threatened.

The Negro baby born in America today, regardless of the section of the nation in which he is born, has about one half as much chance of completing high school as a white baby, one third as much chance of completing college, one third as much chance of becoming a professional, twice as much chance of becoming unemployed, a life expectancy which is seven years shorter, and the prospects of earning only half as much.

This is not a sectional issue. Difficulties over segregation and discrimination exist in every city, in every state of the Union. Nor is this a partisan issue. This is not even a legal or legislative issue alone. New laws are needed at every level, but law alone cannot make men see right. We are confronted primarily with a moral issue.

The heart of the question is whether all Americans are to be afforded equal rights and equal opportunities, whether we are going to treat our fellow Americans as we want to be treated. If an American, because his skin is dark, cannot eat lunch in a restaurant open to the public, if he can not send his children to the best public school available, if he cannot vote for the public officials who represent him, if, in short, he cannot enjoy the full and free life which all of us want, then who among us would be content to have the color of his skin changed and stand in his place? Who among us would be content with the counsels of patience and delay?

Now the time has come for this nation to fulfill its promise. The events in Birmingham and elsewhere have so increased the cries for equality that no city or state or legislative body can prudently choose to ignore them.

Next week I shall ask the Congress of the United States to act, to make a commitment it has not fully made in this century to the proposition that race has no place in American life or law. I am, therefore, asking the Congress to enact legislation giving all Americans the right to be served in facilities which are open to the public – hotels, restaurants, theaters, retail stores, and similar establishments. I am also asking Congress to authorize the federal government to participate more fully in lawsuits designed to end segregation in public education. Other features will also be requested, including greater protection for the right to vote. But legislation, I repeat, cannot solve this problem alone. It must be solved in the homes of every American in every community across our country.

> Dr King praised Kennedy's speech, calling it "one of the most eloquent, profound and unequivocal pleas for justice and freedom of all men ever made by any President." Kennedy, unfortunately, would be assassinated several months later (as King would be five years later). The comprehensive Civil Rights Act that Kennedy proposed was passed by Congress the next year, in 1964, under the leadership of a southerner, President Lyndon B. Johnson.

Study questions

1 How did King answer the charge that his actions were "untimely" – that he should wait for a more opportune moment?
2 How did King describe the difference between just and unjust laws? How did he define and justify civil disobedience?
3 How did King answer the charge that he was an extremist?
4 How did King's religious beliefs influence his thinking and his actions?
5 Was King happy about how the white church dealt with racism? Explain why or why not.

6   How did Kennedy apply the golden rule to racism?
7   What political action did Kennedy call for? Did he think that the whole problem would be solved by political action?
8   What effect have King's demands for desegregation had on schools and other institutions in the United States?

For further study

This selection has excerpts from Dr Martin Luther King's "Letter from the Birmingham Jail." The various collections of King's writings include *A Testament of Hope: The Essential Writings and Speeches of Martin Luther King, Jr.*, edited by James Melvin Washington (San Francisco: Harper, 1991). Harry Gensler's *Ethics: A Contemporary Introduction* (London and New York: Routledge, 1998) discusses racism in Sections 7.4 and 9.3.

Related readings in this anthology include the Bible (the source of many of King's ideas); Nietzsche (who opposes Christian values); and Benedict, Gensler and Tokmenko, Hare, and Singer (on racism).

Notes

1   King is referring to the "Brown vs. the Topeka Board of Education" case.
2   King is referring to the 1956 revolt against the Soviet occupation of Hungary.

LAWRENCE KOHLBERG
Moral Education

Lawrence Kohlberg, an American psychologist who lived from 1927 to 1987, was a major figure in the development of moral psychology. Since he was unhappy with the relativistic slant of many social scientists, he tried to gather psychological support for a more objective approach to morality.

On the basis of extensive studies, Kohlberg claimed that, regardless of our culture, we all develop in our moral thinking through a series of set stages. As young children, we begin by thinking of morality in terms of punishment and obedience; "bad" is what we get punished for. Later, we move to cultural relativism, where "good" is what is socially approved; Kohlberg sees this as an immature approach, typical of teenagers and young adults. If we progress far enough, we begin to criticize accepted norms using rational principles of justice – like the golden rule and the regard for the equal value and dignity of all. Kohlberg argued that moral education should help children develop in their moral thinking toward more advanced stages.

As you read the selection, consider your own experience of how children develop in their moral thinking. Does Kohlberg's description of the process make sense to you? How can we best promote growth in moral thinking?

Moral philosophy and moral psychology

Moral philosophy and moral psychology represent the two basic areas of inquiry into moral education. Moral psychology studies what moral development *is*. Moral philosophy considers what moral development *ought to be*. Because the two types of inquiry – the "is" of psychology and the "ought" of philosophy – must be integrated before one can have a reasoned basis for moral education, I shall try to speak from both points of view throughout this article.

Central to moral education is the problem of relativity of values: Are there universal values that children should develop? Our solution to this problem rests on recent psychological research that shows culturally universal stages of moral development. These findings help generate a philosophy of moral education as the stimulation of moral development, rather than the direct teaching of fixed moral rules. We present, then, a theory of moral education that is both psychological and philosophical.

Overview of theories

The theory of moral psychology we shall use is basically that of John Dewey, more recently elaborated by Jean Piaget and myself. The moral *philosophy* of education is also basically that of Dewey as we have elaborated it in terms of contemporary philosophic thought.

The progressive-educational psychologists and philosophers of the 1930's elaborated Dewey's goals of education but neglected certain of his key assumptions. These were (1) that intelligent thought about the education of social traits and values required a philosophical concept of morality and *moral* development, a very different concept from "social adjustment" or "mental health"; (2) that moral development passed through invariant qualitative stages; and (3) that the stimulation of moral development, like other forms of development, rested on the stimulation of thinking and problem-solving by the child.

These are the core assumptions of the "cognitive-developmental" theory of moral education presented in this article. Before presenting our theory, we shall briefly consider and criticize two other theories of moral education. The first is the "common-sense" theory behind traditional moral education. According to this theory, "everyone knows what's right and wrong," or at least most law-abiding adults do. Adults know a set of facts about morality of which children are ignorant, facts like "stealing is always wrong" or "helping others is good." These facts may be taught on the basis of the teacher's superior knowledge and authority, just as the facts of arithmetic are taught. Not only are children ignorant of moral facts; they are weak and easily tempted to lie, cheat, fight, disobey, and so forth. Children, then, need not only to be taught moral facts; they need to be taught to practice moral behavior and habits, and to be appropriately rewarded for moral behavior and punished for yielding to temptation.

In opposition to this traditional view, another has developed: the relativistic-emotional approach, which is popularly considered *the* view of child psychology. The child is seen as primarily a creature of emotions and needs. Morality, in turn, is no absolute which the child must be measured against, but represents the relativistic rules and standards of the child's culture. The child must adjust to these rules in a realistic manner as part of his mental health, and will do so if his home and school environment are meeting his inner needs.

The cognitive-developmental view starts philosophically from a different view of morality. It claims that, at heart, morality represents a set of *rational principles of judgment and decision* valid for every culture, the principles of human welfare and justice. The lists of rules drawn up by cultures and schools are more or less arbitrary, and hence their teaching tends to rely upon authority rather than reason. Moral principles, however, represent a rational organization of the child's own moral experience. We customarily attempt to deal with other adults as reasonable creatures in moral matters, and we need also to see that the child can be a reasonable being. Although the child does reason, he reasons in a different way than the adult. His way of thinking about fairness or human welfare is not the adult's; it represents a *different stage* of moral reason.

Our research into the stages of moral reasoning provides the key to moral education as the stimulation of children's moral judgment to the next stage of development, and as the stimulation of the child's ability to act consistently in accordance with his own moral judgment. This approach generates a new "Socratic" way for the teacher to conduct discussions about values. It also gives the democratic school a way to foster moral development through increasing the child's participation and responsibility in a community he perceives as *just*.

The principle of justice

Both psychology and philosophy support the claim that there are, in fact, universal human ethical values and principles. A key word here is "principles," for a moral principle is not the same as a rule. "Thou shalt not commit adultery" is a rule for specific behavior in a monogamous society. By contrast, the categorical imperative (act only as you would be willing that everyone should act in the same situation) is a principle – not a prescription for behavior, but a guide for choosing among behaviors. As such it is free from culturally defined content; it both transcends and subsumes particular social laws and hence has universal application.

The principle central to the development of moral judgment is that of *justice*. Justice, the primary regard for the value and equality of all human beings, and for reciprocity in human relations, is a basic and universal standard. Using justice as the organizing principle for moral education meets all the criteria which any such plan must satisfy: It guarantees freedom of belief, it employs a philosophically justifiable concept of morality, and it is based on the psychological facts of human development.

As social psychologists, my colleagues and I have gathered considerable evidence that the concepts of justice inhere in human experience, instead of being the product of a particular world-view. In this we follow Piaget, who says, "In contrast to a given rule imposed upon the child from outside, the rule of justice is an immanent condition of social relationships or a law governing their equilibrium." Social life entails assuming a variety of roles, taking other people's perspectives, and participating in reciprocal relationships, so that arriving at the principle of human equality is simply the effect of maturity in interpersonal relations. It is a normal (if not frequent) result of social existence, rather than a quirk of personality or an act of faith.

Stages of moral judgment

Individuals acquire and refine the sense of justice through a sequence of *invariant* developmental stages. In 1957, we began testing the moral judgment of a group of 72 boys aged 10 through 16 by asking them questions involving moral dilemmas. A typical question raises the issue of stealing a drug to save a dying woman. The inventor of the drug is selling it for 10 times what it costs him to make it. The woman's husband cannot raise the money, and the seller refuses to lower the price or wait for payment. What should the husband do? From the answers given by the group we distinguished six basic types of moral judgment which correspond to developmental stages. Subsequent retesting of the group at three-year intervals has shown growth proceeding through the same stages in the same order.

The stages are:

1. Orientation to punishment and reward, and to physical and material power.
2. Hedonistic orientation with an instrumental view of human relations. Beginning notions of reciprocity, but with emphasis on exchange of favors – "You scratch my back and I'll scratch yours."
3. "Good boy" orientation; seeking to maintain expectations and win approval of one's immediate group.
4. Orientation to authority, law, and duty, to maintaining a fixed order, whether social or religious, assumed as a primary value.
5. Social-contract orientation, with emphasis on equality and mutual obligation within a democratically established order; for example, the morality of the American Constitution.
6. Principles of conscience that have logical comprehensiveness and universality. Highest value placed on human life, equality, and dignity.

These stages are defined by ways of thinking about moral matters. Stages 1 and 2, typical of young children and delinquents, are described as "premoral," since decisions are made largely on the basis of self-interest. The group-oriented Stages 3 and 4 are the "conventional" ones at which most of the adult population operates. The final "principled" stages are characteristic of 20 to 25 per cent of the adult population, with perhaps 5 to 10 per cent arriving at Stage 6.

Each stage is itself defined by values or issues that enter into moral decisions. One such issue is the value placed on life. At Stage 1, life is valued in terms of the power or possessions of the person involved; at Stage 2, for its usefulness in satisfying the needs of the individual in question or others; at Stage 3, in terms of the individual's relations with others and their valuation of him; at Stage 4, in terms of social or religious law. Only at Stage 6 is each life seen as inherently worthwhile, aside from all other considerations.

Another factor defining the stage is motivation for moral action. At the lowest stages, the individual acts to avoid punishment or to obtain exchange of favors; at the highest level, to avoid self-condemnation. Stage-2 thinking in this area is apparent in Jimmy, age 13, who was asked whether a boy should tell his father about a brother's misdeed: "I think he should keep quiet. If he squeals on Alex, Alex might squeal on him." A Stage-3 answer to this question might be that the boy should tell because his father trusts him.

Most people are consistent in their use of a single type of thinking. About 50 per cent of an individual's moral statements correspond to a dominant stage and the rest fall generally into the stages immediately above and below. Stage of thinking usually holds constant regardless of the content of the dilemma – a delinquent at a premoral stage will regard all norms in the same way, whether they are the norms of society or of his gang, conforming only to avoid punishment.

The same stages of development are also found in other cultures, although average progress is faster and farther in some than in others. We have tested youngsters in the US, Great Britain, Mexico, Turkey, Taiwan, and Malaysia, and distinguished the same patterns of thought in the same developmental sequence. When Taiwanese village boys, for example, were asked whether a man should steal food for his starving wife, a typical answer from a preadolescent was, "Yes, because otherwise he will have to pay for her funeral and that costs a lot." A Malaysian child of the same age was likely to say, "Yes, because he needs her to cook his food." Funerals are less important in Malaysia than in Taiwan, so the cultural content of the reply changes, but the Stage-2 orientation of young children remains constant.

Conditions for moral development

What spurs progress from one stage to another? Moral judgment is primarily a function of rational operations. Affectional factors such as the ability to empathize and the capacity for guilt enter in, but moral situations are defined cognitively by the judging individual. Moral development is therefore a result of an increasing ability to perceive social reality or to organize and integrate social experience. One necessary – but not sufficient – condition for principled morality is the ability to reason logically (represented by stages of formal operations).

The main experiential determinants of moral development seem to be amount and variety of social experience, the opportunity to take a number of roles and to encounter other perspectives. Thus middle-class and popular children progress farther and faster than do lower-class children and social isolates. Similarly, development is slower in semiliterate village cultures. Being able, through wide practice, to take another's viewpoint, to "put yourself in his place," is the source of the principled sense of equality and reciprocity. Perhaps the best summary of the situation in everyday language comes from E. M. Forster, who thought that most of the trouble in the world is due to "the inability to imagine the innerness of other lives."

An example of the power of such experiences comes from an experiment by Dowell, who helped high school students counsel one another in the "nondirective" manner. The experience led to a significant upward-stage movement in moral reasoning, presumably stimulated by the intense effort to take the view of the other. In contrast, being counseled or being a member of a self-answer group does not generate moral movement because it does not entail new experiencing of the perspectives of others.

The opportunity for moral role-taking appears to be what is most important in the contribution of the family to moral development. A study by Holstein indicates that children who were advanced in moral judgment had parents who were also advanced in moral judgment. Quite separately, however, the parents' tendency to stimulate reciprocal role-taking was also related to the child's maturity. The parent who sought the child's view, who elicited comparison of views in dialogue, had more advanced children.

Planned moral education in the public schools

Studies by Blatt and Kohlberg indicate that educational efforts to stimulate moral development can have a significant effect. Sixth- and 10th-graders in groups of 10 met twice a week for three months to discuss moral dilemmas. A majority of the students in the classes moved ahead almost one full stage, a substantial change for that period of time. Furthermore, those who had advanced after the 12 weeks remained advanced one year later as compared to a control group without the moral-discussion experience. By using procedures available to any teacher, it is possible to raise children's moral level significantly and in a way that is sustained over time.

While the moral discussion procedures used by Blatt are available to teachers, they are quite different from those that teachers ordinarily use. The procedures rely upon both the induction of cognitive conflict about moral issues and exposure to the stage of thinking next above the student's own.

The first procedure focuses upon moral dilemmas which the instructor and students discuss. The dilemmas are selected because they generate cognitive conflict – uncertainty about what is right, about the adequacy of the current moral beliefs the student holds – or because they generate disagreement between students.

The second procedure elicits discussion between students at two adjacent stages. Since the children were not all at the same stage, the arguments they used were different. In the discussions among the students, the teacher first supported and clarified those arguments one stage above the lowest stage among the children – for example, the teacher supported Stage 3 rather than Stage 2. When it seemed that these arguments were understood by the students, the teacher then challenged that stage, using new situations, and clarified the arguments one stage above the previous one – Stage 4 rather than Stage 3. As noted earlier, at the end of the semester all the students were retested; they showed significant upward change and maintained the change one year later.

The teacher must help the child to consider genuine moral conflicts, see inconsistencies and inadequacies in his way of thinking, and find ways of resolving them. To do this, the teacher must know the child's level of thought, communicate at the level directly above, focus on reasoning, and help the child experience the type of conflict that leads to an awareness of the greater adequacy of the next stage.

This classroom-discussion program is only one example of how the cognitive-developmental approach can be applied in the school. The classroom discussion approach should be part of a broader involvement of students in the social and moral functioning of the school. Rather than attempting to inculcate a predetermined and unquestioned set of values, teachers should challenge students with the moral issues faced by the school community as problems to be solved.

At present, schools are not especially moral institutions. Institutional relationships tend to be based more on authority than on ideas of justice. Adults are often less interested in discovering *how* children are thinking than in telling them *what* to think. The school atmosphere is generally a blend of Stage 1, punishment morality, and Stage 4, "law and order," which fails to impress – or stimulate – children involved in their own Stage-2 or Stage-3 moral philosophies. Children and adults stop communicating with one another, horizons are narrowed, and development is stunted.

If schools wish to foster morality, they have to provide an atmosphere in which interpersonal issues are settled on the basis of principle rather than power. They have to take moral questions seriously, and provide food for thought instead of conventional "right answers."

In summary, then, developmental findings on moral stages, moral-philo-sophic conceptions of principles, and the tenets of constitutional democracy cohere to define a philosophically and psychologically viable conception of moral education. Though outlined in 1909 by John Dewey, this conception has only recently gained the research support needed to make it truly convincing. The concept still remains to be tried by American schools.

Study questions

1 How does moral philosophy differ from moral psychology? Which is needed for a theory about moral education?
2 Explain these three approaches to moral education, as well as their phi-losophical and psychological presuppositions: the common sense ap-proach, the relativistic-emotional approach, and the cognitive-develop-mental approach.
3 How do moral *principles* differ from moral *rules*? Give examples. Are moral principles valid only relative to a particular culture?
4 What empirical methods establish the stage-sequence of moral develop-ment?
5 Explain the two preconventional stages, the two conventional stages, and the two postconventional (principled) stages.
6 Which stages are typical of children? Which are typical of adults?
7 If you reach a given moral stage, do you do all your moral thinking at that stage? Or, will you sometimes use higher or lower stages? Explain.
8 Do the stages differ in different cultures?
9 How does logical ability relate to the stage of moral thinking?
10 How does role-taking ability relate to stage of moral thinking? Which stimulates more growth in moral thinking: counseling another or being counseled? Why?
11 What classroom procedures can stimulate moral development?
12 Summarize how adults can stimulate the growth of moral thinking in children.

For further study

This selection has excerpts from Lawrence Kohlberg's "A Cognitive-Devel-opmental Approach to Moral Education," published in the *Humanist* 32 (November-December 1972): 13–16. For a longer discussion, see his *Essays on Moral Development (The Philosophy of Moral Development* and *The*

Psychology of Moral Development), vols 1 and 2 (San Francisco: Harper & Row, 1981 and 1984). See also Jean Piaget's *The Moral Judgment of the Child* (Glencoe, IL: Free Press, 1948), translated by Marjorie Gabain. For a contrasting view, see Michael Schulman and Eva Mekler's *Bringing Up a Moral Child* (New York: Doubleday, 1994). Carol Gilligan's *In a Different Voice* (Cambridge, MA: Harvard University Press, 1982) accuses Kohlberg's view of having a male bias. Harry Gensler's *Ethics: A Contemporary Introduction* (London and New York: Routledge, 1998) discusses moral education in Section 9.4.

Many readings in this anthology discuss the issue that Kohlberg sees as central to moral education: the objectivity of values. Ayer, Benedict, Hume, and Mackie reject objective values; Moore and Ross adopt the "common sense" intuitionist approach to objective values; and Frankena, Gensler and Tokmenko, Habermas, Hare, Hertzler, Kant, Nagel, and Rawls support ways of reasoning about values that roughly accord with Kohlberg's Stage 6.

PART IV

NORMATIVE THEORY: CONSEQUENTIALISM, NONCONSEQUENTIALISM, DISTRIBUTIVE JUSTICE, AND VIRTUE

JOHN STUART MILL
Utilitarianism

John Stuart Mill, a British philosopher who lived from 1806 to 1873, has had a great influence on contemporary moral and political philosophy. So we thought it helpful to include excerpts from his *Utilitarianism*. His other writings include *On Liberty*, *Considerations on Representative Government*, and *The Subjection of Women*.

Mill defends a consequentialist ethics. He argues that the rightness or wrongness of an act is determined only by its consequences – more specifically, by whether it maximizes happiness.

As you read the selection, ask yourself whether acts should be evaluated by consequences alone. Could an act ever be wrong if it produced the best consequences possible under the circumstances? If you are familiar with Kant's theory, ask yourself how it differs from Mill's and which of the two seems better.

The greatest happiness principle

Utility, or the Greatest Happiness Principle, holds that actions are right in proportion as they tend to promote happiness, wrong as they tend to produce the reverse of happiness. By happiness is intended pleasure and the absence of pain; by unhappiness, pain and the privation of pleasure. Pleasure, and freedom from pain, are the only things desirable as ends; and all desirable things are desirable either for the pleasure inherent in themselves, or as means to the promotion of pleasure and the prevention of pain.

Such a theory excites in many minds dislike. To suppose that life has no higher end than pleasure they designate as a doctrine worthy only of swine, to whom the followers of Epicurus were compared.

The Epicureans answered that it is the accusers who represent human nature in a degrading light, since they suppose human beings to be capable of no pleasures except those of which swine are capable. Humans have faculties more elevated and do not regard anything as happiness which does not include their gratification.

Some kinds of pleasure are more desirable and valuable than others. If I am asked what I mean by quality in pleasures, or what makes one pleasure more valuable than another, there is but one answer. Of two pleasures, if there be one to which almost all who have experienced both give a preference, irrespective of any feeling of moral obligation, that is the more desirable pleasure. If one is, by those acquainted with both, placed above the other, we are justified in ascribing to it a superiority in quality.

Those equally capable of appreciating and enjoying both, do give a marked preference to their higher faculties. Few human creatures would consent to be changed into a lower animal for a promise of its pleasures. A being of higher faculties requires more to make him happy and is capable of more acute suffering; but he can never wish to sink into what he feels to be a lower grade of existence.

It is better to be a human being dissatisfied than a pig satisfied; better to be Socrates dissatisfied than a fool satisfied. And if the fool or pig are of a different opinion, it is because they only know their own side. The other party knows both sides.

Many capable of the higher pleasures, under the influence of temptation, postpone them to the lower. But this is compatible with an appreciation of the intrinsic superiority of the higher. Men often, from infirmity of character, make their election for the nearer good. They pursue sensual indulgences to the injury of health, aware that health is the greater good.

From the verdict of competent judges, there can be no appeal. There is no other tribunal, even on the question of quantity. What means are there of determining which is the acutest of two pains, except the feelings and judgment of the experienced?

The good of everyone

The utilitarian standard is not the agent's greatest happiness, but the greatest amount of happiness altogether.

The ultimate end is an existence exempt as far as possible from pain, and as rich as possible in enjoyments, in quantity and quality. The standard of morality may be defined as the rules for human conduct, by the observance of which an existence such as has been described might be, to the greatest extent possible, secured to all mankind; and not to them only, but to the whole sentient creation.

The utilitarian morality recognizes in human beings the power of sacrificing their own greatest good for the good of others. It only refuses to admit that sacrifice is in itself a good. A sacrifice which does not increase the sum total of happiness, it considers as wasted.

The happiness which forms the utilitarian standard is not the agent's own happiness, but that of all concerned. As between his own happiness and that of others, utilitarianism requires him to be as impartial as a disinterested and benevolent spectator. In the golden rule of Jesus, we read the complete spirit of the ethics of utility. To do as you would be done by, and to love your neighbor as yourself, constitute the ideal perfection of utilitarian morality.

The objectors to utilitarianism sometimes say it is too much to require that people shall always act from the inducement of promoting the interests of society. But this is to confound the rule with the motive. The motive has nothing to do with the morality of the action, though much with the worth of the agent. He who saves a fellow creature from drowning does what is morally right, whether his motive be duty, or the hope of being paid.

Sometimes utility is called a godless doctrine. The question depends upon what idea we have formed of the moral character of the Deity. If God desires, above all things, the happiness of his creatures, and this was his purpose in their creation, utility is not only not a godless doctrine, but more profoundly religious than any other. A utilitarian who believes in the perfect goodness and wisdom of God, necessarily believes that whatever God has revealed on morality must fulfill the requirements of utility in a supreme degree.

Utility is often given the name Expediency, to contrast with Principle. But the Expedient generally means what is expedient for the agent himself or for some temporary purpose, but violates the greater good. The Expedient in this sense is hurtful. It would often be expedient to tell a lie. But the cultivation of a sensitive feeling on veracity is very useful. The violation, for a present advantage, of such a rule is not expedient. Yet even this sacred rule admits of exceptions, as when the withholding of information from a malefactor would prevent evil, and this can only be effected by denial. The principle of utility can weigh these conflicting utilities against one another.

The proof of the principle

The utilitarian doctrine is that happiness is desirable, and the only thing desirable, as an end; all other things being only desirable as means to that end.

The only proof that an object is visible is that people see it. The only proof that a sound is audible is that people hear it. In like manner, the sole evidence that anything is desirable is that people desire it. If the end which the utilitarian doctrine proposes were not, in theory and in practice, acknowledged to be an end, nothing could ever convince any person that it was so. No reason can be given why the general happiness is desirable, except that each person, so far as he believes it to be attainable, desires his own happiness. This, being a fact, we have not only all the proof which the case admits of, but all which it is possible to require, that happiness is a good, that each person's happiness is a good to that person, and the general happiness, therefore, a good to the aggregate of all persons. Happiness has made out its title as one of the ends of conduct and criteria of morality.

But it has not proved itself to be the sole criterion. To do that, it would need to show, not only that people desire happiness, but that they never desire anything else. Now they seem to desire things distinguished from happiness, for example, virtue and the absence of vice. And hence the opponents of the utilitarian standard infer that there are other ends of human action besides happiness, and that happiness is not the sole standard.

Utilitarianism maintains that virtue is to be desired, disinterestedly, for itself. The mind is not in the state most conducive to the general happiness, unless it loves virtue as a thing desirable in itself. The ingredients of happiness are various, and each of them is desirable in itself. Virtue, according to the utilitarian doctrine, is not originally part of the end, but it can become so.

There is nothing originally more desirable about money than about any heap of pebbles. Its worth is solely that of the things which it will buy. Yet money is, in many cases, desired for itself; the desire to possess it is often stronger than the desire to use it. From being a means to happiness, it has come to be a principal ingredient of the individual's conception of happiness. The person thinks he would be made happy by its mere possession. It is included in his happiness.

Virtue is a good of this description. And with this difference between it and the love of money – that there is nothing which makes a person so much a blessing to others as the cultivation of the disinterested love of virtue. The utilitarian standard, while it approves other acquired desires, up to the point where they would be more injurious to the general happiness than promoting of it, requires the cultivation of the love of virtue to the greatest strength possible, as being above all things important to the general happiness.

So there is nothing desired except happiness. Whatever is desired otherwise than as a means to some end beyond itself, is desired as a part of happiness. Those who desire virtue for its own sake desire it either because the consciousness of it is a pleasure, or because the consciousness of being without it is a pain, or for both reasons united.

We have now an answer to the question, of what sort of proof the principle of utility is susceptible. If human nature is so constituted as to desire nothing which is not either a part of happiness or a means of happiness – we can have no other proof, and we require no other, that these are the only things desirable. If so, happiness is the sole end of human action, and the promotion of it the test to judge of human conduct.

Whether this is so can only be determined by observation. This evidence will declare that desiring a thing and finding it pleasant, aversion to it and thinking of it as painful, are two different modes of naming the same psychological fact; to think of an object as desirable (unless for the sake of its consequences) and to think of it as pleasant are one and the same thing.

But if this doctrine be true, the principle of utility is proved. Whether it is so or not must now be left to the consideration of the thoughtful reader.

Study questions

1 Formulate the greatest happiness principle. Use an example to illustrate how it works.
2 How does Mill respond to those who say that his view is worthy only of swine?
3 On Mill's view, are mental pleasures higher because they contain more pleasure? How do we decide which pleasures are superior?
4 Can some people experience both higher and lower pleasures and yet prefer the lower pleasures?
5 Whose happiness are we to consider when applying the greatest happiness principle?
6 Under what conditions should we perform self-sacrificing acts?
7 Do the golden rule and the "Love your neighbor" principle conflict with utilitarianism?
8 Must all our actions be motivated by the goal of promoting the good of society?
9 How does Mill respond to the charge that utilitarianism is a "godless" doctrine of "mere expediency"?
10 How does Mill argue that (the general) happiness and it alone is desirable as an ultimate end?
11 Is virtue desired only as a means to pleasure?
12 How are these three related: "I desire X for its own sake," "I find X desirable for its own sake," and "I regard X as pleasant"?

For further study

This selection has excerpts, sometimes simplified in wording, from the public domain version of John Stuart Mill's 1863 *Utilitarianism*. For an important opposing view, see Immanuel Kant's 1789 *Groundwork of the Metaphysics of Morals*, edited by H. J. Paton (New York: Harper & Row Publishers, 1948). Harry Gensler's *Ethics: A Contemporary Introduction* (London and New York: Routledge, 1998) examines consequentialism in Chapter 10.

Related readings from this anthology include Singer and Smart (who defend utilitarianism); Finnis, Kant, Rawls, Ross, Williams, and O'Neill (who oppose it); Brandt (who defends rule utilitarianism); and Nagel and Slote (who challenge Mill's claim that we need to consider everyone's happiness on an equal basis).

J. J. C. SMART
Defending Utilitarianism

J. J. C. Smart, an Australian philosopher born in 1920, works in ethics and philosophy of science. His *Philosophy and Scientific Realism* defended a physicalist view of mind. This present selection is taken from his defense of utilitarianism in *Utilitarianism: For and Against,* co-authored with Bernard Williams.

After distinguishing various types of utilitarianism, Smart opts for act-utilitarianism. He hopes that our widely shared desires to promote everyone's happiness may lead others to become act-utilitarians too.

As you read the selection, note the different types of utilitarianism. Do you find Smart's argument for act- over rule-utilitarianism convincing? Ought consequences alone to determine whether individual acts are right or wrong? Should other factors be considered?

Method

Act-utilitarianism is the view that the rightness of an action depends only on the total goodness or badness of its consequences, i.e. on the effect on the welfare of all human beings (or perhaps all sentient beings). The best exposition of act-utilitarianism is Sidgwick's *Methods of Ethics,* but Sidgwick stated it within the framework of a cognitivist[1] metaethics which supposed that act-utilitarian principles could be known to be true by intellectual intuition. I reject Sidgwick's metaethics for familiar reasons, and will assume the truth of some such "noncognitivist" analysis as that of Hare's *Language of Morals,* or possibly that of D. H. Monro in his *Empiricism and Ethics.* Both imply that ultimate ethical principles depend on attitudes or feelings. In adopting such a metaethics, I renounce the attempt to *prove* the act-utilitarian system. I shall be concerned with stating it in a form which may appear persuasive to some people, and to show how it may be defended against objections.

In setting up a system of normative ethics, the utilitarian must appeal to ultimate attitudes which he holds in common with those whom he is addressing. The sentiment to which he appeals is generalized benevolence, the disposition to seek happiness or good consequences for all mankind, or perhaps for all sentient beings. His audience may not initially be in agreement with the utilitarian position. For example, they may have a propensity to obey the rules of some traditional moral system into which they have been indoctrinated in youth. Nevertheless the utilitarian will have some hope of persuading the audience to agree with his system of normative ethics. He can appeal to the sentiment of generalized benevolence, which is surely present in any group with whom it is profitable to discuss ethical questions. He may be able to convince some people that their previous disposition to accept non-utilitarian principles was due to conceptual confusions. He will not be able to convince everybody, but that is not an objection. It may well be that there is no ethical system which appeals to all people.

Act- and rule-utilitarianism

I am here concerned to defend act-utilitarianism. Act-utilitarianism is to be contrasted with rule-utilitarianism. Act-utilitarianism is the view that the rightness of an action is to be judged by the consequences, good or bad, of the action itself. Rule-utilitarianism is the view that the rightness of an action is to be judged by the goodness and badness of the consequences of a rule that everyone should perform the action in like circumstances.

I have argued elsewhere the objections to rule-utilitarianism. Briefly they boil down to the accusation of rule worship: the rule-utilitarian advocates his principle because he is ultimately concerned with human happiness: why then should he advocate abiding by a rule when he knows that it will not in the present case be beneficial to abide by it? To refuse to break a rule in cases in which it is not beneficial to obey it seems irrational and to be a case of rule worship.

Hedonistic and non-hedonistic utilitarianism

An act-utilitarian judges the rightness of actions by the goodness and badness of their consequences. But is he to judge the goodness and badness of consequences solely by their pleasantness and unpleasantness? Bentham, who thought that quantity of pleasure being equal, the experience of playing pushpin was as good as that of reading poetry, could be classified as a hedonistic act-utilitarian. Moore, who believed that some states of mind, such as knowledge, had intrinsic value independent of their pleasantness, can be called an ideal utilitarian. Mill seemed to occupy an intermediate position. He held that there are higher and lower pleasures. This seems to imply that pleasure is a necessary condition for goodness but that goodness depends on other qualities of experience than pleasantness and unpleasantness. I propose to call Mill a quasi-ideal utilitarian.

The utilitarian addresses himself to people who likely agree with him as to what consequences are good ones, but who disagree that what we ought to do is to produce the best consequences. The difference between ideal and hedonistic utilitarianism in most cases will not lead to disagreement about what ought to be done.

Let us consider Mill's contention that it is "better to be Socrates dissatisfied than a fool satisfied." A hedonistic utilitarian, like Bentham, might agree with Mill in preferring the experiences of discontented philosophers to those of contented fools. His preference for the philosopher's state of mind, however, would not be an *intrinsic* one. He would say that the discontented philosopher is useful in society and that the existence of Socrates is responsible for an improvement in the lot of humanity generally.

Again, a man who enjoys pushpin is likely eventually to become bored with it, whereas the man who enjoys poetry is likely to retain this interest throughout his life. Moreover reading poetry may develop imagination and sensitivity, and so as a result a man may be able to do more for the happiness of others than if he had played pushpin and let his brain deteriorate. In short, both for the man immediately concerned and for others, the pleasures of poetry are, to use Bentham's word, more *fecund* than those of pushpin.

Average and total happiness

Another disagreement can arise over whether we should try to maximize the *average* happiness or the *total* happiness. I have not yet elucidated the concept of total happiness, and you may regard it as a suspect notion. But for present purposes I shall put it in this way: Would you be quite indifferent between (a) a universe containing one million happy sentient beings, all equally happy, and (b) a universe containing two million happy beings? Or would you, as a humane and sympathetic person, give a preference to the second universe? I myself feel a preference for the second universe. But if someone feels the other way I do not know how to argue with him.

This disagreement might have practical relevance. It might be important in discussions of birth control. But in most cases the difference will not lead to disagreement in practice. For in most cases the most effective way to increase the total happiness is to increase the average happiness, and vice versa.

Rightness of actions

I shall now state the act-utilitarian doctrine. For simplicity of exposition I shall put it forward in a hedonistic form. If anyone values states of mind such as knowledge independently of their pleasurableness he can make appropriate verbal alterations to convert it from hedonistic to ideal utilitarianism.

Let us say, then, that the only reason for performing an action A rather than an alternative action B is that doing A will make mankind (or, perhaps, all sentient beings) happier than will doing B. This is so simple and natural a doctrine that we can expect that many readers will have some propensity to agree. For I am talking, as I said earlier, to sympathetic and benevolent men, that is, to men who desire the happiness of mankind. Since they have a favorable attitude to the general happiness, surely they have a tendency to submit to an ultimate moral principle which expresses this attitude. It is possible, then, that many sympathetic and benevolent people depart from a utilitarian ethical principle only under the stress of tradition, of superstition, or of unsound philosophical reasoning.

The utilitarian's ultimate moral principle, let it be remembered, expresses the sentiment not of altruism but of benevolence, the agent counting himself neither more nor less than any other person.

Suppose we could predict the future consequences of actions with certainty. In order to help someone to decide whether to do A or to do B we could say to him: "Envisage the total consequences of A, and think them over carefully and imaginatively. Now envisage the total consequences of B, and think them over. As a benevolent and humane man, and thinking of yourself just as one man among others, would you prefer the consequences of A or those of B?" That is, we are asking for a comparison of one (present and future) *total* situation with another (present and future) *total* situation. So far we are not asking for a *summation* or *calculation* of pleasures or happiness. We are asking only for a comparison of total situations. And it seems clear that we can frequently make such a comparison and say that one total situation is better than another.

When we look at our ordinary decisions, we see that most people think that we can weigh up probabilities and advantages. A man deciding whether to migrate to a tropical country may well say to himself, for example, that he can expect a pleasanter life for himself and his family in that country, unless there is a change in the system of government there, which is not likely, or unless one of his children catches an epidemic disease, which is perhaps more likely, and so on, and thinking over all these advantages and disadvantages and probabilities and improbabilities he may come out with the statement that on the whole it seems preferable for him to go there.

Maybe we have not any precise methods for deciding what to do, but then our imprecise methods must serve.

The place of rules

The utilitarian position is here put forward as a criterion of rational choice. We may choose to habituate ourselves to behave in accordance with certain rules, such as to keep promises, in the belief that behaving in accordance with these rules is generally optimific, and in the knowledge that we often do not have time to work out pros and cons. The act-utilitarian will regard these rules as mere rules of thumb and will use them only as rough guides. He acts in accordance with rules when there is no time to think. When he has to think what to do, then there is a question of deliberation or choice, and it is for such situations that the utilitarian criterion is intended.

There is no inconsistency in an act-utilitarian's schooling himself to act, in normal circumstances, habitually and in accordance with rules. He knows that we would go mad if we went in detail into the probable consequences of keeping or not keeping every trivial promise: we will do the most good if we habituate ourselves to keep promises in all normal situations. Moreover he may suspect that on some occasions personal bias may prevent him from reasoning in a correct utilitarian fashion. If he trusts to the accepted rules he is more likely to act in the way that an unbiased act-utilitarian would recommend than if he tried to evaluate the consequences himself.

This is not the law worship of the rule-utilitarian, who would say that we ought to keep to a rule that is the most generally optimific, even though we *knew* that obeying it in this instance would have bad consequences.

Nor is this utilitarian doctrine incompatible with a recognition of the importance of warm and spontaneous expressions of emotion. Consider a case in which a man sees that his wife is tired, and from a spontaneous feeling of affection he offers to wash the dishes. Does utilitarianism imply that he should have stopped to calculate the various consequences of his different possible courses of action? Certainly not. This would make married life a misery and the utilitarian knows well as a rule of thumb that on occasions of this sort it is best to act spontaneously and without calculation. There are good utilitarian reasons why we should cultivate in ourselves the tendency to certain types of warm and spontaneous feeling.

Some further examples

We are here considering utilitarianism as a *normative* system. The fact that it has consequences which conflict with some of our particular moral judgments need not be decisive against it. The utilitarian can contend that since his principle rests on something so simple and natural as generalized benevolence it is more securely founded than our particular feelings, which may be subtly distorted by traditional and uncritical ethical thinking.

The chief argument in favor of utilitarianism has been that any deontological [rule-based] ethics will always, on some occasions, lead to misery that could, on utilitarian principles, have been prevented. Thus if the deontologist says that promises always should be kept (or even if, like Ross, he says that there is a *prima facie* duty to keep them) we may confront him with a situation like the well-known "desert island promise": I have promised a dying man on a desert island, from which subsequently I alone am rescued, to give his hoard of gold to the South Australian Jockey Club. On my return I give it to the Royal Adelaide Hospital, which badly needs it for a new X-ray machine. Could anybody deny that I had done rightly without being open to the charge of heartlessness? (Remember that the promise was known only to me, and so my action will not weaken the general confidence in the social institution of promising.) Think of the persons dying of painful tumors who could have been saved by the desert island gold!

Normally the utilitarian is able to assume that the remote effects of his actions tend rapidly to zero, like the ripples on a pond after a stone has been thrown into it. Suppose that a man is deciding whether to seduce his neighbor's wife. On utilitarian grounds it seems obvious that such an act would be wrong, for the unhappiness which it is likely to cause in the short term will be obvious. The man need not consider the possibility that one of his remote descendants, if he seduces the woman, will be a great benefactor of the human race. Such a possibility is not that improbable, considering the number of descendants after many generations, but it is no more probable than that one of his remote descendants will do great harm, or that one from a more legitimate union would benefit the human race. It seems plausible that the long-term probable benefits and costs of his alternative actions are likely to be negligible or to cancel one another out.

Killing the innocent

It is not difficult to show that utilitarianism could, in exceptional circumstances, have horrible consequences. H. J. McCloskey has considered such a case.[2] Suppose that the sheriff of a small town can prevent serious riots (in which hundreds of people will be killed) only by "framing" and executing (as a scapegoat) an innocent man. In actual cases of this sort the utilitarian will usually be able to agree with our normal moral feelings. He will point out that there would be some possibility of the sheriff's dishonesty being found out, with consequent weakening of confidence and respect for law and order in the community, the consequences of which would be far worse even than the painful deaths of hundreds of citizens. But as McCloskey is ready to point out, the case can be presented in such a way that these objections do not apply. For example, it can be imagined that the sheriff could have first-rate empirical evidence that he will not be found out. Someone like McCloskey can always strengthen his story to the point that we would have to admit that if utilitarianism is correct, then the sheriff must frame the innocent man.

Now though a utilitarian might argue that it is empirically unlikely that some such situation would ever occur, McCloskey will point out that it is *logically* possible that such a situation will arise. If the utilitarian rejects the unjust act he is giving up his utilitarianism. McCloskey remarks: "As far as I know, only J. J. C. Smart among the contemporary utilitarians is happy to adopt this 'solution.'" Here I must lodge a mild protest. McCloskey's use of the word "happy" makes me look reprehensible. Even in my most utilitarian moods I am not *happy* about this consequence of utilitarianism. Nevertheless, however unhappy about it he may be, the utilitarian must admit that he might find himself in circumstances where he ought to be unjust. Let us hope that this is a logical possibility and not a factual one.

No, I am not happy to draw the conclusion that McCloskey quite rightly says that the utilitarian must draw. But neither am I happy with the anti-utilitarian conclusion. For if a case *did* arise in which injustice was the lesser of two evils (in terms of human happiness and misery), then the anti-utilitarian conclusion is a very unpalatable one too, namely that in some circumstances one must choose the greater misery, perhaps the *very much* greater misery, such as that of hundreds of people suffering painful deaths.

Among possible options, utilitarianism does have its appeal. With its empirical attitude to means and ends it is congenial to the scientific temper and it has flexibility to deal with a changing world. This last consideration is, however, more self-recommendation than justification. For if flexibility is a recommendation, this is because of the utility of flexibility.

Study questions

1 Does Smart believe in objective moral truths? How does he propose to defend utilitarianism?
2 Explain the difference between act- and rule-utilitarianism. Construct an example that illustrates this difference.
3 Why does Smart reject rule-utilitarianism?
4 How do hedonistic and ideal utilitarianism differ? Is there much difference between them in practice?
5 Why does Smart call Mill a "quasi-ideal" utilitarian?
6 How does Smart formulate and apply act-utilitarianism?
7 Explain why Smart thinks it is consistent for one who is an act-utilitarian to habituate oneself to follow certain rules.
8 Explain the objection to utilitarianism illustrated in McCloskey's "sheriff" example. How does Smart respond to the objection?

For further study

This selection has excerpts, sometimes simplified in wording, from John Jamieson Carswell Smart's *Utilitarianism: For and Against* (Cambridge: Cambridge University Press, 1973), pages 4–5, 7, 9–10, 12–16, 27–8, 30–3, 39–40, 42–5, 56, 62, 64–5, and 69–73; this book was co-authored with Bernard Williams. Harry Gensler's *Ethics: A Contemporary Introduction* (London and New York: Routledge, 1998) examines utilitarianism in Chapter 10.

Related readings in this anthology include Brandt, Mill, and Singer (who defend versions of utilitarianism); Finnis, O'Neill, Rawls, Ross, Slote, and Williams (who criticize utilitarianism); Hume (who also appeals to sympathetic feelings), and Hare (whose analysis of ethical terms Smart assumes).

Notes

1   Smart uses the term "cognitivist" to refer to views that recognize objective moral truths and moral knowledge. Smart rejects such views.

2   H. J. McCloskey, "A note on utilitarian punishment," *Mind* 72 (1963): 599. [Note from Smart]

BERNARD WILLIAMS
Against Utilitarianism

Bernard Williams, a British philosopher born in 1929, has written important works in ethics and philosophy of mind. Those include *Problems of
the Self*, *Ethics and the Limits of Philosophy*, and *Shame and Necessity*.
This selection is taken from his criticism of utilitarianism in *Utilitarianism:
For and Against*, co-authored with J. J. C. Smart.

Williams argues that utilitarianism, when applied to certain cases, has
implications that clash strongly with our intuitions about right and wrong.
He further argues that a utilitarian cannot effectively appeal to "remote
effects" to avoid these counter-intuitive implications.

As you read the selection, ask yourself whether utilitarianism has the
implications that Williams claims about his two cases. Can utilitarians
avoid these implications by appealing to remote effects?

Two examples

Let us look at two examples, to see what utilitarianism might say about
them.

(1) George, who has just taken his Ph.D. in chemistry, finds it difficult to
get a job. He is not robust in health, which cuts down the number of jobs he
might be able to do. His wife has to work, which causes a great deal of
strain, since they have small children. The results of all this, especially on the
children, are damaging. An older chemist says that he can get George a
decently paid job in a laboratory which pursues research into chemical
warfare. George says that he cannot accept this, since he is opposed to
chemical warfare. The older man replies that he is not too keen on it himself,
but George's refusal is not going to make the job or the laboratory go away;
what is more, if George refuses the job, it will certainly go to a contemporary
of George's who is not inhibited by such scruples and is likely to push the
research with greater zeal than George would. What should George do?

(2) Jim finds himself in the central square of a small South American town.
Tied up against the wall are a row of twenty Indians, most terrified. A heavy
man in a khaki shirt turns out to be the captain in charge and explains that
the Indians are a random group of the inhabitants who, after recent acts of

protest against the government, are about to be killed to remind other possible protesters of the advantages of not protesting. However, since Jim is an honored visitor from another land, the captain is happy to offer him a guest's privilege of killing one of the Indians himself. If Jim accepts, then the other Indians will be let off. If Jim refuses, then Pedro will kill them all. The men against the wall, and the other villagers, understand the situation, and are begging him to accept. What should he do?

To these dilemmas, utilitarianism replies, in the first case, that George should accept the job, and in the second, that Jim should kill the Indian. Not only does utilitarianism give these answers but, if there are no further special factors, it regards them as *obviously* the right answers. But many of us would certainly wonder whether, in (1), that could possibly be the right answer; and in the case of (2), even one who came to think that was the answer, might well wonder whether it was obviously the answer. Nor is it just a question of the rightness or obviousness of these answers; it is also a question of what sort of considerations come into finding the answer. Utilitarianism cuts out the idea that each of us is specially responsible for what *he* does, rather than for what other people do. This is an idea closely connected with the value of integrity. It is often suspected that utilitarianism makes integrity as a value more or less unintelligible.

Remote effects

We should first ask whether we are assuming too hastily what the utilitarian answers to the dilemmas will be. In terms of more remote effects, counterweights might be found to enter the utilitarian scales. Thus the effect on George of a decision to take the job might be invoked, or its effect on others who might know of his decision. Such effects are often invoked by utilitarian writers dealing with lying or promise-breaking, and similar considerations might be invoked here.

The certainty that attaches to these hypotheses about possible effects is usually pretty low; in some cases, the hypothesis is so implausible that it would scarcely pass if it were not being used to deliver the respectable moral answer, as in the standard fantasy that one of the effects of telling a particular lie is to weaken the disposition of the world at large to tell the truth.

Effects on the agent

I want to consider two types of effect that are often invoked by utilitarians. First, there is the psychological effect on the agent. Our descriptions have not taken account of how George or Jim will be after they have taken the one course or the other; it might be that if they take the course which seemed at first the utilitarian one, the effects on them will be bad enough to cancel out the initial utilitarian advantages of that course. Now there is one version of this effect in which some confusion must be involved, namely that in which the agent feels bad, his subsequent conduct and relations are crippled and so on, *because he thinks that he has done the wrong thing* – for if the balance of outcomes was as it appeared to be *before* invoking this effect, then he has not (from the utilitarian view) done the wrong thing. So such feelings, which are from a utilitarian view irrational, cannot, consistently, have any great weight in a utilitarian calculation. I shall consider in a moment an argument to suggest that they should have no weight at all. But short of that, the utilitarian could reasonably say that such feelings should not be encouraged and that to give them a lot of weight is to encourage them. Or, at the very best, their weight must be small: they are after all one man's feelings.

There is a powerful appeal that can be made on this point: that a refusal by Jim to do what he has been invited to do would be a self-indulgent squeamishness. The "squeamishness" appeal is not an argument which adds a hitherto neglected consideration. Rather, it is an invitation to consider the situation, and one's own feelings, from a utilitarian view. If one is really going to regard one's feelings from a strictly utilitarian view, Jim should give very little weight to his.

There is an argument, and a strong one, that a utilitarian should give not merely small weight to feelings of this kind, but that he should give absolutely no weight to them. This is based on the point that if a course of action is, before taking these sorts of feelings into account, utilitarianly preferable, then bad feelings about that kind of action will be from a utilitarian view irrational. Now it might be thought that even if that is so, it would not mean that in a utilitarian calculation such feelings should not be taken into account. While a utilitarian will no doubt seek to diminish the incidence of feelings which are utilitarianly irrational, he might be expected to take them into account while they exist. This is classical utilitarian doctrine, but there is good reason to think that utilitarianism cannot stick to it without embracing results which are startlingly unacceptable and perhaps self-defeating.

Suppose that there is in a certain society a racial minority. Considering merely the ordinary interests of the other citizens, as opposed to their sentiments, this minority does no particular harm. Its presence is in those terms neutral or mildly beneficial. However, the other citizens have such prejudices that they find this group very disagreeable. Proposals are made for removing this minority. If we assume various quite plausible things (as that programs to change the majority sentiment are likely to be ineffective) then even if the removal would be unpleasant for the minority, a utilitarian calculation might well end up favoring this step, especially if the minority were a rather small minority and the majority were made very severely uncomfortable by the presence of the minority.

A utilitarian might find that conclusion embarrassing; and not merely because of its nature, but because of the grounds on which it is reached. He might wonder whether the unpleasant experiences of the prejudiced people should be allowed, *merely as such,* to count. If he does count them, then he has once more separated himself from a body of ordinary moral thought which he might have hoped to accommodate; he may also have started on the path of defeating his own view of things. These sentiments are from the utilitarian view irrational, and a thoroughly utilitarian person would either not have them, or if he found that he did have them, would seek to discount them. Since the sentiments are such that a rational utilitarian would discount them in himself, it is reasonable to suppose that he should discount them in his calculations about society.

The precedent effect

The psychological effect on the agent was the first of two general effects considered by utilitarians. The second is the *precedent effect.* This effect can be important: that one morally *can* do what someone has actually done, is a psychologically effective principle, if not a deontically valid one.

For the precedent effect to make a difference to a utilitarian calculation, it must be based upon a confusion. Suppose that there is an act which would be the best in the circumstances, except that doing it will encourage by precedent other people to do things which will not be the best things to do. Then the situation of those other people must be relevantly different from that of the original agent. But if the situations are relevantly different, it must be a confused perception which takes the first situation as an adequate precedent for the second.

However, the fact that the precedent effect is based on a confusion, does not mean that it is not perfectly real, nor that it is to be discounted. What it does emphasize is that calculations of the precedent effect have to be realistic. In the present examples, it is implausible to think that the precedent effect could be invoked to make any difference. Jim's case is extraordinary, and it is hard to imagine who the recipients of the effect might be supposed to be; while George is not in a sufficiently public situation for the question to arise, and in any case one might suppose that the motivations of others on such an issue were quite likely to be fixed one way or another already.

No appeal, then, to these other effects is going to make a difference to what the utilitarian will decide about our examples.

Study questions

1   Explain the examples of George and Jim. How does Williams use these to argue that utilitarianism has counter-intuitive results?
2   Identify and explain the two remote effects that Williams examines. How might utilitarians use these to try to avoid the counter-intuitive results?
3   Explain why, according to Williams, the appeal to remote effects fails to avoid the counter-intuitive results.
4   Construct an example of your own where utilitarianism seems to have counter-intuitive results. How might utilitarians try to use remote effects to avoid the counter-intuitive results? How would Williams argue that the appeal to remote effects doesn't avoid these results?
5   What is the "precedent effect"? Though based on a confusion, why is it nonetheless, according to Williams, not to be discounted?

For further study

This selection has excerpts, sometimes simplified in wording, from Bernard Williams's *Utilitarianism: For and Against* (Cambridge: Cambridge University Press, 1973), pages 96–107; this book was co-authored with J. J. C. Smart. For more on Williams's view, see that work and his *Ethics and the Limits of Philosophy* (Cambridge, MA: Harvard University Press, 1985). Harry Gensler's *Ethics: A Contemporary Introduction* (London and New York: Routledge, 1998) examines utilitarianism in Chapter 10.

Related readings in this anthology include Brandt, Mill, Singer, and Smart (who defend versions of utilitarianism); and Finnis, O'Neill, Rawls, Ross, and Slote (who criticize utilitarianism).

RICHARD B. BRANDT
Rule Utilitarianism

Richard B. Brandt, an American philosopher who lived from 1910 to 1997, contributed to various areas of moral philosophy, including the ideal observer view, the theory of rational desires, cross-cultural ethical studies, and utilitarianism. He introduced the distinction between act- and rule-utilitarianism.

Act-utilitarians apply the utility test to individual actions. For example, I ought to lie if this individual act would have the best consequences. Brandt instead proposes that we apply the utility test to moral *rules*. The rules about lying that we should follow are those whose acceptance by society would have the best consequences. This shift would likely bring stricter guidelines and results that harmonize better with common sense.

As you read the selection, ask yourself if you find Brandt's approach plausible. Does he give strong objections to act-utilitarianism? Does his rule-utilitarianism avoid the objections? Does it accord better with our moral intuitions?

Act and rule utilitarianism

"Act-utilitarianism" holds that the rightness of an act is fixed by the utility of *its* consequences, as compared with those of other acts the agent might perform instead. Act-utilitarianism is an atomistic theory: the value of the effects of a single act on the world is decisive for its rightness. "Rule-utilitarianism," in contrast, applies to views according to which the rightness of an act is not fixed by *its* relative utility, but by conformity with general rules; the correctness of these rules is fixed by the utility of their general acceptance. Rule-utilitarianism is an organic theory: the rightness of individual acts can be ascertained only by assessing a whole social policy.

Act-utilitarianism has implications difficult to accept. It implies that if you have employed a boy to mow your lawn and he has finished the job and asks for his pay, you should pay him what you promised only if you cannot find a better use for your money. When you bring home your monthly pay-check, you should use it to support your family and yourself only if it cannot be used more effectively to supply the needs of others. If your father is ill and has no prospect of good in his life, and maintaining him is a drain on the enjoyments of others, then, if you can end his life without provoking public scandal or setting a bad example, it is your duty to bring his life to a close. Rule-utilitarianism avoids some of these objectionable implications.

Urmson's formulation

It is convenient to begin by taking some statements from an interesting article by J. O. Urmson.[1] Urmson suggested that John Stuart Mill should be interpreted as a rule-utilitarian; and Urmson's opinion was that Mill's view would be more plausible if so interpreted. Urmson summarized the rule-utilitarian interpretation of Mill in four propositions, of which I quote the first two:

A.   A particular action is justified as being right by showing that it is in accord with some moral rule. It is shown to be wrong by showing that it transgresses some moral rule.
B.   A moral rule is shown to be correct by showing that the recognition of that rule promotes the ultimate end.

Urmson's first proposition could be taken in two ways. When it speaks of a "moral rule," it may refer to one accepted in the society of the agent. Alternatively, it may refer to a *correct* moral rule, one the recognition of which promotes the ultimate end. I think it more promising to try the second interpretation.

An empty rule-utilitarianism

I shall now digress to bring out the importance of avoiding a form of rule-utilitarianism which at first seems attractive: "An act is right if and only if it conforms with that set of moral rules, general conformity with which would have the best consequences." This sounds like our above formulation. It is, however, different in a very important way: for its test of whether an act is right, or a general rule correct, is what would happen if people *really all did act* in a certain way.

This theory has identically the same consequences for behavior as does act-utilitarianism. And since it does, it is a mistake to advocate it as a theory preferable to act-utilitarianism. Let us see how this is.

What would a set of moral prescriptions be like, such that general conformity with it would have the best consequences? The answer is that the set would contain just one rule, the prescription of the *act-utilitarian:* "Perform an act, among those open to you, which will have at least as good consequences as any other." There cannot be a moral rule, conformity with which could have better consequences. The two theories, then, have identical consequences for behavior.

A second approximation

So rule-utilitarianism is different from act-utilitarianism only when it speaks of something like *"recognition* of a rule having the best consequences" instead of something like *"conformity* with a rule having the best consequences." With this in mind, we can see clearly one of the virtues of Urmson's proposal, which we interpreted as: "An act is right if and only if it conforms with that set of moral rules, *the recognition of which* would have the best consequences."

But the formulation we suggested is open to interpretations that may lead to problems. How may we construe Urmson's proposal, so that it is unambiguous and credible? We do not wish to take "recognition of" to mean merely "doffing the hat to" without attempt to practice. But how shall we take it? I suggest the following as a second approximation.

First, let us speak of a set of moral rules as being "learnable" if people of ordinary intelligence are able to learn its provisions. Next, let us speak of "the adoption" of a moral code by a person as meaning "the learning and belief and conformity of behavior to the extent we may expect people of ordinary conscientiousness to conform their behavior to rules about right or obligatory behavior." Finally, let us use the phrase "maximizes intrinsic value" to mean "would produce at least as much intrinsic good as would be produced by any alternative action." With these stipulations, we can propose the following rule-utilitarian thesis: "An act is right if and only if it conforms with that learnable set of rules, the adoption of which by everyone would maximize intrinsic value."

This principle gives expression to at least part of our practice in trying to find out what is right or wrong. For when we are in doubt about such matters, we often try to think out how it would work in practice to have a moral code which prohibited or permitted various actions. If someone shows us that a specific injunction would not work out in view of other provisions necessary to an ideal code, we should revise our thinking accordingly.

In order to get a clearer idea of the "set of rules" which could satisfy this rule-utilitarian principle, let us note some general features such a set presumably would have. First, it would contain rules giving directions for recurrent situations which involve conflicts of human interests. Presumably, it would contain rules rather similar to W. D. Ross's list of prima facie obligations: rules about the keeping of promises and contracts, rules about debts of gratitude such as we may owe to our parents, and, of course, rules about not injuring other persons and about promoting the welfare of others where this does not work a comparable hardship on us. Second, such a set of rules would not include petty restrictions. Third, the rules would not be very numerous; an upper limit on quantity is set by the ability of ordinary people to learn them. Fourth, such a set of rules would not include unbearable demands; for their inclusion would only serve to bring moral obligation into discredit. Fifth, the rules could not leave too much to discretion. Ordinary people are not capable of fine discriminations and have a tendency to abuse a rule where it suits their interest. A college dormitory rule like "Don't play music in such a way as to disturb the study or sleep of others" would be ideal if people were perfect; since they aren't, we have to settle for a rule like "No music after 10 p.m." The same thing is true for a moral code.

Further refinements

Our "second approximation" proposed that an act is right if and only if it conforms with a learnable moral code, the adoption of which by *everyone* would maximize utility – meaning by "adoption of a code" the learning and belief that the code lays down the requirements for moral behavior, and conformity to it to the extent we may expect from people of *ordinary conscientiousness*.

The italicized words in the preceding paragraph indicate two respects in which the proposed test departs from reality. First, the proposal is to test rightness by the desirability of a rule among people of ordinary conscientiousness. Now, in a community of people of ordinary conscientiousness we do not have either saints or great sinners. In such a community, we could get along with a minimal police force. Similarly, there would be no value in a moral prescription like "Resist evil men." In the community envisaged, problems of a certain sort would not arise, and therefore the moral code need not have features designed to meet those problems. Very likely, for instance, a moral code near to that of extreme pacifism would work.

More serious is the flaw in the other feature: that the test of rightness is compatibility with the moral code, adoption of which *by everyone* would maximize utility. This permits behavior which would be desirable if everyone agreed, but which might be objectionable and undesirable if not everyone agreed. For instance, it may have the best consequences if the children are regarded as responsible for an elderly parent who is ill or needy; but it would be most unfortunate if the members of a Hopi man's native household decided that their presently recognized obligation had no standing on this account, since the result would be that no one would take the responsibility. Again, if everyone recognized an obligation to share in duties pertaining to national defense, it would be morally acceptable to require this legally; but it would hardly be morally acceptable to do so if there are pacifists who on moral grounds are ready to die rather than bear arms. And similarly for other matters about which there are existing and pronounced moral convictions.

Some modification must be made if our rule-utilitarian proposal is to have implications consistent with the moral convictions of thoughtful people. First, we must drop that part which assumes that people in our hypothetical societies are of ordinary conscientiousness. We want to allow for the existence of both saints and sinners and to have a moral code to cope with them. We had better drop the notion of "adoption" and replace it by his term "recognition," meaning by "recognition by all" simply "belief by all that the rules formulate moral requirements." Second, we must avoid the acceptance by *everybody* and replace it by something short of this, something which does not rule out problems created by actual convictions about morals.

The principle with which we end is this: "An act is right if and only if it conforms with that learnable set of rules the recognition of which as morally binding – roughly at the time of the act – by everyone in the society of the agent, except for the retention by individuals of already formed and decided moral convictions, would maximize intrinsic value."

If the proposed principle is correct, we can give at least a partial answer to a person who asks *why* he ought to perform actions he is obligated to perform, if they conflict with his self-interest. We can say to him that by doing so he plays the game of living according to the rules which will maximize welfare.

Study questions

1 What is Brandt's distinction between act- and rule-utilitarianism? Explain one of his objections to act-utilitarianism and indicate how he thinks rule-utilitarianism avoids the objection.

2 What ambiguity does Brandt see in Urmson's formulation of rule-utilitarianism? What does Brandt think that we should do about the ambiguity?

3 Brandt formulates a version of rule-utilitarianism that he claims is identical in its implications to act-utilitarianism. Explain the problem and how Brandt avoids it.

4 To what kind of rules does Brandt think his rule-utilitarianism would lead? Why would the rules not leave too much to discretion?

5 What problems are there with the view that we should follow the rules whose *adoption* would maximize utility? Explain how Brandt avoids the problem.

For further study

This selection has excerpts, sometimes simplified in wording, from Richard B. Brandt's "Toward a credible form of utilitarianism," in *Morality and the Language of Conduct* (Detroit: Wayne State University Press, 1965), edited by Hector-Neri Castañeda and George Nakhnikian, pages 107–43. Other works by Brandt include "The definition of an 'ideal observer' theory in ethics" and "Some comments on Professor Firth's reply," in *Philosophy and Phenomenological Research* 15 (1955): 407–13 and 422–3; *Ethical Theory* (Englewood Cliffs, NJ: Prentice-Hall, 1959); "Rational desires," in *Proceedings and Addresses of the American Philosophical Association* 43 (1970): 43–64; "Rationality, egoism, and morality," in *Journal of Philosophy* 69 (1972): 681–97; "The psychology of benevolence and its implications for philosophy," *Journal of Philosophy* 73 (1976): 429–53; *A Theory of the Good and the Right* (Oxford: Clarendon Press, 1979); and "The concept of rational action," *Social Theory and Practice* 9 (1983): 143–65. For an attempt to combine the best features of act- and rule-utilitarianism, see R. M. Hare's *Moral Thinking* (Oxford: Clarendon Press, 1981). Harry Gensler's *Ethics: A Contemporary Introduction* (London and New York: Routledge, 1998) discusses rule-utilitarianism in Chapter 10 (Sections 10.5 and 10.6).

Related readings in this anthology include Mill (the classic utilitarian); Smart (who prefers act- over rule-utilitarianism); and Finnis, Rawls, Ross, Slote, O'Neill, and Williams (who criticize utilitarianism).

Note

1   J. O. Urmson, "The Interpretation of the Philosophy of J. S. Mill," *Philosophical Quarterly* 3 (1953): 33–9. [Note from Brandt]

W. D. ROSS
Objective *Prima Facie* Duties

Ross's earlier reading selection on page 90 gave a classic defense of two views of different sorts:

1   the intuitionist view that the basic moral principles are self-evident truths known through our moral intuitions,

2   the nonconsequentialist view that some kinds of action (such as breaking a promise) are wrong in themselves, and not just wrong because they have bad consequences.

His first view proposes an intuitionist method for picking out moral principles. Since this fits best in Part II, we put his reading selection there. But his second view, which proposes specific nonconsequentialist moral principles, fits better into Part IV – where we are now. So you might at this point want to look at Ross's earlier reading selection again, but this time for its defense of nonconsequentialism and criticism of utilitarianism.

JOHN FINNIS
Goods and Absolutes

John Finnis, an Australian philosopher born in 1940, works in ethics, law, and legal philosophy. He carries on the "natural law" tradition of St Thomas Aquinas.

Finnis argues that the basic goods of human life include not just pleasure, but a variety of things, such as life, knowledge, and play. Since basic goods cannot be measured meaningfully on a common scale and totaled, the consequentialist duty to "maximize" total value is senseless. Instead, we are free to choose whatever basic goods we want to emphasize in our lives. Choosing directly against a basic good, however, is always wrong; this leads to exceptionless norms (for example, against murder, which contravenes the basic good of life). Thus Finnis arrives at a non-consequentialist ethics.

As you read the selection, ask yourself how a hedonist (who believes that only pleasure is ultimately worthwhile) would respond to Finnis's list of basic goods. Which of the two views do you see as more plausible? How do you evaluate Finnis's defense of exceptionless duties?

Seven basic forms of human good

What *are* the basic aspects of my well-being? Here each of us is alone with his intelligent grasp of the indemonstrable first principles of his own practical reasoning.[1] There is no inference from fact to value. What, then, are the basic forms of good for us?

A first basic value, corresponding to the drive for self-preservation, is the value of life. "Life" here signifies every aspect of the vitality which puts a human being in good shape for self-determination. Hence, life here includes bodily (including cerebral) health, and freedom from the pain that betokens organic malfunctioning or injury. And the recognition, pursuit, and realization of this basic human purpose are as various as the crafty struggle and prayer of a man overboard seeking to stay afloat; the teamwork of surgeons and the whole network of supporting staff; road safety laws and programs; famine relief; farming and fishing; food marketing; the resuscitation of suicides; watching out as one steps off the curb.

The second basic value I have already discussed:[2] it is knowledge, considered as desirable for its own sake, not merely instrumentally.

The third basic aspect of human well-being is play. A moralist analyzing human goods may overlook this basic value, but an anthropologist will observe this large element in human culture. Each one of us can see the point of engaging in performances which have no point beyond the performance itself, enjoyed for its own sake. The performance may be solitary or social, intellectual or physical, strenuous or relaxed, highly structured or relatively informal. An element of play can enter into any human activity, but is always analytically distinguishable from its "serious" context; and some activities, enterprises, and institutions are entirely or primarily pure play. Play, then, has and is its own value.

The fourth basic component in our flourishing is aesthetic experience. Many forms of play, such as dance or song or football, are the occasion of aesthetic experience. But beauty is not an indispensable element of play. Moreover, beautiful form can he found and enjoyed in nature. Aesthetic experience, unlike play, need not involve an action of one's own; what is sought after and valued for its own sake may simply be the beautiful form "outside" one, and the "inner" appreciation of its beauty. But often enough the valued experience is found in the creation or active appreciation of some *work* of significant and satisfying form.

Fifthly, there is the value of sociability which ranges through the forms of human community to its strongest form in full friendship. Some collaboration is no more than instrumental to the realization of individual purposes. But friendship involves acting for the sake of one's friend's well-being. To be in friendship with at least one other person is a fundamental form of good, is it not?

Sixthly, there is the basic good of being able to bring one's own intelligence to bear effectively (in practical reasoning) on the problems of choosing one's actions and lifestyle and shaping one's own character. Negatively, this involves that one has a measure of effective freedom; positively, it involves that one seeks to bring an intelligent and reasonable order into one's own actions and habits and practical attitudes. This value is thus complex, involving freedom and reason, integrity and authenticity. But it has a sufficient unity to be treated as one; and for a label I choose "practical reasonableness."

Seventhly, and finally in this list, there is the value of what we call "religion." One of the basic human values is the establishment and maintenance of proper relationships between oneself and the divine. There are those who doubt or deny that the universal order-of-things has any origin beyond the "origins" known to the natural sciences. But is it reasonable to deny that it is important to have thought reasonably and (where possible) correctly about these questions of the origins of cosmic order and of human freedom and reason – whatever the answer turns out to be? And does not that importance in large part consist in this: that if there is a transcendent origin of the universal order-of-things and of human freedom and reason, then one's life and actions are in fundamental disorder if they are not brought into harmony with whatever can be known or surmised about that transcendent other and its lasting order?

But are there just seven basic values, no more and no less? There is no magic in the number seven, and others have produced slightly different lists, usually longer. There is no need for the reader to accept the present list as it stands, still less its nomenclature. Still, it seems to me that those seven are all of the basic purposes of human action, and that any other purpose which you or I might recognize and pursue will turn out to represent, or be constituted of, some aspect(s) of some or all of them.

All equally fundamental

More important than the number and description of these values is the sense in which each is basic. First, each is equally self-evidently a form of good. Secondly, none can be reduced to being merely an aspect of any of the others, or to being merely instrumental in the pursuit of any of the others. Thirdly, each one, when we focus on it, can reasonably be regarded as the most important. Hence there is no objective hierarchy amongst them. Let me amplify this third point.

Knowledge can be regarded as the most important thing; life can be regarded as merely a pre-condition, of lesser or no intrinsic value; play can be regarded as frivolous; one's concern about "religious" questions can seem just an aspect of the struggle against error, superstition, and ignorance; friendship can seem worth forgoing, or be found exclusively in sharing and enhancing knowledge; and so on. But one can shift one's focus. If one is drowning, or, again, if one is thinking about one's child who died soon after birth, one is inclined to shift one's focus to the value of life simply as such. The life will not be regarded as a mere pre-condition of anything else; rather, play and knowledge and religion will seem secondary. We can focus on play, and reflect that we spend most of our time working simply in order to afford leisure; play is performances enjoyed for their own sake and thus can seem to be the point of everything; knowledge and religion and friendship can seem pointless unless they issue in the playful mastery of wisdom, or participation in the play of the divine puppetmaster, or in the playful intercourse of mind or body that friends enjoy.

Thus I have illustrated this point in relation to life, truth, and play; the reader can easily test it in relation to the other basic values. Each is fundamental. None is more fundamental than the others, for each, when focused upon, claims a priority of value. Hence there is no objective priority of value amongst them.

Each of us can reasonably *choose* to treat one of the values as of more importance in *his* life. A scholar chooses to dedicate himself to the pursuit of knowledge, and thus gives its demands priority, to a greater or lesser degree, over friendships, worship, games, art and beauty. He might have been out saving lives through medicine or famine relief, but he chooses not to. But he may change his priorities; he may risk his life to save a drowning man, or give up his career to nurse a sick wife or to fight for his community. The change is in his chosen life-plan. His new choice changes the status of that value for *him*. Each of us has a subjective order of priority amongst the basic values; this ranking is no doubt partly shifting and partly stable, but is in any case essential if we are to act to some purpose. But one's reasons for choosing some particular ranking are reasons that properly relate to one's temperament, upbringing, capacities, and opportunities, not to differences of intrinsic value between the basic values.

Is pleasure the point of it all?

Carry out the thought-experiment skillfully proposed by Robert Nozick.[3] Suppose you could be plugged into an "experience machine" which, by stimulating your brain while you lay floating in a tank, would afford you all the experiences you choose, with all the variety you could want: but you must plug in for a lifetime or not at all. On reflection, is it not clear that you would not choose a lifetime of "thrills" or "pleasurable tingles"? The fact is, is it not, that if one were sensible one would not choose to plug into the experience machine *at all*. For, as Nozick rightly concludes, one wants to *do* certain things (not just have the experience of doing them); one wants to *be* a certain sort of person, through one's own authentic, free self-determination and self-realization; one wants to *live* oneself, making a real world through a real pursuit of values.

The experiences of discovery ("Eureka!") or creative play or living through danger are pleasurable, satisfying, and valuable; but it is because we want to make the discovery or create or "survive" that we want the experiences. If these give pleasure, this experience is one aspect of their reality as human goods, which are not participated in fully unless their goodness is experienced as such. But a participation in basic goods which is emotionally unsatisfying nevertheless is good and meaningful as far as it goes.

Absolute human rights

Are there "absolute" rights, rights that are not to be limited or overridden for the sake of any conception of the good life in community, not even "to prevent catastrophe"?

The answer of utilitarians, of course, is clear: there are no absolute human rights, for there are no ways of treating a person of which it can be said, by a consistent utilitarian, "Whatever the consequences, nobody must ever be treated in this way." What is more striking is the fact that no contemporary government manifests in its practice any belief in absolute human rights. For every government that has the physical capacity to make its threats credible says this to its potential enemies: "If you attack us and threaten to defeat us, we will incinerate or dismember as many of your old men and women and children, and poison as many of your mothers and their unborn offspring, as it takes to persuade you to desist." Those who say this, and have been preparing elaborately for years to act upon their threat (and most of them acted upon it massively, between 1943 and 1945), cannot be said to accept that anyone has, in virtue of his humanity, any absolute right. These people subscribe to Bills of Rights which, like the Universal Declaration and its successors, clearly treat the right not to be tortured as (unlike most of the other "inalienable" rights there proclaimed) subject to no exceptions. But their military policy involves courses of action which in all but name are torture on an unprecedented scale, inflicted for the same motive as an old-fashioned torturer seeking to change his victim's mind or the minds of those next in line for the torture.

The tradition of natural law has never maintained that what I have called the requirements of practical reasonableness,[4] as distinct from the basic human values, are clearly recognized by all or even most people – on the contrary. So we too need not hesitate to say that, notwithstanding the substantial consensus to the contrary, there are absolute human rights. For the seventh of the requirements of practical reasonableness that I identified is this: that it is always unreasonable to choose directly against any basic value, whether in oneself or in one's fellow human beings. And the basic values are not mere abstractions; they are aspects of the real well-being of flesh-and-blood individuals. Correlative to the exceptionless duties entailed by this requirement are, therefore, exceptionless or absolute human claim-rights – most obviously, the right not to have one's life taken directly as a means to any further end; but also the right not to be positively lied to in any situation (e.g. teaching, preaching, research publication, news broadcasting) in which factual communication (as distinct from fiction, jest, or poetry) is reasonably expected; and the related right not to be condemned on knowingly false charges; and the right not to be deprived of one's procreative capacity; and the right to be taken into respectful consideration in any assessment of the common good.

Because these are claim-rights strictly correlative to duties entailed by the requirements of practical reasonableness, the difficult task of giving precision to the specification of these rights has usually been undertaken in terms of a casuistry of duties.[5] And because an unwavering recognition of the immeasurable value of human personality requires us to discount the apparently measurable evil of looming catastrophes which threaten the common good and the enjoyment by others of *their* rights, that casuistry is more complex, difficult, and controvertible in its details than can be indicated in the foregoing summary list of absolute rights. That casuistry may be framed in terms of "direct" choices or intentions, as against "indirect" effects, and of "means" as against "incidents." Such judgments are arrived at by a steady determination to respect human good in one's own existence and the equivalent humanity or human rights of others, when that human good and those human rights fall directly into one's care and disposal – rather than trade off that good and those rights against some vision of future "net best consequences," consequences which overall, both logically and practically, one cannot know, cannot control or dispose of, and cannot evaluate.

Study questions

1   How does Finnis justify principles about basic goods? Does he derive such principles from claims about human inclinations?
2   Explain what is included under Finnis's basic value of life. Give a few examples of human activities that are efforts to promote this value.
3   List Finnis's seven basic forms of human well-being. Can you think of any further form of human well-being that Finnis omits?
4   Explain in detail how Finnis would answer this question: "Which of the basic forms of human well-being is the most important?"
5   According to Finnis, which of the basic values should we emphasize in our own individual lives?
6   Explain Nozick's "experience machine" example and what it is supposed to show.
7   How does Finnis argue for absolute human rights and exceptionless duties? Give some examples of such rights and duties.

For further study

This selection has excerpts, sometimes simplified in wording, from John Mitchell Finnis's *Natural Law and Natural Rights* (Oxford: Oxford University

Press, 1980), pages 85–97 and 224–6; for more on his approach, you might consult this book or his *Foundations of Ethics* (Washington: Georgetown University Press, 1983) or *Moral Absolutes* (Washington: Catholic University of America Press, 1991). For a somewhat similar view, see T. D. J. Chappell's *Understanding Human Goods: A Theory of Ethics* (Edinburgh: Edinburgh University Press, 1999). Harry Gensler's *Ethics: A Contemporary Introduction* (London and New York: Routledge, 1998) examines basic values in Section 10.5 and exceptionless duties in Section 11.3.

Related readings in this anthology include Moore and Ross (who also appeal to self-evident truths about what is good in itself); Mill and Smart (utilitarians who appeal to human inclinations to justify claims about what is good in itself); and Nozick and Rawls (who discuss human rights).

Notes

1   Finnis thinks his claims about basic goods are "indemonstrable first principles"; they are self-evident truths that need no further demonstration or proof. On this point, Finnis separates himself from those followers of Aquinas who appeal to natural human inclinations to establish basic goods.

2   Finnis discusses the basic value of knowledge in a previous section not included in this anthology.

3   *Anarchy, State and Utopia* (Oxford: 1974), pages 42–5. [Note from Finnis]

4   Chapter V of Finnis's book distinguishes nine requirements of practical reasonableness that shape one's participation in the basic human values: (1) One must have a coherent plan of life. (2) One must utilize no arbitrary preferences amongst values. (3) One must entertain no arbitrary preferences amongst persons (here the classical golden rule formulation is a help). (4) One needs a certain detachment from all the specific and limited projects that one undertakes. (5) One needs a balance between fanaticism and apathy (one must not abandon one's general commitments lightly). (6) One must bring about good in the world by actions that are efficient for their reasonable purpose (but this is not an endorsement of utilitarianism, since it cannot explain a "greatest net good"). (7) One should not choose to do any act which of itself does nothing but damage or impede a realization or participation of any one or more of the basic forms of human good. (8) One ought to favor and foster the common good of one's communities. (9) One should not do what one judges or thinks or feels all-in-all should not be done (one must act according to one's conscience).

5   Finnis uses the term "casuistry" to refer to a method of refining general ethical principles by applying them to a series of specific cases.

JOHN RAWLS
A Theory of Justice

John Rawls, an American philosopher who lived from 1921 to 2002, was one of the most important political philosophers of the last hundred years. He defended liberal democratic ideas in *A Theory of Justice* (from which this selection is taken) and *Political Liberalism*.

Rawls here asks what basic principles of justice ought to regulate society. He suggests that we adopt the principles we would agree to under certain hypothetical conditions ("the original position"). Imagine that we were free and rational but did not know our own place in society (whether rich or poor, black or white, male or female). The knowledge limitation is meant to insure impartiality; if we did not know our race, for example, then we could not manipulate the principles to favor our race. The principles of justice are those that we would agree to under these conditions.

Rawls argues that we would in the original position agree to the "equal liberty principle," which insures things like freedom of religion and freedom of speech. We also would agree to the "difference principle"; this promotes the equal distribution of wealth, except for inequalities that serve as incentives to benefit everyone (including the least advantaged group) and are open to everyone on an equal basis.

As you read the selection, ask yourself if you find the original position to be a plausible framework for selecting principles of justice. Do Rawls's two principles of justice make sense to you? Are they the principles that we would select under the conditions Rawls describes?

The role of justice

Justice is the first virtue of social institutions, as truth is of systems of thought. A theory however elegant and economical must be rejected or revised if it is untrue; likewise laws and institutions no matter how efficient and well-arranged must be reformed or abolished if they are unjust. Each person possesses an inviolability founded on justice that even the welfare of society as a whole cannot override. For this reason justice denies that the loss of freedom for some is made right by a greater good shared by others. Being first virtues of human activities, truth and justice are uncompromising.

These propositions seem to express our intuitive conviction of the primacy of justice. No doubt they are expressed too strongly. In any event I wish to inquire whether these contentions or others similar to them are sound, and if so how they can be accounted for. To this end it is necessary to work out a theory of justice in the light of which these assertions can be interpreted and assessed.

The original position

My aim is to present a conception of justice which generalizes and carries to a higher level of abstraction the familiar theory of the social contract as found, say, in Locke, Rousseau, and Kant. In order to do this we are not to think of the original contract as one to enter a particular society or to set up a particular form of government. Rather, the guiding idea is that the principles of justice for the basic structure of society are the object of the original agreement. They are the principles that free and rational persons concerned to further their own interests would accept in an initial position of equality as defining the fundamental terms of their association. These principles are to regulate all further agreements; they specify the kinds of social cooperation that can be entered into and the forms of government that can be established. This way of regarding the principles of justice I shall call justice as fairness.

In justice as fairness the original position of equality corresponds to the state of nature in the traditional theory of the social contract. This original position is not, of course, thought of as an actual historical state of affairs, much less as a primitive condition of culture. It is understood as a purely hypothetical situation characterized so as to lead to a certain conception of justice. Among the essential features of this situation is that no one knows his place in society, his class position or social status, nor does any one know his fortune in the distribution of natural assets and abilities, his intelligence, strength, and the like. The principles of justice are chosen behind a veil of ignorance. This ensures that no one is advantaged or disadvantaged in the choice of principles by the outcome of natural chance or the contingency of social circumstances. Since all are similarly situated and no one is able to design principles to favor his particular condition, the principles of justice are the result of a fair agreement or bargain. This explains the propriety of the name "justice as fairness": it conveys the idea that the principles of justice are agreed to in an initial situation that is fair.

Justice as fairness begins, as I have said, with one of the most general of all choices which persons might make together, namely, with the choice of the first principles of a conception of justice which is to regulate all subsequent criticism and reform of institutions. Then, having chosen a conception of justice, we can suppose that they are to choose a constitution and a legislature to enact laws, and so on, all in accordance with the principles of justice initially agreed upon. Our social situation is just if it is such that by this sequence of hypothetical agreements we would have contracted into the general system of rules which defines it. Moreover, assuming that the original position does determine a set of principles, it will then be true that whenever social institutions satisfy these principles those engaged in them can say to one another that they are cooperating on terms to which they would agree if they were free and equal persons whose relations with respect to one another were fair. The general recognition of this fact would provide the basis for a public acceptance of the corresponding principles of justice. No society can, of course, be a scheme of cooperation which men enter voluntarily in a literal sense; each person finds himself placed at birth in some particular position in some particular society, and the nature of this position materially affects his life prospects. Yet a society satisfying the principles of justice as fairness comes as close as a society can to being a voluntary scheme, for it meets the principles which free and equal persons would assent to under circumstances that are fair. In this sense its members are autonomous and the obligations they recognize self-imposed.

Once the principles of justice are thought of as arising from an original agreement in a situation of equality, it is an open question whether the principle of utility would be acknowledged. Offhand it hardly seems likely that persons who view themselves as equals, entitled to press their claims upon one another, would agree to a principle which may require lesser life prospects for some simply for the sake of a greater sum of advantages enjoyed by others. Since each desires to protect his interests, no one has a reason to acquiesce in an enduring loss for himself in order to bring about a greater net balance of satisfaction. In the absence of strong and lasting benevolent impulses, a rational man would not accept a basic structure merely because it maximized the algebraic sum of advantages irrespective of its permanent effects on his own basic rights and interests. Thus it seems that the principle of utility is incompatible with the conception of social cooperation among equals for mutual advantage.

I shall maintain instead that the persons in the initial situation would choose two rather different principles: the first requires equality in the assignment of basic rights and duties, while the second holds that social and economic inequalities, for example inequalities of wealth and authority, are just only if they result in compensating benefits for everyone, and in particular for the least advantaged members of society.

One should not be misled by the somewhat unusual conditions which characterize the original position. The idea here is simply to make vivid to ourselves the restrictions that it seems reasonable to impose on arguments for principles of justice, and therefore on these principles themselves.

Two principles of justice

I shall now state in a provisional form the two principles of justice that I believe would be agreed to in the original position. As we go on I shall consider several formulations and approximate step by step the final statement to be given much later.

The first statement of the two principles reads as follows.

> First: each person is to have an equal right to the most extensive scheme of equal basic liberties compatible with a similar scheme of liberties for others.

> Second: social and economic inequalities are to be arranged so that they are both (a) reasonably expected to be to everyone's advantage, and (b) attached to positions and offices open to all.

The final version of the two principles is given in § 46.[1]

These principles primarily apply to the basic structure of society and govern the assignment of rights and duties and regulate the distribution of social and economic advantages. Their formulation presupposes that, for the purposes of a theory of justice, the social structure may be viewed as having two more or less distinct parts, the first principle applying to the one, the second principle to the other. Thus we distinguish between the aspects of the social system that define and secure the equal basic liberties and the aspects that specify and establish social and economic inequalities. Now it is essential to observe that the basic liberties are given by a list of such liberties. Important among these are political liberty (the right to vote and to hold public office) and freedom of speech and assembly; liberty of conscience and freedom of thought; freedom of the person, which includes freedom from psychological oppression and physical assault and dismemberment (integrity of the person); the right to hold personal property and freedom from arbitrary arrest and seizure as defined by the concept of the rule of law. These liberties are to be equal by the first principle.

The second principle applies, in the first approximation, to the distribution of income and wealth and to the design of organizations that make use of differences in authority and responsibility. While the distribution of wealth and income need not be equal, it must be to everyone's advantage, and at the same time, positions of authority and responsibility must be accessible to all. One applies the second principle by holding positions open, and then, subject to this constraint, arranges social and economic inequalities so that everyone benefits.

These principles are to be arranged in a serial order with the first principle prior to the second. This ordering means that infringements of the basic equal liberties protected by the first principle cannot be justified, or compensated for, by greater social and economic advantages. These liberties have a central range of application within which they can be limited and compromised only when they conflict with other basic liberties. Since they may be limited when they clash with one another, none of these liberties is absolute; but however they are adjusted to form one system, this system is to be the same for all.

The two principles are rather specific in their content, and their acceptance rests on certain assumptions that I must eventually try to explain and justify. For the present, it should be observed that these principles are a special case of a more general conception of justice that can be expressed as follows.

> All social values – liberty and opportunity, income and wealth, and the social bases of self-respect – are to be distributed equally unless an unequal distribution of any, or all, of these values is to everyone's advantage.

Injustice, then, is simply inequalities that are not to the benefit of all.

Study questions

1 What does Rawls mean when he writes "Justice is the first virtue of social institutions"? Explain the uncompromising role of justice.
2 Explain the original position and its role in Rawls's theory of justice. What is the veil of ignorance and what is its purpose?
3 Does Rawls believe that society originated long ago in a contract or agreement between individuals? If not, then what is the present usefulness of the social contract notion?
4 Does Rawls think that people in the original position would adopt the principle of utility? Why or why not?
5 What are Rawls's two principles of justice? Give an example of how each one would apply.
6 Rawls's difference principle has been criticized by both Marxists and capitalists. What criticism do you suppose each would make?

For further study

This selection has excerpts, sometimes simplified in wording, from John Rawls's *A Theory of Justice* (Cambridge, MA: Harvard University Press, 1999), revised version, pages 3–4, 10–13, 16, 52–4, and 266. This selection corresponds to pages 3–4, 11–15, 18, 60–2, and 302 of the original 1971 version of his book, which sometimes differs in wording. For Rawls's later ideas, see his

Political Liberalism (New York: Columbia University Press, 1993). For a critical discussion, see *Reading Rawls: Critical Studies on Rawls' "A Theory of Justice,"* edited by Norman Daniels (New York: Basic Books, 1975). Harry Gensler's *Ethics: A Contemporary Introduction* (London and New York: Routledge, 1998) briefly discusses Rawls in Chapter 11 (Section 11.4).

Related readings in this anthology include Frankena, Hare, and Kant (who also give "rational choice" approaches to ethics); Brandt, Mill, and Smart (whose utilitarianism Rawls opposes); and Nozick (who gives a sharp alternative to Rawls's principles of justice).

Note

1   In § 46 of *A Theory of Justice*, Rawls's first principle is virtually unchanged, but his second principle is modified using ideas developed in the intervening sections:

Second: Social and economic inequalities are to be arranged so that they are both: (a) to the greatest benefit of the least advantaged, consistent with the just savings principle, and (b) attached to offices and positions open to all under conditions of fair equality of opportunity.

ROBERT NOZICK
Justice and Goods

Robert Nozick, an American philosopher who lived from 1938 to 2002, wrote *Philosophical Explanations* and *Anarchy, State, and Utopia*. In the latter work, he argued for a minimal state; to protect the rights of individuals, a state's authority to regulate private property ought to be severely restricted.

Nozick explains how and when individuals are entitled to the goods they possess. If a good is justly acquired and transferred, then the individual who possesses it is entitled to that good. The state violates the rights of individuals if it enforces a distribution of goods different from that achieved by just acquisitions and transfers.

As you read the selection, ask yourself whether Nozick has provided an adequate account of distributive justice. Does the manner in which a good is acquired alone determine whether one is entitled to it? If you are familiar with Rawls's theory, ask yourself how it differs from Nozick's and which of the two seems more satisfactory.

Justice in holdings

A distribution is just if it arises from another just distribution by legitimate means. The legitimate means of moving from one distribution to another are specified by the principle of justice in transfer. The legitimate first "moves" are specified by the principle of justice in acquisition.[1] Whatever arises from a just situation by just steps is itself just. The means of change specified by the principle of justice in transfer preserve justice. The fact that a thief's victims voluntarily *could* have presented him with gifts does not entitle the thief to his ill-gotten gains. Justice in holdings is historical; it depends upon what actually has happened.

Not all actual situations are generated in accordance with the principle of justice in acquisition and the principle of justice in transfer. Some people steal from others, or defraud them, or enslave them, seizing their product and preventing them from living as they choose, or forcibly exclude others from competing in exchanges. The existence of past injustice raises the third major topic under justice in holdings: the rectification of injustice in holdings. If past injustice has shaped present holdings in various ways, what now, if anything, ought to be done to rectify these injustices? I do not know of a thorough or theoretically sophisticated treatment of such issues. Idealizing greatly, let us suppose theoretical investigation will produce a principle of rectification.

The holdings of a person are just if he is entitled to them by the principles of justice in acquisition and transfer, or by the principle of rectification of injustice. If each person's holdings are just, then the total set (distribution) of holdings is just.

Historical and structural principles

The entitlement theory of justice in distribution is *historical;* whether a distribution is just depends upon how it came about. In contrast, *current time-slice principles* of justice hold that the justice of a distribution is determined by how things are distributed (who has what) as judged by some *structural* principle(s) of just distribution.[2] A utilitarian who judges between any two distributions by seeing which has the greater sum of utility and, if the sums tie, applies some fixed equality criterion to choose the more equal distribution, would hold a current time-slice principle of justice. According to a current time-slice principle, all that needs to be looked at, in judging the justice of a distribution, is who ends up with what. No further information need be fed into a principle of justice. It is a consequence of such principles of justice that any two structurally identical distributions are equally just. (Two distributions are structurally identical if they present the same profile, but perhaps have different persons occupying the particular slots. My having ten and your having five, and my having five and your having ten are structurally identical distributions.) Welfare economics is the theory of current time-slice principles of justice. The subject is conceived as operating on matrices representing only current information about distribution.

Most persons do not accept current time-slice principles as constituting the whole story about distributive shares. They think it relevant in assessing the justice of a situation to consider not only the distribution it embodies, but also how that distribution came about. If some persons are in prison for murder or war crimes, we do not say that to assess the justice of the distribution in the society we must look only at what this person has, and that person has, and that person has, at the current time. We think it relevant to ask whether someone did something so that he *deserved* to be punished, deserved to have a lower share. Consider also desired things. One traditional socialist view is that workers are entitled to the product and full fruits of their labor; they have earned it; a distribution is unjust if it does not give the workers what they are entitled to. Such entitlements are based upon some past history.

In contrast to end-result principles of justice, *historical principles* of justice hold that past circumstances or actions of people can create differential entitlements or differential deserts to things. An injustice can be worked by moving from one distribution to another structurally identical one, for the second, in profile the same, may violate people's entitlements or deserts; it may not fit the actual history.

The Wilt Chamberlain example

It is not clear how those holding alternative conceptions of distributive justice can reject the entitlement conception of justice in holdings. For suppose a distribution favored by one of these non-entitlement conceptions is realized. Let us suppose it is your favorite one and let us call this distribution *D1*; perhaps everyone has an equal share, perhaps shares vary in accordance with some dimension you treasure. Now suppose that Wilt Chamberlain is greatly in demand by basketball teams, being a great gate attraction. He signs the following sort of contract with a team: In each home game, twenty-five cents from the price of each ticket of admission goes to him. The season starts, and people cheerfully attend his team's games; they buy their tickets, each time dropping a separate twenty-five cents of their admission price into a special box with Chamberlain's name on it. They are excited about seeing him play; it is worth the total admission price to them.

Let us suppose that in one season one million persons attend his home games, and Wilt Chamberlain winds up with $250,000, a much larger sum than the average income and larger even than anyone else has. Is he entitled to this income? Is this new distribution *D2*, unjust? If so, why? There is *no* question about whether each of the people was entitled to the control over the resources they held in *D1*; because that was the distribution we assumed was acceptable. Each of these persons *chose* to give twenty-five cents of their money to Chamberlain. They could have spent it on going to the movies, or on candy bars. But they all, at least one million of them, converged on giving it to Wilt Chamberlain in exchange for watching him play basketball. If *D1* was a just distribution, and people voluntarily moved from it to *D2*, transferring parts of their shares they were given under *D1*, isn't *D2* also just? If the people were entitled to dispose of the resources to which they were entitled (under *D1*), didn't this include their being entitled to give it to, or exchange it with, Wilt Chamberlain? Can anyone else complain on grounds of justice?

The instability of egalitarian distributions

Why might someone work overtime in a society in which it is assumed their needs are satisfied? Perhaps because they care about things other than needs. I like to write in books that I read, and to have easy access to books for browsing at odd hours. It would be very pleasant and convenient to have the resources of Widener Library in my back yard. No society, I assume, will provide such resources close to each person who would like them as part of his regular allotment (under *D1*). Thus, persons either must do without some extra things that they want, or be allowed to do something extra to get some of these things. On what basis could the inequalities that would eventuate be forbidden?

Notice also that small factories would spring up in a socialist society, unless forbidden. I melt down some of my personal possessions (under *D1*) and build a machine out of the material. I offer you, and others, a philosophy lecture once a week in exchange for your cranking the handle on my machine, whose products I exchange for yet other things, and so on. (The raw materials used by the machine are given to me by others who possess them under *D1*, in exchange for hearing lectures.) Each person might participate to gain things over and above their allotment under *D1*. Some persons even might want to leave their job in socialist industry and work full time in this private sector. Private property even in means of production would occur in a socialist society that did not forbid people to use as they wished some of the resources they are given under the socialist distribution *D1*. The socialist society would have to forbid capitalist acts between consenting adults.

The general point illustrated by the Wilt Chamberlain example and the example of the entrepreneur in a socialist society is that no distributional patterned principle of justice can be continuously realized without continuous interference with people's lives. Any favored pattern would be transformed into one unfavored by the principle, by people choosing to act in various ways; for example, by people exchanging goods and services with other people, or giving things to other people, things the transferrers are entitled to under the favored distributional pattern. To maintain a pattern one must either interfere to stop people from transferring resources as they wish to, or interfere to take from some persons resources that others for some reason chose to transfer to them.

Any distributional pattern with any egalitarian component is overturnable by the voluntary actions of individual persons over time.

Study questions

1   For Nozick, what makes a distribution of goods just?

2   Explain the principles that constitute justice in holdings.
3   Construct an example that illustrates a just holding.
4   Explain the difference between historical and current time-slice theories of distributive justice. Which approach does Nozick favor, and why?
5   What is the Wilt Chamberlain example and what it is meant to illustrate?
6   Why does Nozick think that attempts to enforce equal distributions of goods are inherently unstable?

For further study

This selection has excerpts, sometimes simplified in wording, from Robert Nozick's *Anarchy, State, and Utopia* (New York: Basic Books, 1974), pages 151–64. For the opposing view to which Nozick was responding, see John Rawls's *A Theory of Justice* (Cambridge, MA: Harvard University Press, 1971). Harry Gensler's *Ethics: A Contemporary Introduction* (London and New York: Routledge, 1998) briefly discusses distributive justice, including the views of Nozick and Rawls, in Chapter 11 (Section 11.4).

Related readings in this anthology include Mill and Rawls (both of whom differ from Nozick in their views on distributive justice), and Nietzsche (who also criticizes egalitarian views of justice).

Notes

1   These examples illustrate what Nozick has in mind. (a) Just acquisition: if you find an apple tree that belongs to no one and there are plenty of similar apple trees for others to pick from, then any apples that you pick justly belong to you. (b) Just transfer: if you make your apples into an apple pie and by a fair agreement sell your pie to another person, then the money you earn justly belongs to you and the pie justly belongs to the other person.
2   Some examples of the "structural principles" that Nozick opposes are that wealth should be distributed (a) equally, (b) according to merit, (c) in whatever way maximizes the total pleasure, or (d) equally except for inequalities that serve as incentives to benefit everyone (including the least advantaged group). The last one is Rawls's difference principle (see the Rawls selection in this anthology).

ARISTOTLE

Nicomachean Ethics

Aristotle, an ancient Greek philosopher who lived from 384 to 323 BC, was a dominant figure in Western thought. He started as a student in Plato's Academy. Later, after serving as tutor to Alexander the Great for three years, he founded his own school in Athens called the Lyceum. Besides writing much on philosophy, he was a scientist and a naturalist.

This selection is from his virtue-oriented *Nicomachean Ethics*, the first systematic treatment of ethics in Western philosophy. Aristotle begins with his teleological assumption that all actions aim at a good. For human actions, he argues, this good is happiness (*eudaimonia*), the only end we pursue entirely for its own sake. We gain happiness through "activity in accordance with virtue": rationally-guided actions done with excellence over a complete life. Moral virtues involve actions, desires, and feelings. We attain moral virtue by habitually choosing moderate actions that are neither "too much" nor "too little" for us.

As you read the selection, note how Aristotle describes the relationship between our moral dispositions, or character, and our actions. What does he mean when he says "Virtue is a state of character"?

Preface

Every art and inquiry, and similarly every action and pursuit, is thought to aim at some good; and for this reason the good has rightly been declared to be that at which all things aim.

If there is some end of the things we do, which we desire for its own sake (everything else being desired for the sake of this), and if we do not choose everything for the sake of something else (for at that rate the process would go on to infinity), clearly this must be the good and the chief good. Will not the knowledge of it, then, have a great influence on life? Shall we not, like archers who have a mark to aim at, be more likely to hit upon what is right? If so, we must try to determine what it is, and of which of the sciences or capacities it is the object. It would seem to belong to the most authoritative art. And politics appears to be of this nature; for it is this that ordains which sciences should be studied in a state, and which each class of citizens should learn. For even if the end is the same for a single man and for a state, that of the state seems greater; though it is worthwhile to attain the end merely for one man, it is finer and more godlike to attain it for a nation.

Now each man judges well the things he knows. Hence a young man is not a proper hearer of lectures on political science; for he is inexperienced in the actions that occur in life; and, since he tends to follow his passions, his study will be vain and unprofitable, because the end aimed at is not knowledge but action. And it makes no difference whether he is young in years or youthful in character; the defect does not depend on time, but on his living.

Happiness

Let us state what is the highest of all goods achievable by action. Verbally there is general agreement; for both the general run of men and people of superior refinement say it is happiness, and identify living well and doing well with being happy; but with regard to what happiness is they differ, and the many do not give the same account as the wise. For the former think it is some plain and obvious thing, like pleasure, wealth, or honor; they differ, however, from one another – and often even the same man identifies it with different things, with health when he is ill, with wealth when he is poor.

There is a difference between arguments from and those to the first principles. Plato was right in asking, as he used to do, "are we on the way from or to the first principles?" We must begin with things known to us. Hence anyone who is to listen intelligently to lectures about what is noble and just must have been brought up in good habits. For the fact is the starting-point; and the man who has been well brought up has or can get starting-points.

To judge from the lives that men lead, most men identify the good, or happiness, with pleasure. For there are three prominent types of life – that just mentioned, the political, and the contemplative life. People of superior refinement and active disposition identify happiness with honor; for this is, roughly speaking, the end of the political life. But it seems too superficial to be what we are looking for, since it depends on those who bestow honor rather than on him who receives it, but the good we divine to be proper to a man and not easily taken from him. Further, men seem to pursue honor in order that they may be assured of their goodness; clearly, then, according to them, virtue is better. Perhaps one might even suppose this to be, rather than honor, the end of the political life. But even this appears incomplete; for possession of virtue seems compatible with being asleep, or with lifelong inactivity, and with the greatest sufferings and misfortunes; but a man who was living so no one would call happy, unless he were maintaining a thesis at all costs. Third comes the contemplative life, which we shall consider later.

Let us again return to the good we are seeking, and ask what it can be. It seems different in different actions and arts; it is different in medicine, in strategy, and in the other arts. What then is the good of each? Surely that for whose sake everything else is done. In medicine this is health, in strategy victory, in architecture a house.

Since there is more than one end, and we choose some of these for the sake of something else, clearly not all ends are final ends; but the chief good is evidently something final. Therefore, if there is only one final end, this will be what we are seeking, and if there are more than one, the most final of these will be what we are seeking. We call final without qualification that which is always desirable in itself and never for the sake of something else.

Now such a thing happiness, above all else, is held to be; for this we choose always for itself and never for the sake of something else. Honor, pleasure, reason, and every virtue we choose indeed for themselves (for if nothing resulted from them we should still choose them), but we choose them also for the sake of happiness, judging that by means of them we shall be happy. Happiness, on the other hand, no one chooses for the sake of anything other than itself.

From self-sufficiency the same result follows; for the final good is thought to be self-sufficient. The self-sufficient we define as that which when isolated makes life desirable and lacking in nothing; and such we think happiness to be. Happiness, then, is final and self-sufficient, and is the end of action.

However, to say that happiness is the chief good seems a platitude, and a clearer account of it is desired. This might perhaps be given, if we could first ascertain the function of man. For just as for a flute-player, a sculptor, or an artist, the good is thought to reside in the function, so would it seem to be for man, if he has a function. Have the carpenter, then, and the tanner certain functions, and has man none? Is he born without a function? Or as eye, hand, foot, and in general each of the parts evidently has a function, may one lay it down that man similarly has a function apart from all these? What then can this be? Life seems to be common even to plants, but we are seeking what is peculiar to man. Next would be a life of perception, but it also seems to be common even to the horse and every animal. There remains, then, an active life of the element that has a rational principle. Now if the function of man is an activity of soul which follows or implies a rational principle, and we state the function of man to be a certain kind of life, and the function of a good man to be the good and noble performance of this, and if any action is well performed when it is performed in accordance with the appropriate excellence: if this is the case, human good turns out to be activity of soul in accordance with virtue, and if there is more than one virtue, in accordance with the best and most complete.

But we must add "in a complete life." For one swallow does not make a summer, nor does one day; and so too one day, or a short time, does not make a man blessed and happy.

Virtue

Since happiness is an activity of soul in accordance with perfect virtue, we must consider the nature of virtue; for perhaps we shall thus see better the nature of happiness. Clearly the virtue we must study is human virtue. By human virtue we mean not that of the body but that of the soul; and happiness also we call an activity of soul.

Some virtues are intellectual and others moral, philosophic wisdom and understanding and practical wisdom being intellectual, liberality and temperance moral. For in speaking about a man's character we do not say that he is wise or has understanding but that he is good-tempered or temperate; yet we praise the wise man also with respect to his state of mind; and of states of mind we call those which merit praise virtues.

Virtue, then, being of two kinds, intellectual and moral, intellectual virtue in the main owes both its birth and its growth to teaching, while moral virtue comes about as a result of habit, whence also its name (*ethike*) is one that is formed by a slight variation from the word ethos (habit). We become just by doing just acts, temperate by doing temperate acts, brave by doing brave acts.

It is from playing the lyre that both good and bad lyre-players are produced. This is the case with the virtues also; by doing the acts that we do in our transactions with other men we become just or unjust, and by doing the acts that we do in the presence of danger, and being habituated to feel fear or confidence, we become brave or cowardly. The same is true of appetites and feelings of anger; some men become temperate and good-tempered, others self-indulgent and irascible, by behaving in one way or the other in the appropriate circumstances. It makes no small difference, then, whether we form habits of one kind or of another from our very youth; it makes a very great difference, or rather all the difference.

Since the present inquiry does not aim at theoretical knowledge (for we are inquiring not in order to know what virtue is, but in order to become good), we must examine the nature of actions, namely how we ought to do them; for these determine also the nature of the states of character that are produced. Now, that we must act according to the right rule is a common principle and must be assumed – it will be discussed later, i.e. both what the right rule is, and how it is related to the other virtues.

It is the nature of such things to be destroyed by defect and excess, as we see in the case of strength and of health; both excessive and defective exercise destroys the strength, and similarly drink or food which is above or below a certain amount destroys the health, while that which is proportionate increases and preserves it. So too is it, then, in the case of temperance and courage and the other virtues. For the man who flies from and fears everything and does not stand his ground against anything becomes a coward, and the man who fears nothing at all but goes to meet every danger becomes rash; and similarly the man who indulges in every pleasure becomes self-indulgent, while the man who shuns every pleasure, as boors do, becomes insensible; temperance and courage, then, are destroyed by excess and defect, and preserved by the mean.

We must take as a sign of states of character the pleasure or pain that ensues on acts; for the man who abstains from bodily pleasures and delights in this very fact is temperate, while the man who is annoyed at it is self-indulgent, and he who stands his ground against things that are terrible and delights in this or at least is not pained is brave, while the man who is pained is a coward. For moral excellence is concerned with pleasures and pains; it is on account of the pleasure that we do bad things, and on account of the pain that we abstain from noble ones. Hence we ought to have been brought up in a particular way from our very youth, as Plato says, so as both to delight in and to be pained by the things that we ought; for this is the right education.

If acts are in accordance with the virtues, it does not follow that they are done justly or temperately. The agent also must be in a certain condition when he does them; in the first place he must have knowledge, secondly he must choose the acts for their own sakes, and thirdly his action must proceed from a firm and unchangeable character.

Actions, then, are called just and temperate when they are such as the just or the temperate man would do; but it is not the man who does these that is just and temperate, but the man who also does them as just and temperate men do them. It is well said, then, that it is by doing just acts that the just man is produced, and by doing temperate acts the temperate man; without doing these no one would have even a prospect of becoming good.

Virtue is a state of character

Next we must consider what virtue is. Since things found in the soul are of three kinds – passions, faculties, states of character – virtue must be one of these. By passions I mean appetite, anger, fear, confidence, envy, joy, friendly feeling, hatred, longing, emulation, pity, and in general the feelings that are accompanied by pleasure or pain; by faculties the things in virtue of which we are capable of feeling these, e.g. of becoming angry or being pained or feeling pity; by states of character the things in virtue of which we stand well or badly with reference to the passions, e.g. with reference to anger we stand badly if we feel it violently or too weakly, and well if we feel it moderately.

Now neither the virtues nor the vices are passions, because we are not called good or bad on the ground of our passions, but are so called on the ground of our virtues and our vices. Again, we feel anger and fear without choice, but the virtues are modes of choice or involve choice.

For these reasons also they are not faculties; for we are neither called good nor bad, nor praised nor blamed, for the simple capacity of feeling the passions; again, we have the faculties by nature, but we are not made good or bad by nature. If, then, the virtues are neither passions nor faculties, all that remains is that they should be states of character.

We must, however, not only describe virtue as a state of character, but also say what sort of state it is. The virtue of man is the state of character which makes a man good and which makes him do his own work well.

In everything that is continuous and divisible it is possible to take more, less, or an equal amount, and that either in terms of the thing itself or relatively to us; and the equal is an intermediate between excess and defect. By the intermediate in the object I mean that which is equidistant from each of the extremes; by the intermediate relatively to us that which is neither too much nor too little – and this is not the same for all. For instance, if ten is many and two is few, six is the intermediate according to arithmetical proportion. But the intermediate relatively to us is not to be taken so; if ten pounds are too much for a particular person to eat and two too little, it does not follow that the trainer will order six pounds; for this also is perhaps too much for the person, or too little – too little for Milo, too much for the beginner in athletic exercises. The same is true of running and wrestling. Thus a master of any art avoids excess and defect, but seeks the intermediate and chooses this – the intermediate not in the object but relatively to us.

Virtue must have the quality of aiming at the intermediate. I mean moral virtue; for it is this that is concerned with passions and actions, and in these there is excess, defect, and the intermediate. For instance, both fear and confidence and appetite and anger and pity and in general pleasure and pain may be felt both too much and too little, and in both cases not well; but to feel them at the right times, with reference to the right objects, towards the right people, with the right motive, and in the right way, is what is both intermediate and best, and this is characteristic of virtue. Similarly with regard to actions also there is excess, defect, and the intermediate.

Virtue, then, is a state of character concerned with choice, lying in a mean, i.e. the mean relative to us, this being determined by a rational principle, and by that principle by which the man of practical wisdom would determine it.

But not every action nor every passion admits of a mean; for some have names that already imply badness, e.g. spite, shamelessness, envy, and in the case of actions adultery, theft, murder; for all of these imply by their names that they are themselves bad, and not the excesses or deficiencies of them. It is not possible, then, ever to be right with regard to them; one must always be wrong. Nor does goodness or badness with regard to such things depend on committing adultery with the right woman, at the right time, and in the right way, but simply to do any of them is to go wrong.

Choice

We must next discuss choice; for it is thought to be most closely bound up with virtue and to discriminate characters better than actions do.

Choice, then, seems to be voluntary, but the latter extends more widely. For both children and the lower animals share in voluntary action, but not in choice, and acts done on the spur of the moment we describe as voluntary, but not as chosen.

Choice is not wish, though it seems near to it; for choice cannot relate to impossibles, and if anyone said he chose them he would be thought silly; but there may be a wish even for impossibles, e.g. for immortality. And wish may relate to things that could in no way be brought about by one's own efforts, e.g. that a particular athlete should win in a competition; but no one chooses such things, but only the things that he thinks could be brought about by his own efforts. Again, wish relates rather to the end, choice to the means; for instance, we wish to be healthy, but we choose the acts which will make us healthy; for choice seems to relate to things that are in our power.

We deliberate about things that are in our power and can be done. We deliberate not about ends but about means. For a doctor does not deliberate whether he shall heal, nor an orator whether he shall persuade, nor does anyone else deliberate about his end. They assume the end and consider how and by what means it is to be attained; and if it seems to be produced by several means they consider by which it is most easily and best produced.

The end, being what we wish for, the means what we deliberate about and choose, actions concerning means must be according to choice and voluntary. Now the exercise of the virtues is concerned with means. Therefore virtue also is in our own power, and so too vice. For where it is in our power to act it is also in our power not to act; so that, if to act, where this is noble, is in our power, not to act, which will be base, will also be in our power.

Witness seems to be borne to this both by individuals and by legislators; for these punish and take vengeance on those who do wicked acts (unless they have acted under compulsion or as a result of ignorance for which they are not themselves responsible), while they honor those who do noble acts, as though they meant to encourage the latter and deter the former. But no one is encouraged to do the things that are neither in our power nor voluntary; it is assumed that there is no gain in being persuaded not to be hot or in pain or hungry or the like, since we shall experience these feelings none the less.

But not only are the vices of the soul voluntary, but those of the body also for some men, whom we accordingly blame; while no one blames those who are ugly by nature, we blame those who are so owing to want of exercise and care. So it is, too, with respect to weakness and infirmity; no one would reproach a man blind from birth or by disease or from a blow, but rather pity him, while everyone would blame a man who was blind from drunkenness or some other self-indulgence.

If, then, the virtues are voluntary (for we are ourselves somehow partly responsible for our states of character), the vices also will be voluntary. But actions and states of character are not voluntary in the same way; for we are masters of our actions from the beginning right to the end, but though we control the beginning of our states of character the gradual progress is not obvious any more than it is in illnesses; because it was in our power, however, to act in this way or not in this way, therefore the states are voluntary.

Contemplation

If happiness is activity in accordance with virtue, it is reasonable that it should be in accordance with the highest virtue; and this will be that of the best thing in us. This activity is contemplative.

This would seem to be in agreement both with what we said before and with the truth. Firstly, this activity is the best (since not only is reason the best thing in us, but the objects of reason are the best of knowable objects); and secondly, it is the most continuous, since we can contemplate truth more continuously than we can do anything. And we think happiness has pleasure mingled with it, but the activity of philosophic wisdom is admittedly the pleasantest of virtuous activities; the pursuit of it is thought to offer pleasures marvelous for their purity and enduringness. And self-sufficiency must belong most to the contemplative activity. For while a philosopher, as well as a just man, needs the necessaries of life, the just man needs people towards whom he shall act justly, but the philosopher, even when by himself, can contemplate truth; he can perhaps do so better if he has fellow-workers, but still he is the most self-sufficient. And this activity alone would seem to be loved for its own sake; for nothing arises from it apart from the contemplating, while from practical activities we gain more or less apart from the action.

But such a life would be too high for man; for it is not in so far as he is man that he will live so, but in so far as something divine is present in him. If reason is divine, then the life according to it is divine in comparison with human life. But we must not follow those who advise us, being men, to think of human things, and, being mortal, of mortal things, but must, so far as we can, make ourselves immortal, and strain every nerve to live in accordance with the best thing in us.

Study questions

1 How does Aristotle argue that there is a single "chief good" that is the end of the things we do?

2 What discipline studies this good, and why?

3 On what grounds does Aristotle claim this chief good can be identified neither with pleasure nor honor? Who makes these identifications false?

4 How does Aristotle use the "function of man" to illustrate how happiness is the chief good of humans? How does he define happiness?

5 What are the differences between moral and intellectual virtue? Why do education and character formation play an important role in the development of moral virtue?

6 Aristotle claims that three things are found in the soul: passions, faculties, and states of character. Briefly describe each of these. On what grounds does he claim that virtue is neither a faculty nor a passion, but only a state of character? How does he describe this state of character?

7 Give examples of how virtue aims at an intermediate between excess and deficiency. What are some actions that do not admit of an intermediate?

8 What is choice? How is it distinct from wish? How does it relate to ends and means? How is it related to virtue and vice?

9 Why does Aristotle consider contemplation the highest virtue? What unique reward does this virtue bestow on its possessor?

For further study

This selection has excerpts, sometimes simplified in wording, from William David Ross's translation of the *Nicomachean Ethics* (Oxford: Oxford University Press, 1925). For recent assessments of Aristotle's approach, see W. D. Ross, *Aristotle* (New York: Meridian, 1959); Terence Irwin, *Aristotle's First Principles* (Oxford: Oxford University Press, 1988); Amiele Rorty, ed., *Essays on Aristotle's Ethics* (Berkeley: University of California Press, 1980); J. O. Urmson, *Aristotle's Ethics* (New York: Blackwell, 1988); and Jonathan Barnes, ed., *The Cambridge Companion to Aristotle* (Cambridge: Cambridge University Press, 1995).

Related readings in this anthology include MacIntyre and Slote (who defend virtue ethics) and Hume, Kant, Mill, and Frankena (who criticize some important features of Aristotelian ethics).

ALASDAIR MACINTYRE
Virtue Ethics

Alasdair MacIntyre, a Scottish philosopher born in 1929, is a major exponent of virtue ethics. Critical of the predominant act-centered approach to
ethics, MacIntyre turns to an Aristotelian person-centered approach that
stresses character and social identity.

MacIntyre lays out a theory of virtue consistent with this person-
centered approach. Virtues, on his initial definition, are habits or dispositions that we develop to sustain social practices in which we participate.
Later he brings in the good. The goal of the ethical actor is not just to do
one's duty or maximize utility or contribute to social practices, but to seek
excellence understood, ultimately, in terms of the good.

As you read the selection, ask yourself whether MacIntyre's theory of
virtue recognizes the importance of individual actions, rights, and duties.
Does it provide an adequate guide to action?

The modern self

The modern self, the self I have called emotivist, lacks rational criteria for
evaluation. Everything may be criticized from whatever standpoint the self
has adopted. Whatever evaluative allegiances the emotivist self may profess
are expressions of attitudes, preferences and choices. Inner conflicts are the
confrontation of one contingent arbitrariness by another. It is a self with no
given continuities.

The self thus conceived, utterly distinct from its social embodiments and
lacking any rational history of its own, may seem to have a certain abstract
character. The abstract quality arises from the contrast, indeed the loss, that
comes into view if we compare the emotivist self with its historical predeces-
sors. The emotivist self has suffered a deprivation, a stripping away of
qualities. The self is thought of as lacking any social identity, because the
social identity that it once enjoyed is no longer available; the self is thought
of as criterionless, because the *telos* [goal] in terms of which it once judged
and acted is no longer thought to be credible. What kind of identity and what
kind of *telos* were they?

In traditional societies it is through social groups that the individual identifies himself or herself. I am brother and grandson, member of this household, that village. These characteristics are part of my substance, defining partially my duties. Individuals inherit a particular space within interlocking social relationships; lacking that space, they are nobody, or at best a stranger or an outcast. To know oneself as such a social person is to find oneself placed at a certain point on a journey with set goals; to move through life is to make progress – or to fail to make progress – toward a given end.

The peculiarly modern self, the emotivist self, in acquiring sovereignty in its own realm lost its traditional social identity and view of human life as ordered to a given end. This transformation of the self could not have occurred if the forms of moral discourse had not also been transformed at the same time. Indeed it is wrong to separate the history of the self from the history of the language through which roles are given expression. What we discover is a single history.

In the next few chapters, MacIntyre analyzes various moral traditions, including those of ancient Greece (as expressed in Homer and Aristotle), Christianity (as expressed in the Bible and medieval thinkers), and England and America (as expressed in Jane Austen and Benjamin Franklin). He stresses the diversity of the different approaches to virtue.

The core concept of virtue

Are we able to disentangle from these rival and various claims a core concept of the virtues? I am going to argue that we can.

A virtue requires some prior account of social and moral life in terms of which it has to be explained. So in Homer the concept of a virtue is secondary to that of a *social role*, in Aristotle it is secondary to *the good life for man* and in Franklin it is secondary to utility. The account I am to give provides in a similar way the background against which the concept of a virtue has to be made intelligible.

There are three stages which have to be identified, if the core conception of a virtue is to be understood. The first stage requires an account of what I call a practice, the second an account of the narrative order of a human life and the third an account of a moral tradition.

Practices and internal goods

By a "practice" I mean any coherent and complex form of cooperative human activity through which goods internal to that form of activity are realized in the course of trying to achieve those standards of excellence which are appropriate to, and partially definitive of, that form of activity. Tic-tac-toe is not an example of a practice in this sense, nor is throwing a football with skill; but the game of football is, and so is chess. Bricklaying is not a practice; architecture is. Planting turnips is not a practice; farming is. So are the inquiries of physics, chemistry and biology, and so is the work of the historian, and so are painting and music. Thus the range of practices is wide: arts, sciences, games, politics, family life, all fall under the concept. But the precise range of practices is not of the first importance. Instead let me explain some of the key terms involved in my definition, beginning with the notion of goods internal to a practice.

Consider a child whom I teach to play chess, although the child has no desire to learn. If the child will play chess with me once a week I will give the child 50¢ worth of candy; if the child wins, the child will receive an extra 50¢ worth of candy. Thus motivated, the child plays to win. So long as it is the candy alone which provides the child with a reason for playing chess, the child has every reason to cheat, provided he or she can do so successfully. But, we may hope, there will come a time when the child will find in those goods specific to chess, in the achievement of a certain analytical skill, strategic imagination and competitive intensity, a new set of reasons, reasons now not just for winning on a particular occasion, but for trying to excel in whatever way the game of chess demands. Now if the child cheats, he or she will be defeating not me, but himself or herself.

There are thus two kinds of good to be gained by playing chess. On the one hand there are goods externally and contingently attached to chess-playing – in the case of the imaginary child candy, in the case of real adults prestige, status and money. There are always alternative ways for achieving such goods. On the other hand there are goods internal to the practice of chess which cannot be had in any way but by playing chess. Those who lack the relevant experience are incompetent as judges of internal goods.

External goods are always some individual's possession. Moreover, the more someone has of them, the less there is for other people. This is some-times necessarily the case, as with power and fame, and sometimes the case by contingent circumstance as with money. External goods are therefore objects of competition in which there must be losers as well as winners. Internal goods are a good for the whole community who participate in the practice.

A practice involves standards of excellence. To enter into a practice is to accept the authority of those standards. It is to subject my own attitudes, choices and tastes to the standards which partially define the practice. Practices have a history: games, sciences and arts all have histories. The standards are not immune from criticism, but we cannot be initiated into a practice without accepting their authority. If, on starting to play baseball, I do not accept that others know better than I when to throw a fast ball and when not, I will never learn to appreciate good pitching let alone to pitch. In the realm of practices the authority of both goods and standards operates to rule out all subjectivist and emotivist analyses of judgment.

Virtues promote a practice's internal goods

We are now in a position to formulate a tentative definition of a virtue: *A virtue is an acquired human quality the possession and exercise of which tends to enable us to achieve those goods which are internal to practices and the lack of which effectively prevents us from achieving any such goods.*

There are three ways in which my account is Aristotelian. First it requires for its completion those concepts which Aristotle's account requires: voluntariness, the distinction between intellectual virtues and virtues of character, the relationship to natural abilities and to passions and practical reasoning. On these topics something like Aristotle's view has to be defended, if my account is to be plausible.

Secondly my account can accommodate an Aristotelian view of pleasure. Consider how to reply to someone who, having considered my account of the differences between goods internal to and goods external to a practice, inquired into which class does pleasure fall? The answer is, "Some types of pleasure into one, some into the other."

Thirdly my account links evaluation and explanation in an Aristotelian way. To identify actions as manifesting a virtue is never only to evaluate; it is also to take the first step towards explaining why those actions rather than others were performed. Hence the fate of a city or an individual can be explained by citing the injustice of a tyrant or the courage of its defenders. Indeed without allusion to the place that justice and injustice, courage and cowardice play in human life very little will be genuinely explicable.

Evil practices

I have defined the virtues partly in terms of their place in practices. But some practices are evil. It has been suggested that torture and sado-masochistic sexual activities might be examples. But how can a disposition be a virtue if it is sustains evil practices?

I allow that there *may* be practices which *are* evil. I am far from convinced that there are, and I do not in fact believe that either torture or sado-masochistic sexuality answer to the description of a practice. But I do not want to rest my case on this, since many types of practice may on occasions be productive of evil. For practices include the arts, the sciences and certain types of game. And any of these may be a source of evil: the desire to excel and to win can corrupt, a man may be so engrossed by his painting that he neglects his family.

It is not the case that my account entails *either* that we ought to condone such evils *or* that whatever flows from a virtue is right. Courage sometimes sustains injustice, and loyalty has been known to strengthen a murderous aggressor.

That the virtues are defined, not in terms of good practices, but of practices, does not imply that practices never need moral criticism. And the resources for such criticism are not lacking. There is no inconsistency in appealing to a virtue to criticize a practice.

Identifying actions

We identify a particular action by invoking two kinds of context. We place the agent's intentions with reference to their role in his or her history; and we also place them with reference to their role in the history of the settings to which they belong. In doing this, we ourselves write a further part of these histories. Narrative history turns out to be the essential genre for the characterization of human actions.

The standpoint presupposed by the argument so far is different from that of those analytical philosophers who make central the notion of "a" human action. A course of human events is then seen as a complex sequence of individual actions, and a natural question is: How do we individuate human actions? Now there are contexts in which such notions are at home. In the recipes of a cookery book actions are individuated in the way some analytical philosophers have supposed. "Take six eggs. Then break them into a bowl. Add flour, salt, sugar, etc." But each element is intelligible as an action only as a-possible-element-in-a-sequence. Moreover even such a sequence requires a context to be intelligible. The concept of an intelligible action is more fundamental than that of an action as such.

Narratives

In understanding what someone is doing we place a particular episode in the context of a set of narrative histories, histories both of the individuals and of the settings in which they act. Action has a basically historical character. We all live out narratives in our lives and understand our lives in terms of narratives.

At any given point in a dramatic narrative we do not know what will happen next. Unpredictability is required by the narrative structure of human life, and the generalizations which social scientists discover provide an understanding of human life compatible with that structure. This unpredictability coexists with a second characteristic of lived narratives, a teleological character. We live our lives in the light of a future in which certain possibilities beckon us forward and others repel us. There is no present which is not informed by some image of the future which presents itself in the form of goals – towards which we are either moving or failing to move. Unpredictability and teleology therefore coexist as part of our lives.

Man is a story-telling animal. I can only answer the question "What am I to do?" if I can answer the prior question "Of what stories do I find myself a part?" We enter society with roles into which we have been drafted – and we have to learn what they are in order to understand how others respond to us. It is through stories about wicked stepmothers, lost children, good but misguided kings, and eldest sons who waste their inheritance, that children learn what a child and what a parent is, what the cast of characters may be and what the ways of the world are. Deprive children of stories and you leave them unscripted, anxious stutterers in their actions as in their words. Hence there is no way to understand any society except through the stock of stories which constitute its dramatic resources. The telling of stories has a key part in educating us into the virtues.

Narratives and self-understanding

What the narrative concept of selfhood requires is twofold. On the one hand, I am the *subject* of a history that is my own, that has its own peculiar meaning. When someone complains that his or her life is meaningless, he or she is often complaining that the narrative of their life has become unintelligible to them, that it lacks any point, any movement towards a climax or a *telos*. Hence the point of doing one thing rather than another seems to have been lost.

To be the subject of a narrative is to be accountable for the actions and experiences which compose a narratable life. It is to be open to being asked to give an account of what one did or what happened to one. Personal identity is just that identity presupposed by the unity of the character which the unity of a narrative requires. Without such unity there would not be subjects of whom stories could be told.

The other aspect of narrative selfhood is correlative: I am not only accountable, I can always ask others for an account. I am part of their story, as they are part of mine. The narrative of any one life is part of an interlocking set of narratives. Moreover this asking for and giving of accounts itself plays an important part in narratives. Asking what you did and why, saying what I did and why, pondering the differences between your account and my account, these are essential constituents of narratives. Without accountability narratives would lack that continuity required to make them and the actions that constitute them intelligible.

The good

In what does the unity of an individual life consist? Its unity is the unity of a narrative embodied in a single life. To ask "What is the good for me?" is to ask how best I might live out that unity and bring it to completion. To ask "What is the good for man?" is to ask what all answers to the former question must have in common. It is the systematic asking of these two questions and the attempt to answer them in deed as well as in word which provide the moral life with its unity. The unity of a human life is the unity of a narrative quest. A quest for what?

Without some conception of the final *telos* there could not be any beginning to a quest. Some conception of the good for man is required. Whence is such a conception to be drawn? Precisely from those questions which led us to transcend that limited conception of the virtues which is available in practices. It is in looking for a conception of *the* good which will order other goods, a conception of *the* good which will extend our understanding of the purpose and content of the virtues, that we initially define the quest for the good. But secondly the quest is not a search for something already adequately characterized, as miners search for gold or geologists for oil. It is in the course of the quest that the goal is finally to be understood.

The virtues therefore are to be understood as those dispositions which not only sustain practices and enable us to achieve the goods internal to practices, but which also sustain us in the quest for the good. The catalogue of the virtues will therefore include the virtues required to sustain the households and communities in which men and women can seek for the good together and the virtues necessary for philosophical inquiry about the good.

Study questions

1   What criticism of the modern or emotivist self does MacIntyre offer? Do you agree with his criticism? Why or why not?

2   How does MacIntyre define a practice? What are some examples of practices? Can a practice be evil?
3   What is the difference between an external and an internal good? Give an example of each.
4   How does MacIntyre view standards of excellence?
5   What is his definition of virtue? How is it similar to Aristotle's conception?
6   What is his criticism of how some analytic philosophers identify or individuate actions? What is his alternative?
7   What two core characteristics are narratives claimed to have? Might there be others?
8   MacIntyre claims that the unity of a life is the unity of a narrative quest. How does he appeal to a transcendent good to make this claim? How could a skeptic criticize MacIntyre's claim?

For further study

This selection has excerpts, sometimes simplified in wording, from Alasdair MacIntyre's *After Virtue* (Notre Dame, IN: University of Notre Dame Press, 1981), Chapters 3, 14, and 15. His other ethical writings include *Whose Justice? Which Rationality?* (Notre Dame, IN: University of Notre Dame Press, 1988); and *Three Rival Versions of Moral Inquiry* (Notre Dame, IN: University of Notre Dame Press, 1990). For a good analysis of *After Virtue*, see W. K. Frankena's "MacIntyre and Modern Morality," *Ethics* 93 (1982-3): 579-87. For further readings on virtue theory, see Aristotle's *Nicomachean Ethics*, particularly books I-VI; Anthony Kenny's *Aristotelian Ethics* (Oxford: Clarendon Press, 1978); Peter Geach's *The Virtues* (Cambridge: Cambridge University Press, 1977); and Charles Taylor's *Sources of the Self* (Cambridge, MA: Harvard University Press, 1989). Harry Gensler's *Ethics: A Contemporary Introduction* (London and New York: Routledge, 1998) briefly talks about virtue in Chapter 11 (Section 11.6).

Related readings in this anthology include Aristotle and Slote (who defend virtue ethics); Kant, Mill, and Ross (who discuss whether virtue is good in itself); and Ayer, Hume, and Nietzsche (who make some references to virtues). Most of the readings in this anthology take an act-centered approach to ethics.

MICHAEL SLOTE
Rudiments of Virtue Ethics

Michael Slote, an American philosopher born in 1941, has done much to revive interest in virtue ethics. Virtue ethicists often criticize other approaches as too rationalistic, for wrongly assuming that all duties reduce to a single rule, or for not appreciating the moral value of self-interest. In contrast, virtue ethics emphasizes the role that diverse habits and dispositions play in moral decisions and it recognizes the value of both self-regarding and other-regarding virtues.

Virtue ethicists prefer to describe moral acts not in deontic terms (like "right" or "obligatory") that refer only to acts, but in aretaic terms (like "admirable" and "excellent") that apply equally to the act and to the person performing the act. While Slote defends virtue ethics, he does not argue that it is complete or that it provides specific action-guiding principles. He leaves open the possibility that insights of virtue theory can be incorporated into other systems of morality.

As you read this section, ask yourself whether Slote's claims about "our ordinary sense of what is admirable" fit how you evaluate actions. Is the incompleteness of virtue ethics a strength or a weakness?

Distinctive features of virtue ethics

Virtue ethics is commonly regarded as involving two distinctive or essential elements. A virtue ethics in the fullest sense must treat aretaic notions (like "good" or "excellent") rather than deontic notions (like "morally wrong," "ought," "right," and "obligation") as primary, and it must put a greater emphasis on the ethical assessment of agents and their motives and character traits than on the evaluation of acts and choices. If we understand the notion in this rough manner, then much of ancient ethics – Aristotle, the Epicureans, and the Stoics, for example – constitute forms of virtue ethics. However, these instances of virtue ethics are less radically different from familiar deontology and utilitarianism than some advocates of a virtues approach may have hoped for.

Thus although Aristotle and I both make consideration of the virtues and of virtuous or admirable individuals central to our ethical views, neither of us altogether eschews the ethical evaluation of acts and neither makes the ethical assessment of acts strictly derivative from the evaluation of persons or traits. For Aristotle, an action will be noble if it is one that a noble or virtuous individual would perform. But he also allows that people can perform good or virtuous acts even if they are not themselves virtuous or good and, in addition, he characterizes the virtuous individual as one who *sees* or *perceives* what it is good or right or proper to do in any given situation. Such language clearly implies that the virtuous individual does what is noble or virtuous because it is the noble thing to do, rather than its being the case that what is noble to do has this status simply because the virtuous individual will choose it.

So for Aristotle, as well as for the view defended here, the ethical status of acts is not *entirely derivative* from that of traits, motives, or individuals, even though traits and individuals are the *major focus*. Some philosophers recently advocating an ethics of virtue have advocated the more radical form of theory that would treat the evaluation of acts as entirely derivative, and on some occasions this has been done because of a conflation of the notions just mentioned and consequent misidentification of the ethical position of virtue theorists like Aristotle. The fact that Aristotle makes virtues and the virtuous individual the center of ethics in no way entails that he treats act-evaluation as derivative from agent-, motive-, or trait-evaluation.

Egoism

Traits of character can qualify as virtues through what they enable their possessors to do for themselves as well as through what they enable their possessors to do for others, and so our ordinary notion of a virtue gives fundamental significance to the well-being of the self and to the well-being of others. So our refusal to use specifically moral concepts doesn't force our virtue ethics in the direction of egoism. In the absence of deontic and / or moral concepts, egoism is roughly the virtue-ethical view that traits are virtues to the extent they favor their possessors / agents. Few of us would maintain an egoistic view of what counts as a virtue, and we have more than one reason for avoiding egoism in favor of a more even-handed common-sense view.

Given that we are thinking critically and theoretically about ethics, we may well wish to avoid asymmetry whenever other things are equal, and clearly egoism is asymmetric in a way common-sense views about admirability and virtue-status are not. But, more important, we have every reason to make only those large-scale or radical shifts from ordinary ways of thinking that we need to avoid problems and inconsistencies. A properly conservative approach seems to dictate, therefore, that we prefer a common-sense account of the virtues to the sort of egoistic view which, despite its predominance in the ancient world, e.g., among the Stoics and Epicureans, is out of keeping with what we (post-)Judeo-Christians typically think. And I will therefore largely ignore egoism and attempt, instead, to articulate a common-sense form of virtue ethics.

Although Aristotle does advocate both self-regarding and other-regarding virtues (as well as mixed virtues), his fundamental doctrine of the mean seems ill adapted to helping us understand or justify duties of promise-keeping and truth-telling, so I think we have reasons of common-sense plausibility to avoid the doctrine of the mean. Freed of that doctrine, our intuitive virtue ethics will readily allow us to criticize promise-breaking and lying, but there will, nonetheless, be much that is reminiscent of Aristotle in what follows. Furthermore, our approach all along has been much more explicit about issues of self-other symmetry than anything to be found in Aristotle. Here we have had to be explicit about issues of symmetry in an attempt to explain how a common-sense virtue-ethical approach may be superior to common-sense, Kantian, and even utilitarian forms of ethics.

Some issues of terminology

The observant reader may have noted my tendency to focus on the evaluation of traits (of character) as virtues and to treat the evaluation of actions as a matter of subsuming them under virtues. I have been doing this simply as a matter of convenience, as a means to streamlining our discussion, and I certainly want to leave room for the direct evaluation of actions. To say of an act that it exemplifies a certain virtue, is typically to evaluate it indirectly, through its relation to a certain trait regarded as valuable or admirable, but there is no reason why one can't also assess an act itself in virtue-ethical terms. If we admire or think highly of an act (which may or may not obviously exemplify some familiar virtue), we can simply say that the act is admirable or that we think well of it, and in so doing, it is not at all obvious that we must base such an act-evaluation on some prior or implicit evaluation of certain general traits.

The aretaic term "admirable" can be as readily applied to traits of character (and people) as to particular actions. By the same token, what is done for others and what is done for the agent are both ordinarily taken to be relevant to the admirability of a particular act, so the term "admirable" is not only more broadly usable than the expression "is a virtue" but also possesses the highly desirable self-other symmetry that so clearly characterizes the latter expression.

The virtue ethics I will be describing is largely based on our common-sense ideas and intuitions about what counts as a virtue and, more generally, as admirable. The idea of excellent acts or actions – however much Greek usage pushes us in the direction of such neologism – is much less natural as English than similar talk using the concept of admirability – consider the difference between "I found what he did admirable" and "I found what he did excellent." And I think something similar can be said in connection with the concept of good(ness), even though one may be initially inclined to hold that it is the most generally useful of our virtue-ethical aretaic notions. But to say "I found his actions good" is to invite a request for further clarification in a way that use of "admirable" seems not to do. And part of the problem here may be that "good" also suggests moral goodness more strongly than we wish to do in the version of virtue ethics to be developed here. And so for purposes of our present foundational discussion, I will for the most part avoid "good" and "excellent" and use "admirable" as the canonical general term of virtue-ethical commendation.

The last point raises the problem of how to express the opposite of admirability. If we wish to express an attitude that is as fully negative as "admirable" is positive, it is not enough to speak of a less-than-admiring attitude or of behavior as less-than-admirable. "Blameworthy," "reprehensible," and "culpable" are all specifically moral – Winston Churchill may have been careless or foolish, when on an early trip to the United States he stepped off a curb looking the wrong way and was injured by an oncoming car, but we wouldn't ordinarily regard him as even the least bit blameworthy, culpable, or reprehensible for such self-neglect. So what term can be used for expressing the opposite of admirability?

I think our best bet is "deplorable." Although it can be predicated of accidents, events, or states of affairs, the term "deplorable" can be used in other contexts to imply the kind of non-moral criticism we make when we accuse someone of careless or foolish behavior. If Churchill was sufficiently warned of the dangers for Britons of the American rule of the road, then we may regard his failure to look left as open to criticism, as deplorable; we may deplore his inattention, even if "blame" seems the wrong word for our critical attitude. But someone can also be considered deplorable for the harm he negligently or intentionally does to others, and so I think we can treat "deplorable" as the opposite of "admirable."

Modes of symmetry

Under utilitarianism, the welfare or preferences of every individual are given equal weight. So utilitarianism embodies an ideal of equal concern for all persons (or sentient beings): the calculations that determine the obligations of each agent are based on a reckoning that treats the welfare of each and every person other than the agent as no more or less important than that of the agent. Utilitarianism embodies an ideal of uniform or symmetrical concern toward *every* individual that is *self-other* symmetric.

The form of symmetry we attributed to utilitarianism is clearly absent from common-sense morality. The judgments made by the latter are not predicated on any ideal of equal concern for everyone; on the contrary, the agent counts for *less* than others and *greater* concern for those near and dear as opposed to distant others is morally incumbent upon her. To be sure our ordinary thinking about the virtues treats benefit to the possessor of a trait as relevant to its status as a good trait of character. But nothing in our ordinary understanding of the virtues precludes the admirability of traits or acts that involve giving preference to certain people over others, and in fact it seems contrary to our usual understanding of the virtues, seems out and out deplorable, for one's actions and character not to give greater concern, for example, for one's spouse and children than for random others.

Yet that ethics embodies another sort of self-other symmetry we have not yet considered. Traits admired for other-regarding reasons are not normally considered to have precedence over self-regarding virtues. Kindness, justice, and generosity are not usually viewed as greater or more important virtues than self-regarding virtues such as prudence, fortitude, sagacity, and equanimity or "mixed" virtues like courage, self-control, and practical wisdom; indeed the language of common-sense ethics includes as many terms for self-regarding or "mixed" virtues as for other-regarding virtues. To that degree, our ordinary thinking about the virtues gives equal emphasis to virtues helping others and virtues helping their possessors, and this embodies a kind of equality or symmetry of concern for self and others.

I am not saying that virtue ethics requires us to have an equal concern for every single individual. Rather, I am saying that our ordinary thinking about the virtues treats the category of trait-possessor and the category of "other people" as of roughly equal importance. Our ordinary understanding of what is admirable and what counts as a virtue embodies equal concern for self and others, where "others" is to be understood *in sensu composito*, that is, applying to other people as a class; whereas, by contrast, utilitarianism's ethical ideal expresses equality or symmetry of concern for self and others in a sense that understands "others" *in sensu diviso*, as applying to each and every other individual as compared to the concern shown for the self (the agent / possessor herself).[1] And this means that utilitarianism and common-sense virtue ethics differ as regards the importance and evaluation of purely self-regarding traits and actions.

Utilitarian evaluation reflects an equality of concern for the self and for every single other individual, and where enough other people can be affected by a trait or activity, concern for the given self may be practically insignificant by comparison with the sum of concern for other people. Since over a lifetime, most of us can affect thousands of other people, the self is likely to be submerged in the sea of concern for others that gives rise to utilitarian ethical judgments. But our ordinary thinking about the virtues – though it may not rule out the possibility of self-sacrifice – seems less committed to evaluations that take such little account of the agent / possessor's self-regarding concerns. If its ideal involves an equality as between the self as a category, on the one hand, and other people taken as a category, rather than individually, on the other, then an evaluative balance is established between self-concern and concern for all others put together, and it is such a (two-way) balance that on my view constitutes the backbone of our ordinary thinking about what is and is not admirable. The idea of a merely two-way balance between any given self and the totality or class of others also expresses an ethical ideal of symmetry, one that utilitarianism clearly and necessarily fails to embody.

In effect, I am saying that "equality of concern for self and other people" has two natural readings embodying two incompatible but attractive ideals of self-other symmetry. Both are understandable, natural ways of ascribing symmetry, but neither utilitarianism nor common-sense virtue ethics allows both of them to be exemplified or adhered to. As a result, the choice between utilitarianism and a virtue ethics that remains as close as possible to our ordinary sense of what is admirable entails a choice between two kinds of self-other symmetry.

Study questions

1   Does Slote view the evaluation of actions as derivative from the evaluation of agents, motives, or traits? Why or why not?
2   How do egoistic and common-sense views of virtue differ?
3   On what grounds does Slote reject Aristotle's "doctrine of the mean"?
4   From Slote's perspective, what is the advantage to describing actions as "admirable" rather than as "virtuous" or as "good"? What is the opposite of "admirable"?
5   On Slote's view, why can an admirable action give preference to some persons over others? Contrast Slote's position with the utilitarian view.
6   How does Slote's view of the self-other symmetry differ from that of the usual utilitarian view? How do these two views differ in their understanding of how oneself and others have equal moral importance?

For further study

This selection has excerpts, sometimes simplified in wording, from Chapter 5 of Michael Slote's *From Morality to Virtue* (New York: Oxford University Press,

1992). See also his *Goods and Virtue* (New York: Oxford University Press, 1983); *Common Sense Morality and Consequentialism* (London: Routledge and Kegan Paul, 1985); *Beyond Optimizing: A Study of Rational Choice* (Cambridge: Harvard, 1989); "Some Advantages of Virtue Ethics," in *Identity, Character, and Morality,* edited by O. Flanagan and A. Rorty (London and Cambridge, MA: MIT Press, 1990), pages 429–48; and "Virtue Ethics," in *The Blackwell Guide to Ethical Theory,* edited by H. LaFollette (Malden, MA: Blackwell, 2000), pages 325–47. Slote has recently developed an ethics of caring that relates to how to deal with those close to us and those distant from us; see his "The Justice of Caring," *Social Philosophy and Policy* 15 (1998): 171–95, and *Morals from Motives* (New York: Oxford University Press, 2001). For other late twentieth-century versions of virtue ethics, see G. E. M. Anscombe, "Modern Moral Philosophy," *Philosophy* 33 (1958): 1–19; Rosalind Hursthouse, "Virtue Theory and Abortion," *Philosophy and Public Affairs* 20 (1991): 223–46; and Martha Nussbaum, *The Fragility of Goodness* (New York: Cambridge University Press, 1986).

Related readings in this anthology include Aristotle and MacIntyre (who also develop theories of virtue ethics), Kant (who emphasizes the moral worth of an action), and the utilitarians Mill and Singer (whose self-other symmetry Slote criticizes).

Note

1   Here is an example to illustrate Slote's distinction. Suppose you say "All these shirts cost $20." You could mean that it costs $20 to buy the group of shirts (*sensu composito*) or that it costs $20 to buy each shirt (*sensu diviso*). Similarly, suppose you say "My concern for myself is equal to my concern for others." You could mean that your concern for yourself equals your total concern for everyone else (*sensu composito*) or that it equals your concern for each other person (*sensu diviso*).

PART V

APPLIED ETHICS: ABORTION AND OTHER ISSUES

JUDITH JARVIS THOMSON
A Defense of Abortion

Judith Jarvis Thomson, an American philosopher born in 1929, works in ethics and philosophy of mind. Her article on abortion is one of the most widely reprinted essays of contemporary moral philosophy.

Opponents of abortion generally claim that a fetus is a person with a right to life. Thomson argues that, even if we grant this, abortion would still be morally permissible in cases of rape or contraceptive failure.

As you read the selection, ask yourself whether Thomson has given a convincing defense of abortion. What do you think of her analogy between a pregnant woman and a woman plugged into a violinist? Is her analogy strong or weak? Can you think of moral considerations that her argument overlooks?

A slippery-slope argument

Most opposition to abortion relies on the premise that the fetus is a human being, a person, from the moment of conception. The premise is argued for, but not well. We are asked to notice that the development of a human being from conception through birth into childhood is continuous; to draw a line, to choose a point in this development and say "before this point the thing is not a person, after this point it is a person" is to make an arbitrary choice for which no good reason can be given. It is concluded that the fetus is, or anyway that we had better say it is, a person from the moment of conception.

But this conclusion does not follow. Similar things might be said about the development of an acorn into an oak tree, and it does not follow that acorns are oak trees, or that we had better say they are. Arguments of this form are called "slippery slope arguments" and opponents of abortion rely on them uncritically.

I am inclined to agree, however, that the prospects for "drawing a line" in the development of the fetus look dim. We shall probably have to agree that the fetus has already become a human person well before birth. Indeed, it comes as a surprise when one first learns how early in its life it begins to acquire human characteristics. By the tenth week, for example, it already has a face, arms and legs, fingers and toes; it has internal organs, and brain activity is detectable. On the other hand, I think that the fetus is not a person from the moment of conception. A newly fertilized ovum, a newly implanted clump of cells, is no more a person than an acorn is an oak tree. But I shall not discuss any of this. For it seems to me to be of great interest to ask what happens if, for the sake of argument, we allow the premise.

The violinist case

I propose that we grant that the fetus is a person from the moment of conception. How does the [pro-life] argument go from here? Something like this. Every person has a right to life. So the fetus has a right to life. No doubt the mother has a right to decide what shall happen in and to her body. But surely a person's right to life is stronger than the mother's right to decide what happens in and to her body. So the fetus may not be killed; an abortion may not be performed.

It sounds plausible. But imagine this. You wake up in the morning and find yourself in bed with a famous unconscious violinist. He has a fatal kidney ailment, and the Society of Music Lovers has found that you alone have the right blood type to help. They have therefore kidnapped you, and the violinist's circulatory system was plugged into yours, so your kidneys can be used to extract poisons from his blood. The director of the hospital tells you, "Look, we're sorry the Society of Music Lovers did this to you – we would never have permitted it if we had known. But still, they did it, and the violinist now is plugged into you. To unplug you would be to kill him. But it's only for nine months. By then he will have recovered from his ailment, and can safely be unplugged from you." Is it morally incumbent on you to accede to this situation? No doubt it would be very nice of you if you did, a great kindness. But do you *have* to accede to it? What if it were not nine months, but nine years? What if the director says, "Tough luck, but you've got to stay in bed, with the violinist plugged into you, for the rest of your life. Because remember this. All persons have a right to life, and violinists are persons. A person's right to life outweighs your right to decide what happens in and to your body. So you cannot ever be unplugged from him." I imagine you would regard this as outrageous, which suggests that something is wrong with that plausible-sounding argument I mentioned a moment ago.

The pro-life argument and rape cases

In this case, you were kidnapped; you didn't volunteer for the operation that plugged the violinist into your kidneys. Can those who oppose abortion on the ground I mentioned make an exception for a pregnancy due to rape?

Certainly. They can say that persons have a right to life only if they didn't come into existence because of rape; or they can say that all persons have a right to life, but those who came into existence because of rape have less. But these statements have a rather unpleasant sound. Surely the question of whether you have a right to life, or how much of it you have, shouldn't turn on whether you are the product of a rape. The people who oppose abortion on the ground I mentioned do not make an exception in case of rape.

Nor do they make an exception for a case in which the mother has to spend the nine months of her pregnancy in bed. They would agree that would be a great pity, and hard on the mother; but all persons have a right to life, the fetus is a person, and so on. I suspect that they would not make an exception for a case in which the pregnancy went on for nine years, or even the rest of the mother's life.

The mother's right to self-defense

Let us call the view that abortion is impermissible even to save the mother's life "the extreme view." I want to suggest first that it does not issue from the argument I mentioned earlier without the addition of some fairly powerful premises. Suppose a woman has become pregnant, and now learns that she has a cardiac condition such that she will die if she carries the baby to term. What may be done for her? The fetus, being a person, has a right to life, but as the mother is a person too, so has she a right to life. Presumably they have an equal right to life. How is it supposed to come out that an abortion may not be performed? If mother and child have an equal right to life, shouldn't we perhaps flip a coin? Or should we add the mother's right to decide what happens in and to her body, which everybody seems ready to grant – the sum of her rights now outweighing the fetus' right to life?

The most familiar argument here is the following. Performing the abortion would be directly killing the child, whereas doing nothing would not be killing the mother, but only letting her die. Moreover, in killing the child, one would be killing an innocent person, for the child has committed no crime, and is not aiming at his mother's death. Thus an abortion may not be performed.

Suppose you find yourself trapped in a tiny house with a growing child. I mean a very tiny house, and a rapidly growing child – you are already up against the wall of the house and in a few minutes you'll be crushed to death. The child on the other hand won't be crushed to death; if nothing is done to stop him from growing, he'll simply burst open the house and walk out a free man. Now I could well understand it if a bystander were to say, "We cannot choose between your life and his, we cannot intervene." But it cannot be concluded that you too can do nothing, that you cannot attack it to save your life. However innocent the child may be, you do not have to wait passively while it crushes you to death. Perhaps a pregnant woman is vaguely felt to have the status of house, to which we don't allow the right of self-defense. But if the woman houses the child, it should be remembered that she is a person who houses it.

I am not claiming that people have a right to do anything whatever to save their lives. There are limits to the right of self-defense. If someone threatens you with death unless you torture someone else to death, you have not the right, even to save your life, to do so. But the case under consideration here is very different. In our case there are only two people involved, one whose life is threatened, and one who threatens it. Both are innocent. For this reason we may feel that we bystanders cannot intervene. But the person threatened can.

In sum, a woman surely can defend her life against the threat to it posed by the unborn child, even if doing so involves its death. And this shows that the extreme view of abortion is false.

The people-seeds case

Suppose a woman voluntarily indulges in intercourse, knowing of the chance it will issue in pregnancy, and she does become pregnant; is she not in part responsible for the presence of the unborn person inside her? No doubt she did not invite it in. But doesn't her partial responsibility for its being there itself give it a right to the use of her body?

It is not at all plain that this argument really does go even as far as it purports to. If the room is stuffy, and I therefore open a window to air it, and a burglar climbs in, it would be absurd to say, "Ah, now he can stay, she's given him a right to the use of her house – for she is partially responsible for his presence there, having voluntarily done what enabled him to get in, in full knowledge that there are such things as burglars." It would be still more absurd to say this if I had had bars installed outside my windows, precisely to prevent burglars from getting in, and a burglar got in only because of a defect in the bars. Again, suppose it were like this: people-seeds drift about in the air like pollen, and if you open your windows, one may drift in and take root in your carpets or upholstery. You don't want children, so you fix up your windows with fine mesh screens, the very best you can buy. As can happen, one of the screens is defective; and a seed drifts in and takes root. Does the person-plant who now develops have a right to the use of your house? Surely not – despite the fact that you voluntarily opened your windows and you knew that screens were sometimes defective. Someone may argue that you are responsible for its rooting, that it does have a right to your house, because after all you *could* have lived out your life with bare floors and furniture, or with sealed windows and doors. But this won't do – for by the same token anyone can avoid a pregnancy due to rape by having a hysterectomy, or anyway by never leaving home without a (reliable!) army.

It seems to me that the argument we are looking at can establish at most that there are *some* cases in which the unborn person has a right to the use of its mother's body, and therefore *some* cases in which abortion is unjust killing. There is room for much discussion and argument as to precisely which, if any. At any rate the argument certainly does not establish that all abortion is unjust killing.

Moral decency

There may be cases in which it would be morally indecent to detach a person from your body at the cost of his life. Suppose you learn that what the violinist needs is not nine years of your life, but only one hour: all you need do to save his life is to spend one hour with him. Admittedly you were kidnapped. Admittedly you did not give anyone permission to plug him into you. Nevertheless it seems to me plain you *ought* to allow him to use your kidneys for that hour – it would be indecent to refuse.

Again, suppose pregnancy lasted only an hour, and constituted no threat to life or health. And suppose that a woman becomes pregnant as a result of rape. Admittedly she did not voluntarily do anything to bring about the existence of a child. Admittedly she did nothing at all which would give the unborn person a right to the use of her body. All the same it might well be said, as in the newly emended violinist story, that she *ought* to allow it to remain for that hour – that it would be indecent to refuse.

My own view is that even though you ought to let the violinist use your kidneys for the one hour, we should not conclude that he has a right to do so – we should say that if you refuse, you are self-centered and callous, indecent in fact, but not unjust. And similarly, that even supposing a case in which a woman pregnant due to rape ought to allow the unborn person to use her body for the hour he needs, we should not conclude that he has a right to do so; we should conclude that she is self-centered, callous, indecent, but not unjust, if she refuses. The complaints are no less grave; they are just different.

Except in such cases as the unborn person has a right to demand it – and we were leaving open the possibility that there may be such cases – nobody is morally *required* to make large sacrifices, of health, of all other interests and concerns, for nine years, or even for nine months, in order to keep another person alive.

Assuming responsibility

Following the lead of the opponents of abortion, I have been speaking of the fetus merely as a person. But it may be said that what is important is not merely that the fetus is a person, but that it is a person for whom the woman has a special responsibility issuing from the fact that she is its mother. And it might be argued that all my analogies are therefore irrelevant – for you do not have that special kind of responsibility for that violinist.

If parents do not try to prevent pregnancy, do not obtain an abortion, and then at the birth of the child do not put it out for adoption, but rather take it home, then they have assumed responsibility for it, they have given it rights, and they cannot *now* withdraw support from it at the cost of its life because they now find it difficult to go on providing for it. But if they have taken all reasonable precautions against having a child, they do not simply by virtue of their biological relationship to the child who comes into existence have a special responsibility for it. They may wish to assume responsibility for it, or they may not wish to. I am suggesting that if assuming responsibility for it would require large sacrifices, then they may refuse.

Objections from the pro-choice side

My argument will be found unsatisfactory on two counts by many who want to regard abortion as morally permissible. First, I do not argue that abortion is always permissible. I am inclined to think it a merit of my account that it does *not* give a general yes or a general no. It allows for and supports our sense that, for example, a sick and desperately frightened fourteen-year-old schoolgirl, pregnant due to rape, may *of course* choose abortion, and that any law which rules this out is insane. And it also allows for and supports our sense that in other cases resort to abortion is positively indecent. It would be indecent in the woman to request an abortion, and indecent in a doctor to perform it, if she is in her seventh month, and wants the abortion just to avoid postponing a trip abroad. The fact that the arguments I have been drawing attention to treat all cases of abortion as morally on a par ought to have made them suspect at the outset.

Secondly, while I am arguing for the permissibility of abortion in some cases, I am not arguing for the right to secure the death of the unborn child. It is easy to confuse these two things in that up to a certain point the fetus is not able to survive outside the mother's body; hence removing it from her body guarantees its death. But they are importantly different. I have argued that you are not morally required to spend nine months in bed, sustaining the life of that violinist; but to say this is by no means to say that if, when you unplug yourself, there is a miracle and he survives, you then have a right to turn round and slit his throat. You may detach yourself even if this costs him his life; you have no right to his death. Some people will feel dissatisfied by this. A woman may be utterly devastated by the thought of a child, a bit of herself, put out for adoption and never seen or heard of again. She may therefore want not merely that the child be detached from her, but that it die. Some opponents of abortion regard this as beneath contempt – thereby showing insensitivity to a powerful source of despair. All the same, I agree that the desire for the child's death is not one which anybody may gratify, should it turn out to be possible to detach the child alive.

At this place, it should be remembered that we have only been pretending that the fetus is a human being from the moment of conception. A very early abortion is surely not the killing of a person, and so is not dealt with by anything I have said here.

Study questions

1 How do opponents of abortion argue that the fetus is a human being? How does Thomson criticize their argument?
2 How does the pro-life argument use the premise that the fetus is a person? Does Thomson base her defense of abortion on the claim that a fetus is not a person?
3 Explain the violinist case and how Thomson argues that it is like a pregnancy resulting from rape. How is the violinist case supposed to show that abortion is morally permissible in rape cases?
4 Explain how Thomson argues for a mother's right to self-defense.
5 Does Thomson deny that humans have a right to life?
6 Explain the people-seeds case and how it is analogous to a pregnancy resulting from failed contraception. What conclusion does Thomson draw from the analogy?
7 Explain how Thomson addresses moral decency. What demands does it place on those considering abortions?
8 Explain how Thomson thinks pro-choice advocates would object to her position and how she responds to those objections.

For further study

This selection has excerpts, sometimes simplified in wording, from Judith Jarvis Thomson's "A Defense of Abortion" in *Philosophy and Public Affairs* 1 (1971): 47–66. Further works by Thomson include *Acts and Other Events* (Ithaca, NY: Cornell University Press, 1977) and *The Realm of Rights* (Cambridge, MA: Harvard University Press, 1990). Harry Gensler's *Ethics: A Contemporary*

Introduction (London and New York: Routledge, 1998) examines abortion in Chapter 12.

For further study of the pro-abortion side, see Peter Singer's *Practical Ethics* (Cambridge: Cambridge University Press, 1993), second edition, Chapter 6; and Michael Tooley's *Abortion and Infanticide* (Oxford: Oxford University Press, 1983). On the anti-abortion side, see Stephen D. Schwarz's *The Moral Question of Abortion* (Chicago: Loyola University Press, 1990); and Baruch Brody's *Abortion and the Sanctity of a Human Life: A Philosophical View* (Cambridge, MA: MIT Press, 1975). Anthologies on abortion include *The Abortion Controversy* (Belmont, CA: Wadsworth, 1998), second edition, edited by Louis P. Pojman and Francis J. Beckwith; and *The Ethics of Abortion* (Buffalo: Prometheus Books, 1993), revised edition, edited by Robert M. Baird and Stuart E. Rosenbaum. Both anthologies have an uncut version of Thomson's paper; for criticisms of her paper, see Beckwith (in the first anthology), Wilcox (in the second), and Gensler (in both).

Related readings in this anthology include Callahan (who argues that abortion is wrong) and Singer (who regards both fetuses and infants as having very little inherent right to life).

SIDNEY CALLAHAN
Pro-life Feminism

Sidney Callahan, an American psychologist born in 1933, works in psychology, ethics, and religion. While vigorously pro-life, she is married to the pro-choice ethicist Daniel Callahan; the two have collaborated on works that explore differing perspectives on abortion.

While many feminists defend abortion, Callahan criticizes their arguments and their underlying views on sexuality. She argues that a more authentic feminism would nurture life and oppose abortion.

As you read the selection, ask yourself whether Callahan successfully refutes the pro-choice arguments. Does she convince you that feminists should be pro-life?

Pro-choice feminism

The abortion debate continues. In the latest development, pro-life feminists are contesting pro-choice feminist claims that abortion rights are prerequisites for women's full development and social equality. Pro-life feminists, like myself, argue on good feminist principles that women can never achieve the fulfillment of feminist goals in a society permissive toward abortion.

The opposing arguments can best be seen when presented in turn. The feminist case for abortion can be analyzed in terms of four central moral claims: (1) the moral right to control one's body; (2) the moral necessity of autonomy and choice; (3) the moral claim for the contingent value of fetal life; (4) the moral right of women to social equality.

1. The moral right to control one's body. Pro-choice feminism argues that a woman choosing an abortion is exercising a basic right of bodily integrity granted in our common law tradition. If she does not choose to be physically involved in a pregnancy and birth, she should not be compelled to be so against her will. Just because it is *her* body which is involved, a woman should have the right to terminate any pregnancy. No one can be forced to donate an organ or submit to other invasive physical procedures for however good a cause. Thus no woman should be subjected to "compulsory pregnancy." Since hers is the body, hers the risk, hers the burden, she alone should be free to decide on pregnancy or abortion.

2. The moral necessity of autonomy and choice. A woman must be able to make yes or no decisions about a specific pregnancy, according to her present situation, resources, prior commitments, and life plan. Only with such reproductive freedom can a woman have the moral autonomy necessary to make mature commitments, in the area of family, work, or education. Contraception provides a measure of personal control, but contraceptive failure or other chance events can too easily result in involuntary pregnancy.

3. The moral claim for the contingent value of fetal life. The value of fetal life is contingent upon the woman's free consent and subjective acceptance. If a woman does not consent to invest her pregnancy with meaning or value, then the merely biological process can be freely terminated. Moreover, in cases of voluntary pregnancy, a woman can withdraw consent if fetal genetic defects or some other problem emerges at any time before birth. Late abortion should thus be granted without legal restrictions.

4. The moral right of women to social equality. Social equality depends upon being able to participate as freely as males can in educational and economic life. If a woman cannot control when and how she will be pregnant or rear children, she is at a distinct disadvantage. No less than males, women should be able to be sexually active without the fear of pregnancy.

How does a pro-life feminist respond to these arguments? Pro-life feminists grant the good intentions of their pro-choice counterparts but protest that the pro-choice position is flawed, morally inadequate, and inconsistent with feminism's demands for justice. Pro-life feminists champion a more encompassing moral ideal.

1. From the right to one's body to a wider justice

The moral right to control one's body does apply to organ transplants, mastectomies, contraception, and sterilization; but it is not a conceptualization adequate for abortion. The abortion dilemma is caused by the fact that 266 days following a conception in one body, another body will emerge. One's body is engendering another organism's life. This dynamic passage from conception to birth is genetically ordered and universally found in the human species. Pregnancy is not like the growth of cancer or infestation by a biological parasite; it is the way every human being enters the world. Strained philosophical analogies fail to apply: having a baby is not like rescuing a drowning person, being hooked up to a famous violinist's artificial life-support system, donating organs for transplant – or anything else.

As embryology and fetology advance, it becomes clear that human development is a continuum. Within such a continuous growth process, it is hard to defend logically any demarcation point after conception as the point at which an immature form of human life is so different from the day before or the day after, that it can be morally or legally discounted as a non-person. Even the moment of birth can hardly differentiate a nine-month fetus from a newborn. It is not surprising that those who countenance late abortions are logically led to endorse selective infanticide.

The same legal tradition which guarantees the right to control one's body firmly recognizes the wrongfulness of harming other bodies, however immature, dependent, different looking, or powerless. The handicapped, the retarded, and newborns are legally protected from deliberate harm. Pro-life feminists reject the suppositions that would except the unborn from this protection.

Debates similar to those about the fetus were once conducted about feminine personhood. Just as women, or blacks, were considered too different, too underdeveloped, too "biological," to have souls or to possess legal rights, so the fetus is now seen as "merely" biological life, subsidiary to a person. A woman was once viewed as incorporated into the "one flesh" of her husband's person; she too was a form of bodily property. In all patriarchal unjust systems, lesser orders of human life are granted rights only when wanted, chosen, or invested with value by the powerful.

Justice demands that the powerless and dependent be protected against the uses of power wielded unilaterally. No human can be treated as a means to an end without consent. The fetus is an immature, dependent form of human life which needs time and protection to develop. Surely, immaturity and dependence are not crimes.

In an effort to think about the requirements of a just society, philosophers like John Rawls recommend imagining yourself in an "original position," in which your position in the society to be created is hidden by a "veil of ignorance." You have to weigh the possibility that any inequalities inherent in that society's practices may rebound upon you in the worst, as well as in the best, conceivable way. This thought experiment helps ensure justice for all.

Beverly Harrison argues that in such an envisioning of society everyone would institute abortion rights in order to guarantee that if one turned out to be a woman one would have reproductive freedom. But surely in the original position and behind the "veil of ignorance," you would have to contemplate the possibility of being the particular fetus to be aborted. Since everyone has passed through the fetal stage, it is false to refuse to imagine oneself in this state when thinking about a potential world in which justice would govern. Would it be just that an embryonic life – in half the cases, a female life – be sacrificed to the right of a woman's control over her body? A woman may be pregnant without consent and experience a great many penalties, but a fetus killed without consent pays the ultimate penalty.

It does not matter whether the fetus being killed is fully conscious or feels pain. We do not sanction killing the innocent if it can be done painlessly or without the victim's awareness. Consciousness becomes important to the abortion debate because it is used as a criterion for the "personhood" so often seen as the prerequisite for legal protection. Yet certain philosophers set the standard of personhood so high that half the human race could not meet the criteria during most of their waking hours (let alone their sleeping ones). Sentience, self-consciousness, rational decision-making, social participation? Surely no infant, or child under two, could qualify. Either our idea of person must be expanded or another criterion, such as human life itself, be employed to protect the weak in a just society.

It also seems a travesty of just procedures that a pregnant woman acts as sole judge of her own case, under the most stressful conditions. It has never been thought right to have an interested party, especially the more powerful party, decide his or her own case when there may be a conflict of interest. If one considers the matter as a case of a powerful versus a powerless, silenced claimant, the pro-choice feminist argument can rightly be inverted: since hers is the body, hers the risk, and hers the greater burden, then how in fairness can a woman be the sole judge of the fetal right to life?

Human ambivalence, a bias toward self-interest, and emotional stress have always been recognized as endangering judgment. In the case of a woman's involuntary pregnancy, a complex, long-term solution requiring effort and energy has to compete with the immediate solution offered by a morning's visit to an abortion clinic. The speed, ease, and privacy of abortion, combined with the small size of the embryo, tend to make early abortions seem less morally serious – even though speed, size, technical ease, and the private nature of an act have no moral standing.

As the most recent immigrants from non-personhood, feminists have traditionally fought for justice. Women rally to feminism as a new and better way to live. Rejecting male aggression and destruction, feminists seek peaceful means to resolve conflicts while respecting human potentiality. It is a chilling inconsistency to see pro-choice feminists demanding continued access to assembly-line, technological methods of fetal killing. It is a betrayal of feminism, which has built the struggle for justice on the bedrock of women's empathy. After all, "maternal thinking" receives its name from a mother's unconditional acceptance and nurture of dependent, immature life.

2. From autonomy to an expanded responsibility

A distorted idea of morality overemphasizes individual autonomy and active choice. Thus if one does not choose to be pregnant or cannot rear a child, who must be given up for adoption, then better to abort the pregnancy.

But morality also consists of the acceptance of the unexpected events that life presents. Response-ability to things unchosen are also instances of the highest human moral capacity. Morality is not confined to contracted agreements of isolated individuals. Yes, one is obligated by explicit contracts freely initiated, but human beings are also obligated by implicit compacts and involuntary relationships in which persons simply find themselves. To be embedded in a family, a neighborhood, a social system, brings moral obligations which were never entered into with informed consent.

Parent-child relationships are one instance of implicit moral obligations arising by virtue of our being part of the interdependent human community. A woman, involuntarily pregnant, has a moral obligation to the now-existing dependent fetus whether she explicitly consented to its existence or not. No pro-life feminist would dispute the forceful observations of pro-choice feminists about the extreme difficulties that bearing an unwanted child in our society can entail. But the stronger force of the fetal claim presses a woman to accept these burdens. The woman's moral obligation arises both from her status as a human being embedded in the interdependent human community and her unique lifegiving female reproductive power. To follow the pro-choice feminist ideology of insistent individualistic autonomy and control is to betray a fundamental basis of the moral life.

3. From the contingent to the intrinsic value of life

The feminist pro-choice position which claims that the value of the fetus is contingent upon the pregnant woman's bestowal of humanbood is seriously flawed. Pro-life feminism takes a very different stance to life and nature.

Human life from the beginning to the end of development *has* intrinsic value, which does not depend on meeting the selective criteria set up by powerful others. A fundamental humanist assumption is at stake here. Either we are going to value embodied human life and humanity as a good thing, or take some variant of the nihilist position that assumes that each instance of human life must explicitly be justified to prove itself worthy to continue.

In a sound moral tradition, human rights arise from human needs, and it is the very nature of a right, or valid claim upon another, that it cannot be denied, conditionally delayed, or rescinded by more powerful others, at their behest. It seems fallacious to hold that in the case of the fetus it is the pregnant woman alone who gives or removes its right to life and human status solely through her subjective conscious investment or "humanization." Surely no pregnant woman has created her own human nature by an individually willed act of consciousness, nor for that matter been able to guarantee her own human rights. Membership in the species, or collective human family, is the basis for human solidarity, equality, and natural human rights.

4. The right of women to social equality

Pro-life feminists and pro-choice feminists are totally agreed on the moral right of women to the full social equality so far denied them. The disagreement between them concerns the definition of the desired goal and the best means to get there. Permissive abortion laws do not bring women reproductive freedom, social equality, sexual fulfillment, or full personal development.

Pitting women against their offspring is not only morally offensive, it is psychologically and politically destructive. Women will never climb to equality and social empowerment over mounds of dead fetuses, numbering now in the millions. Women stand to gain from the same attitudes and institutions that also protect the fetus in the woman's womb – and they stand to lose from the cultural assumptions that support permissive abortion.

Women's rights and liberation are pragmatically linked to fetal rights. Society in general, and men in particular, have to provide women more support in rearing the next generation, or our devastating feminization of poverty will continue. But if a woman claims the right to decide by herself whether the fetus becomes a child, what does this do to paternal and communal responsibility? Why should men share responsibility for child support or childrearing if they cannot share in what is asserted to be the woman's sole decision? Furthermore, if explicit intentions and consciously accepted contracts are necessary for moral obligations, why should men be held responsible for what *they* do not voluntarily choose to happen? By pro-choice reasoning, a man who does not want to have a child, or whose contraceptive fails, can be exempted from the responsibilities of fatherhood and child support. Traditionally, many men have been laggards in assuming parental responsibility and support for their children; ironically, ready abortion legitimizes male irresponsibility and paves the way for even more male detachment and lack of commitment.

For that matter, why should the state provide day-care or child support, or require workplaces to accommodate women's maternity and the needs of childrearing? Permissive abortion, granted in the name of women's privacy and reproductive freedom, ratifies the view that pregnancies and children are a woman's private individual responsibility. If she refuses to get rid of it, it's her problem. The larger community is relieved of moral responsibility.

A feminine model of sexuality

There are far better goals for feminists to pursue. First, women have to insist upon a different, woman-centered approach to sex and reproduction. In our male-dominated world, what men don't do, doesn't count. Pregnancy, childbirth, and nursing have been characterized as passive, debilitating, animal-like. This female disease or impairment naturally handicaps women in the "real" world of hunting, war, and the corporate fast track. Many pro-choice feminists adopt the male perspective when they cite the "basic injustice that women have to bear the babies," instead of seeing injustice in the fact that men cannot. Women's biologically unique capacity and privilege has been denied, despised, and suppressed under male domination.

Childbirth often appears in pro-choice literature as a painful, traumatic, life-threatening experience. Yet giving birth is accurately seen as an arduous but normal exercise of lifegiving power, a violent and ecstatic peak experience, which men can never know. The obstetrician Niles Newton herself a mother has written of the extended threefold sexuality of women, who can experience orgasm, birth, and nursing as passionate pleasure-giving experiences. Only orgasm, which males share, has been glorified as nature's great gift; the feminine processes of childbirth and nursing have been seen as bondage to biology.

Women can never have the self-confidence and self-esteem they need until a more holistic, feminine model of sexuality becomes the dominant cultural ethos. Men and women differ in the domain of sexual functioning. Males have been more physically aggressive and more likely to fuse sexuality with aggression and dominance. Females have a greater capacity than men for repeated orgasm and a more tenuous path to arousal and orgasmic release. Women also have a far greater sociobiological investment in the act of human reproduction. On the whole, women as compared to men possess a sexuality which is more complex, more intense, more extended in time, involving higher investment, risks, and psychosocial involvement.

Considering the differences in sexual functioning, it is not surprising that men and women have often constructed different sexual ideals. In Western culture, most women have espoused a version of sexual functioning in which sex acts are embedded within deep emotional bonds and secure long-term commitments. Within these committed "pair bonds" males assume parental obligations. In the idealized version of the Christian sexual ethic, culturally endorsed and maintained by women, the double standard was not countenanced. Men and women did not need to marry to be whole persons, but if they did engage in sexual functioning, they were to be equally chaste, faithful, responsible, loving, and parentally concerned. A culturally dominant demand for monogamy, self-control, and emotionally bonded and committed sex works well for women. When love, chastity, fidelity, and commitment for better or worse are the ascendant cultural prerequisites for sexual functioning, young girls and women expect protection from rape and seduction, adult women justifiably demand male support in childrearing, and older women are more protected from abandonment as their biological attractions wane.

These feminine sexual ideals always coexisted in competition with another view. A more male-oriented model of erotic sexuality endorses sexual permissiveness without long-term commitment or reproductive focus. Erotic sexuality emphasizes pleasure, play, passion, self-expression, and romantic games of courtship and conquest. A variety of partners and sexual experiences are necessary to stimulate romantic passion. This erotic model has often worked satisfactorily for men. But for the average woman, it is quite destructive. Women can only play the erotic game successfully when they are young, physically attractive, economically powerful, and fulfilled enough in a career to be willing to sacrifice family life. Abortion is also required. As our society increasingly endorses this male-oriented, permissive view of sexuality, it is all too ready to give women abortion on demand. Abortion helps a woman's body be more like a man's.

The modern feminist movement made a mistaken move. Rightly rebelling against unequal education, restricted work opportunities, and women's downtrodden political status, feminists also rejected the older feminine sexual ethic of love and fidelity. A permissive, erotic view of sexuality is assumed to be the only option. The male-oriented sexual orientation has been harmful to women and children. It has helped bring us epidemics of venereal disease, pornography, sexual abuse, adolescent pregnancy, divorce, displaced older women, and abortion. Will these signals of something amiss stimulate pro-choice feminists to rethink what kind of sex ideal really serves women's best interests? While the erotic model cannot encompass commitment, the committed model can – happily – encompass and encourage romance, passion, and playfulness. In fact, within the security of long-term commitments, women may be more likely to experience sexual pleasure and fulfillment.

New feminist efforts to rethink the meaning of sexuality, femininity, and reproduction are all the more vital as new techniques for artificial reproduction, surrogate motherhood, and the like present a whole new set of dilemmas. In the long run, the abortion debate may be merely the opening round in a series of far-reaching struggles over the role of human sexuality and the ethics of reproduction. What kind of people are we going to be? Pro-life feminists pursue a vision for their sisters, daughters, and granddaughters. Will their great-granddaughters be grateful?

Study questions

1 Explain the "right to one's body" argument and Callahan's criticism.
2 Explain the "autonomy" argument and Callahan's criticism.
3 Explain the "contingent value of fetal life" argument and Callahan's criticism.
4 Explain the "right of women to equality" argument and Callahan's criticism.
5 What is Callahan's "feminine model" of sexuality and how does it differ from the "male model"? How do these relate to abortion?

For further study

This selection has excerpts, sometimes simplified in wording, from Sidney Cornelia Callahan's "Abortion and the sexual agenda: A case for pro-life feminism" in *Commonweal* 113 (25 April 1986): 232–8. Further works by Callahan include *Abortion: Understanding Differences* (New York: Plenum Press, 1984), co-edited with her husband Daniel Callahan; *The Illusion of Eve: Modern Woman's Quest for Identity* (New York: Sheed and Ward, 1965); and *In Good Conscience: Reason and Emotion in Moral Decision Making* (San Francisco: Harper, 1991). Harry Gensler's *Ethics: A Contemporary Introduction* (London and New York: Routledge, 1998) examines abortion in Chapter 12.

For further study of the pro-abortion side, see Peter Singer's *Practical Ethics* (Cambridge: Cambridge University Press, 1993), second edition, Chapter 6; and Michael Tooley's *Abortion and Infanticide* (Oxford: Oxford University Press, 1983). On the anti-abortion side, see Stephen D. Schwarz's *The Moral Question of Abortion* (Chicago: Loyola University Press, 1990); and Baruch Brody's *Abortion and the Sanctity of a Human Life: A Philosophical View* (Cambridge, MA: MIT Press, 1975). Anthologies on abortion include *The Abortion Controversy* (Belmont, CA: Wadsworth, 1998), second edition, edited by Louis P. Pojman and Francis J. Beckwith; and *The Ethics of Abortion* (Buffalo: Prometheus Books, 1993), revised edition, edited by Robert M. Baird and Stuart E. Rosenbaum. Both anthologies have essays by Callahan.

Related readings in this anthology include Thomson (who argues that abortion is often morally permissible) and Singer (who regards both fetuses and infants as having very little inherent right to life).

PETER SINGER
Animal Liberation

Peter Singer, an Australian philosopher born in 1946, may be the most controversial philosopher alive today. Many praise him for having fathered the "animal liberation" movement (his book of that title sold 400,000 copies and led to improved treatment of animals) and for promoting famine relief (for which he donates a fifth of his income). Others attack him as an evil neo-Nazi who rejects the sanctity of human life and has a permissive attitude toward killing handicapped infants.

In this reading, Singer contends that racism and sexism are wrong because they give greater weight to the interests of those of one's own race or sex. Similarly, he claims, "speciesism" is wrong because it gives greater weight to the interests of those of one's own species. The only non-arbitrary approach is to consider equally the interests of *any* sentient being – and thus to give an animal's suffering the same weight as an equal suffering of a human.

As you read the selection, ask yourself how you would live differently if you followed Singer's ideas. Do you see any way to evade his arguments? What do you think of his rejection of the sanctity of human life?

The basis for equality

"Animal Liberation" may sound like a parody of liberation movements. "The Rights of Animals" was once used to parody women's rights. If the argument for equality was sound when applied to women, why should it not be applied to dogs, cats, and horses?

To explain the case for equality of animals, it will be helpful to start with equality of women. Let us assume that we wish to defend women's rights. How should we reply?

We might reply that the case for equality between men and women cannot validly be extended to nonhuman animals. Women have a right to vote, for instance, because they are just as capable of making rational decisions as men are; dogs, on the other hand, are incapable of voting, so they cannot have the right to vote. Men and women resemble each other closely, while humans and animals differ greatly. So, it might be said, men and women should have similar rights, while humans and nonhumans should not have equal rights.

This reply is correct up to a point, but it does not go far enough. There are important differences between humans and other animals, and these must give rise to differences in rights. Recognizing this fact, however, is no barrier to extending the basic principle of equality to nonhuman animals. Differences between men and women are equally undeniable. Many feminists hold that women have the right to an abortion on request. It does not follow that they must support the right of men to have abortions too. Since a man cannot have an abortion, it is meaningless to talk of his right to have one. Since dogs can't vote, it is meaningless to talk of their right to vote. The basic principle of equality does not require equal or identical *treatment;* it requires equal consideration. Equal consideration for different beings may lead to different treatment and different rights.

So there is a way of replying that does not deny obvious differences between human beings and nonhumans but concludes that the basic principle of equality applies to so-called brutes. Such a conclusion may appear odd; but we would be on shaky ground if we were to demand equality for blacks, women, and other oppressed humans while denying equal consideration to nonhumans. To make this clear we need to see why racism and sexism are wrong. When we say that all human beings, whatever their race, creed, or sex, are equal, what are we asserting? Those who defend inegalitarian societies point out that not all humans are equal. Humans come in different shapes and sizes; they come with different moral capacities and intellectual abilities. In short, if the demand for equality were based on the actual equality of all human beings, we would have to stop demanding equality.

Still, it may be said, there are no differences between the races and sexes as such. Although there are differences among individuals, some blacks are superior to some whites in all of the capacities that could conceivably be relevant. The opponent of sexism would say the same: a person's sex is no guide to his or her abilities, and this is why it is unjustifiable to discriminate on the basis of sex.

The existence of individual variations that cut across lines of race or sex, however, provides us with no defense against a more sophisticated opponent of equality, one who proposes that, say, the interests of all those with IQ scores below 100 be given less consideration. Perhaps those scoring below the mark would be made slaves. Would a hierarchical society of this sort really be so much better than one based on race or sex? I think not. But if we tie the moral principle of equality to factual equality, our opposition to racism and sexism does not provide us with any basis for objecting to this inegalitarianism.

There is a second reason why we ought not to base our opposition to racism and sexism on factual equality: we can have no guarantee that capacities are distributed evenly. There do seem to be measurable differences both among races and between sexes. These do not appear in every case, but only when averages are taken. We do not yet know how many of these differences are due to the different genetic endowments of the races and sexes, and how many are due to poor schools, poor housing, and other factors that are the result of discrimination. Perhaps all important differences will eventually prove to be environmental rather than genetic. Anyone opposed to racism and sexism will certainly hope that this will be so, for it will make the task of ending discrimination easier; nevertheless, it would be dangerous to rest the case on the belief that all significant differences are environmental in origin. The opponent of racism who takes this line will be unable to avoid conceding that if differences in ability did prove to have some genetic connection with race, racism would be defensible.

Equal consideration as a moral ideal

Fortunately there is no need to pin the case for equality to one particular outcome of a scientific investigation. The claim to equality does not depend on intelligence, moral capacity, or similar matters of fact. Equality is a moral idea, not an assertion of fact. *The principle of the equality of human beings is not a description of an alleged actual equality among humans: it is a prescription of how we should treat human beings.*

Jeremy Bentham, the utilitarian, incorporated moral equality into his ethics by the formula: "Each to count for one and none for more than one." In other words, the interests of every being affected by an action are to be taken into account and given the same weight as the like interests of any other being.[1] A later utilitarian, Henry Sidgwick, put the point in this way: "The good of any one individual is of no more importance, from the point of view of the Universe, than the good of any other." The leading figures in contemporary moral philosophy have specified some similar requirement to give everyone's interests equal consideration.[2]

Our concern for others ought not to depend on what they are like. What our concern requires us to do may vary: concern for the well-being of children in America would require that we teach them to read; concern for the well-being of pigs may require that we leave them with other pigs in a place where there is adequate food and room. The taking into account of interests must be extended to all beings, black or white, masculine or feminine, human or nonhuman.

It is on this basis that the case against racism and sexism must rest; and it is in accordance with this principle that the attitude that we may call "speciesism," by analogy with racism, must also be condemned. Speciesism is a prejudice or bias in favor of the interests of members of one's own species and against those of members of other species. The objections to racism and sexism apply equally to speciesism. If possessing a higher degree of intelligence does not entitle one human to use another for his or her own ends, how can it entitle humans to exploit nonhumans for the same purpose?

If a being suffers there can be no moral justification for refusing to take that suffering into consideration. No matter what the nature of the being, the principle of equality requires that its suffering be counted equally with the like suffering of any other being. If a being is not capable of suffering, or of experiencing enjoyment or happiness, there is nothing to be taken into account. So the capacity to suffer and/or experience enjoyment or happiness is the only defensible boundary of concern for the interests of others.

Racists violate the principle of equality by giving greater weight to the interests of members of their own race. Sexists violate the principle by favoring the interests of their own sex. Similarly, speciesists allow the interests of their own species to override the greater interests of members of other species. The pattern is identical.

Most human beings are speciesists. The majority of humans take part in practices that sacrifice the most important interests of members of other species to promote the most trivial interests of our own.

Do animals feel pain?

We know that we ourselves feel pain. We know this from the experience of pain that we have when, for instance, somebody presses a lighted cigarette against the back of our hand. But how do we know that anyone else feels pain? We cannot directly experience anyone else's pain, whether that "anyone" is our best friend or a stray dog. Pain is a state of consciousness, a "mental event." Behavior like writhing, screaming, or drawing one's hand away from the lighted cigarette is not pain itself; nor are the recordings a neurologist might make of activity within the brain observations of pain itself. Pain is something that we feel, and we can only infer that others are feeling it from various external indications.

Nearly all the external signs that lead us to infer pain in other humans can be seen in other species. The behavioral signs include writhing, facial contortions, moaning, attempts to avoid the source of pain, appearance of fear at the prospect of its repetition, and so on. In addition, we know that animals have nervous systems like ours, which respond physiologically as ours do when the animal is in circumstances in which we would feel pain.

The nervous systems of animals evolved as our own did. A capacity to feel pain enhances a species' survival, since it causes members of the species to avoid sources of injury. It is unreasonable to suppose that nervous systems that are virtually identical physiologically, have a common origin and evolutionary function, and result in similar behavior should actually operate in an entirely different manner on the level of subjective feelings. So there are no good reasons for denying that animals feel pain. If we do not doubt that other humans feel pain we should not doubt that other animals do so too.

Practical consequences

As we saw earlier, there can be no moral justification for regarding the pain (or pleasure) that animals feel as less important than the same amount of pain (or pleasure) felt by humans. But what practical consequences follow from this conclusion?

If I give a horse a hard slap, the horse may start, but it presumably feels little pain. Its skin is thick enough to protect it. If I slap a baby in the same way, the baby will cry and presumably feel pain, for its skin is more sensitive. So it is worse to slap a baby than a horse, if both slaps are administered with equal force. But there must be some kind of blow – perhaps a blow with a heavy stick – that would cause the horse as much pain as we cause a baby by slapping it with our hand. That is what I mean by "the same amount of pain," and if we consider it wrong to inflict that much pain on a baby for no good reason then we must, unless we are speciesists, consider it equally wrong to inflict the same amount of pain on a horse for no good reason.

Other differences between humans and animals cause complications. Normal adult human beings have mental capacities that will, in certain circumstances, lead them to suffer more than animals would. If, for instance, we decided to perform extremely painful or lethal experiments on normal adult humans, kidnapped at random, adults would become fearful that they would be kidnapped. The resultant terror would be additional to the pain of the experiment. The same experiments performed on nonhuman animals would cause less suffering since the animals would not have the anticipatory dread of being kidnapped. This does not mean that it would be *right* to experiment on animals, but only that there is a reason, which is *not* speciesist, for preferring to use animals rather than normal adult human beings, if the experiment is to be done. This same argument gives us a reason for preferring to use human infants – orphans perhaps – or severely retarded human beings for experiments, rather than adults, since infants and retarded humans would also have no idea of what was going to happen to them. So if we use this argument to justify experiments on nonhuman animals we have to ask ourselves whether we are also prepared to allow experiments on human infants and retarded adults; and if we make a distinction between animals and these humans, on what basis can we do it, other than a morally indefensible preference for members of our own species?

Comparisons of suffering between members of different species cannot be made precisely, but precision is not essential. Even if we were to prevent the infliction of suffering on animals only when the interests of humans will not be affected to anything like the extent that animals are affected, we would be forced to make radical changes in our treatment of animals that would involve diet, farming methods, experimental procedures, hunting, the wearing of furs, and areas of entertainment like circuses, rodeos, and zoos. As a result, a vast amount of suffering would be avoided.

Killing

Most human beings are speciesists in their readiness to kill other animals when they would not kill human beings. We need to proceed more cautiously here, however, because people hold differing views about when it is legitimate to kill humans, as the debates over abortion and euthanasia attest. Nor have moral philosophers been able to agree on exactly what it is that makes it wrong to kill human beings.

Let us consider the view that it is always wrong to take an innocent human life. We may call this the "sanctity of life" view. People who take this view oppose abortion and euthanasia. They do not usually oppose the killing of nonhuman animals – so it would be more accurate to describe this as the "sanctity of *human* life" view. The belief that human life, and only human life, is sacrosanct is a form of speciesism. To see this, consider the following example.

Assume that an infant has been born with massive brain damage. The infant can never be more than a "human vegetable," unable to talk, recognize other people, act independently, or develop self-awareness. The parents ask the doctor to kill the infant painlessly. Should the doctor do what the parents ask? Legally, the doctor should not, and in this respect the law reflects the sanctity of life view. The life of every human being is sacred. Yet people who say this do not object to the killing of nonhuman animals. How can they justify their different judgments? Adult chimpanzees, dogs, pigs, and members of many other species far surpass the brain-damaged infant in their ability to relate to others, act independently, be self-aware, and any other capacity that could reasonably be said to give value to life. With the most intensive care possible, some severely retarded infants can never achieve the intelligence level of a dog. Nor can we appeal to the concern of the infant's parents, since they in this example do not want the infant kept alive. The only thing that distinguishes the infant from the animal is that it is a member of the species Homo sapiens. But to use *this* as the basis for granting a right to life to the infant and not to the other animals is pure speciesism.[3] It is the kind of arbitrary difference that the crude racist uses to justify racial discrimination.

To avoid speciesism we must allow that beings similar in all relevant respects have a similar right to life – and mere membership in our own biological species cannot be morally relevant. We could still hold that it is worse to kill a normal adult human, with a capacity for self-awareness and ability to plan for the future, than it is to kill a mouse; or we might appeal to the close personal ties that humans have but mice do not have to the same degree; or we might think that it is the consequences for other humans, who will be put in fear for their lives, that makes the crucial difference.

Whatever criteria we choose we will have to admit that they do not follow precisely the boundary of our own species. There will be some nonhuman animals whose lives, by any standards, are more valuable than the lives of some humans. A chimpanzee, dog, or pig, for instance, will have a higher self-awareness and capacity for meaningful relations with others than a severely retarded infant or someone in a state of advanced senility. So if we base the right to life on these characteristics we must grant these animals a right to life as good as, or better than, such retarded or senile humans.

A rejection of speciesism does not imply that all lives are of equal worth. It is not arbitrary to hold that the life of a self-aware being, capable of abstract thought, of planning for the future, of complex communication, and so on, is more valuable than the life of a being without these capacities. To see the difference between inflicting pain and taking life, consider how we choose within our own species. If we had to choose to save the life of a normal human being or an intellectually disabled human being, we would probably save the life of a normal human being; but if we had to choose between preventing pain in the normal human being or the intellectually disabled one – imagine that both have injuries and we only have enough painkiller for one – it is not so clear how we ought to choose. The same is true when we consider other species. The evil of pain is, in itself, unaffected by the other characteristics of the being who feels the pain; the value of life is affected by these other characteristics. To give just one reason for this difference, to take the life of a being who has been hoping, planning, and working for some future goal is to deprive that being of the fulfillment of those efforts; to take the life of a being with a mental capacity below the level needed to grasp that one is a being with a future cannot involve this kind of loss.

Normally if we have to choose between the life of a human being and the life of another animal we should choose to save the life of the human; but there may be special cases in which the reverse holds true, because the human in question does not have the capacities of a normal human. We should give the same respect to the lives of animals as we give to the lives of humans at a similar mental level.

Animal experimentation and eating meat

The next two chapters explore two examples of speciesism in practice. I have limited myself to two examples, although this means that the book contains no discussion of other practices that exist only because we do not take seriously the interests of other animals – practices like hunting; farming animals for their fur; capturing wild animals and imprisoning them in cages; tormenting animals to make them learn tricks for circuses; slaughtering whales with explosive harpoons, under the guise of scientific research; drowning over 100,000 dolphins annually in nets set by tuna fishing boats; shooting three million kangaroos every year in the Australian outback to turn them into skins and pet food; and generally ignoring the interests of wild animals as we extend our empire of concrete and pollution over the surface of the globe.

I shall have virtually nothing to say about these things, because this book is not a compendium of all the nasty things we do to animals. Instead I have chosen two central illustrations of speciesism. One of them – experimentation on animals – is promoted by the government we elect and is largely paid for out of the taxes we pay. The other – rearing animals for food – is possible only because most people buy and eat the products of this practice. These forms of speciesism cause more suffering to a greater number of animals than anything else that human beings do. To stop them we must change the policies of our government, and we must change our diet. If these forms of speciesism can be abolished, abolition of the other speciesist practices cannot be far behind.

Study questions

1 According to Singer, why are racism and sexism wrong? In your answer, highlight the distinction between factual equality and equal consideration of interests.
2 Does Singer's "principle of equality" require that we treat all beings the same? Give an example to illustrate your answer.
3 How does Singer's "principle of equality" apply to our treatment of animals? What is "speciesism" and why is it wrong?
4 How do we infer that animals feel pain?
5 For Singer, would doing painful experiments on animals be equally bad as doing the same experiments on humans?
6 What is the "sanctity of life" view and why does Singer reject it?
7 Singer criticizes the "sanctity of (human) life" view, in part, by pointing out that people who hold this view often think it permissible to kill animals. Explain Singer's criticism. Do you think this type of criticism is justified?

8   What are Singer's two most important practical suggestions about how we ought to treat animals?

For further study

This selection has excerpts, sometimes simplified in wording, from Peter Singer's *Animal Liberation* (New York: Avon Books, 1990), new revised edition, pages 1–23; the first edition came out in 1975. For further study, see his *Practical Ethics* (Cambridge: Cambridge University Press, 1993); his *Ethics into Action: Henry Spira and the Animal Rights Movement* (Lanham, MD: Rowman & Littlefield, 1999); and *Singer and His Critics* (Oxford: Blackwell publishers, 1999), edited by Dale Jamieson.

Related readings in this anthology include Mill and Smart (who share Singer's utilitarianism); Nagel and Slote (who criticize the equality of consideration principle); Callahan, Finnis, and O'Neill (who support the sanctity of human life); Benedict, Gensler and Tokmenko, Hare, and King (who also discuss racism); and Callicott (who wants to extend our moral concern beyond humans and animals to the wider ecosystem).

Notes

1   Singer, a utilitarian, holds that we ought to do whatever is most likely to maximize the sum total of the interests of every sentient being. What does Singer mean by "interests"? When discussing animals (as in this selection from *Animal Liberation*), he tends to interpret "interests" in terms of pleasure and the absence of pain. When discussing our treatment of humans (as in *Practical Ethics*, second edition, pages 13–14 and 94–5), he defines "interests" sometimes in terms of satisfying actual desires and sometimes in terms of satisfying what we would prefer "after reflection on all the relevant facts." This latter notion is difficult to apply to animals; does it make sense to ask what a goldfish would prefer if it reflected on all the relevant facts?

2   In a footnote, Singer refers to Hare and Rawls; both are in this anthology.

3   I am here putting aside religious views, for example the doctrine that all and only human beings have immortal souls, or are made in the image of God. Historically these have been very important, and no doubt are partly responsible for the idea that human life has a special sanctity. In any case, defenders of the "sanctity of life" view are generally reluctant to base their position on religious doctrines, since these are no longer as widely accepted as they once were. [Note from Singer]

ONORA O'NEILL

A Kantian Approach to Famine Relief

Onora O'Neill, an Irish philosopher born in 1941, teaches in England at the University of Essex. She has made important contributions to the study of Kant, ethics, and social-political philosophy. She is author of *Acting on Principle: An Essay on Kantian Ethics* and *Faces of Hunger: An Essay on Poverty, Justice, and Development*.

O'Neill applies Kantian ethical theory to the problem of famine relief. She examines the demands that Kantian theory makes on us toward starving people in other countries and compares those demands with the demands of utilitarianism. She also compares how the two theories regard the value of human life.

As you read the selection, think about the distinction between treating persons as means and treating them as *mere* means. How does the Kantian prohibition against treating persons as mere means apply to famine relief? What obligations do we have to help those starving in other countries and how do they differ from those prescribed by utilitarianism?

The formula of the end in itself

Kant states the Formula of the End in Itself as follows:

> Act in such a way that you always treat humanity, whether in your own person or in the person of any other, never simply as a means but always at the same time as an end.

To understand this we need to know what it is to treat a person as a means or as an end. According to Kant, each of our acts reflects one or more *maxims*. The maxim of the act is the principle on which one sees oneself as acting. A maxim expresses a person's policy, or if he or she has no settled policy, the principle underlying the particular intention or decision on which he or she acts. Thus, a person who decides "This year I'll give 10 percent of my income to famine relief" has as a maxim the principle of tithing his or her income for famine relief.

Whenever we act intentionally, we have at least one maxim and can, if we reflect, state what it is. When we want to work out whether an act we propose to do is right or wrong, according to Kant, we should look at our maxims. We just have to check that the act we have in mind will not use anyone as a mere means, and, if possible, that it will treat other persons as ends in themselves.

Using persons as mere means

To use someone as a *mere means* is to involve them in a scheme of action *to which they could not in principle consent*. Kant does not say that there is anything wrong about using someone as a means. Evidently we have to do so in any cooperative scheme of action. If I cash a check I use the teller as a means, without whom I could not lay my hands on the cash; the teller in turn uses me as a means to earn his or her living. But in this case, each party consents to her or his part in the transaction. Kant would say that though they use one another as means, they do not use one another as *mere* means. Each person assumes that the other has maxims of his or her own and is not just a thing or a prop to be manipulated.

But there are other situations where one person uses another in a way to which the other could not in principle consent. For example, one person may make a promise to another with every intention of breaking it. If the promise is accepted, then the person to whom it was given must be ignorant of what the promisor's intention (maxim) really is. Successful false promising depends on deceiving the person to whom the promise is made about what one's real maxim is. And since the person who is deceived doesn't know that real maxim, he or she can't in principle consent to his or her part in the proposed scheme of action. The person who is deceived is, as it were, a prop or a tool – a mere means – in the false promisor's scheme. In Kant's view, it is this that makes false promising wrong.

In Kant's view, acts that are done on maxims that require deception or coercion of others, and so cannot have the consent of those others, are wrong. When we act on such maxims, we treat others as mere means, as things rather than as ends in themselves. If we act on such maxims, our acts are not only wrong but unjust: such acts wrong the particular others who are deceived or coerced.

Treating persons as ends in themselves

To treat someone as an end in him or herself requires in the first place that one not use him or her as mere means, that one respect each as a rational person with his or her own maxims. But beyond that, one may also seek to foster others' plans and maxims by sharing some of their ends. To act beneficently is to seek others' happiness, therefore to intend to achieve some of the things that those others aim at with their maxims. Beneficent acts try to achieve what others want. However, we cannot seek everything that others want; their wants are too numerous and diverse, and, of course, sometimes incompatible. It follows that beneficence has to be selective.

There is a sharp distinction between the requirements of justice and of beneficence in Kantian ethics. Justice requires that we act on *no* maxims that use others as mere means. Beneficence requires that we act on *some* maxims that foster others' ends, though it is a matter for judgment and discretion which of their ends we foster. Kantians will claim that they have done nothing wrong if none of their acts is unjust, and that their duty is complete if in addition their life plans have been reasonably beneficent.

Kantian deliberations on famine problems

The theory I have just sketched may seem to have little to say about famine problems. For it is a theory that forbids us to use others as mere means but does not require us to direct our benevolence first to those who suffer most. A conscientious Kantian, it seems, has only to avoid being unjust to those who suffer famine and can then be beneficent to those nearer home. He or she would not be obliged to help the starving, even if no others were equally distressed.

Kant's moral theory does make less massive demands on moral agents than utilitarian moral theory. On the other hand, it is somewhat clearer just what the more stringent demands are, and they are not negligible. We have here a contrast between a theory that makes massive but often indeterminate demands and a theory that makes fewer but less unambiguous demands and leaves other questions, in particular the allocation of beneficence, unresolved.

Kantian duties of justice in times of famine

In famine situations, Kantian moral theory requires unambiguously that we do no injustice. We should not act on any maxim that uses another as mere means, so we should neither deceive nor coerce others. Such a requirement can become quite exacting when the means of life are scarce, when persons can more easily be coerced, and when the advantage of gaining more than what is justly due to one is great.

First, where there is a rationing scheme, one ought not to cheat and seek to get more than one's share – any scheme of cheating will use someone as mere means. Nor may one take advantage of others' desperation to profiteer or divert goods onto the black market or to accumulate a fortune out of others' misfortunes. Transactions that are outwardly sales and purchases can be coercive when one party is desperate. All the forms of corruption that deceive or put pressure on others are also wrong: hoarding unallocated food, diverting relief supplies for private use, corruptly using one's influence to others' disadvantage. Such requirements are far from trivial and frequently violated in hard times. In severe famines, refraining from coercing and deceiving may risk one's own life and require the greatest courage.

Second, justice requires that in famine situations one still try to fulfill one's duties to particular others. For example, even in times of famine, a person has duties to try to provide for dependents. These duties may, tragically, be unfulfillable. If they are, Kantian ethical theory would not judge wrong the acts of a person who had done her or his best. A conscientious attempt to meet the particular obligations one has undertaken may also require of one many further maxims of self-restraint and of endeavor – for example, it may require a conscientious attempt to avoid having (further) children; it may require contributing one's time and effort to programs of economic development. Where there is no other means to fulfill particular obligations, Kantian principles may require a generation of sacrifice.

The obligations of those who live with or near famine are undoubtedly stringent and exacting; for those who live further off it is harder to see what a Kantian moral theory demands. Might it not, for example, be permissible to do nothing at all about those suffering famine? Might one not ensure that one does nothing unjust to the victims of famine by adopting no maxims whatsoever that mention them? To do so would, at the least, require one to refrain from certain deceptive and coercive practices frequently employed during the European exploration and economic penetration of the now underdeveloped world and still not unknown. For example, it would be unjust to "purchase" valuable lands and resources from persons who don't understand commercial transactions or exclusive property rights or mineral rights, and so do not understand that their acceptance of trinkets destroys their traditional economic pattern and way of life. The old adage "trade follows the flag" reminds us to how great an extent the economic penetration of the less-developed countries involved elements of coercion and deception, so was on Kantian principles unjust (regardless of whether or not the net effect has benefited the citizens of those countries).

Few persons in the developed world today find themselves faced with the possibility of adopting on a grand scale maxims of deceiving or coercing persons living in poverty. But at least some people find that their jobs require them to make decisions about investment and aid policies that enormously affect the lives of those nearest to famine. What does a commitment to Kantian moral theory demand of such persons?

It has become common in writings in ethics and social policy to distinguish between one's *personal responsibilities* and one's *role responsibilities*. So a person may say, "As an individual I sympathize, but in my official capacity I can do nothing"; or we may excuse persons' acts of coercion because they are acting in some particular capacity – e.g., as a soldier or a jailer. On the other hand, this distinction isn't made or accepted by everyone. At the Nuremberg trials of war criminals, the defense "I was only doing my job" was disallowed, at least for those whose command position meant that they had some discretion in what they did. Kantians generally would play down any distinction between a person's own responsibilities and his or her role responsibilities. They would not deny that in any capacity one is accountable for certain things for which as a private person one is not accountable. For example, the treasurer of an organization is accountable to the board and has to present periodic reports and to keep specified records. But if she fails to do one of these things for which she is held accountable she will be held responsible for that failure – it will be imputable to her as an individual. When we take on positions, we *add* to our responsibilities those that the job requires; but we do not lose those that are already required of us. Our social role or job gives us, on Kant's view, no license to use others as mere means.

If persons are responsible for all their acts, it follows that it would be unjust for aid officials to coerce persons into accepting sterilization, wrong for them to use coercive power to achieve political advantages (such as military bases) or commercial advantages (such as trade agreements that will harm the other country). Where a less-developed country is pushed to exempt a multinational corporation from tax laws, or to construct out of its meager tax revenues the infrastructure of roads, harbors, or airports (not to mention executive mansions) that the corporation – but perhaps not the country – needs, then one suspects that some coercion has been involved.

The problem with such judgments – and it is an immense problem – is that it is hard to identify coercion and deception in complicated institutional settings. It is not hard to understand what is coercive about one person threatening another with serious injury if he won't comply with the first person's suggestion. But it is not at all easy to tell where the outward forms of political and commercial negotiation – which often involve an element of threat – have become coercive.

Kantian duties of beneficence in times of famine

The grounds of duties of beneficence are that such acts develop or promote others' ends and, in particular, foster others' capacities to pursue ends, to be autonomous beings.

Clearly there are many opportunities for beneficence. But one area in which the *primary* task of developing others' capacity to pursue their own ends is particularly needed is in the parts of the world where extreme poverty and hunger leave people unable to pursue *any* of their other ends. Beneficence directed at putting people in a position to pursue whatever ends they may have has, for Kant, a stronger claim on us than beneficence directed at sharing ends with those who are already in a position to pursue varieties of ends. It would be nice if I bought a tennis racquet to play with my friend who is tennis mad and never has enough partners; but it is more important to make people able to plan their own lives to a minimal extent. It is nice to walk a second mile with someone who requests one's company; better to share a cloak with someone who may otherwise be too cold to make any journey. Though these suggestions are not a detailed set of instructions for the allocation of beneficence by Kantians, they show that relief of famine must stand very high among duties of beneficence.

The limits of Kantian ethics: intentions and results

Kantian ethics differs from utilitarian ethics both in its scope and in the precision with which it guides action. Every action, whether of a person or of an agency, can be assessed by utilitarian methods, provided only that information is available about all the consequences of the act. The theory has unlimited scope, but, owing to lack of data, often lacks precision. Kantian ethics has a more restricted scope. Since it assesses actions by looking at the maxims of agents, it can only assess intentional acts. This means that it is most at home in assessing individuals' acts; but it can be extended to assess acts of agencies that (like corporations and governments and student unions) have decision-making procedures.

It may seem a great limitation of Kantian ethics that it concentrates on intentions to the neglect of results. It might seem that all conscientious Kantians have to do is to make sure that they never intend to use others as mere means, and that they sometimes intend to foster others' ends. And, as we all know, good intentions sometimes lead to bad results, and correspondingly, bad intentions sometimes do no harm, or even produce good. If Hardin is right, the good intentions of those who feed the starving lead to dreadful results in the long run. If some traditional arguments in favor of capitalism are right, the greed and selfishness of the profit motive have produced unparalleled prosperity for many.

But such discrepancies between intentions and results are the exception and not the rule. For we cannot just *claim* that our intentions are good and do what we will. Our intentions reflect what we expect the immediate results of our action to be. Nobody credits the "intentions" of a couple who practice neither celibacy nor contraception but still insist "we never meant to have (more) children." Conception is likely (and known to be likely) in such cases. Where people's expressed intentions ignore the normal and predictable results of what they do, we infer that (if they are not amazingly ignorant) their words do not express their true intentions. The Formula of the End in Itself applies to the intentions on which one acts – not to some prettified version that one may avow. Provided this intention – the agent's real intention – uses no other as mere means, he or she does nothing unjust. If some of his or her intentions foster others' ends, then he or she is sometimes beneficent. It is therefore possible for people to test their proposals by Kantian arguments even when they lack the comprehensive causal knowledge that utilitarianism requires. Conscientious Kantians can work out whether they will be doing wrong by some act even though they know that their foresight is limited and that they may cause some harm or fail to cause some benefit.

Utilitarianism and respect for life

Utilitarians value happiness and the absence or reduction of misery. As a utilitarian one ought (if conscientious) to devote one's life to achieving the best possible balance of happiness over misery. If one's life plan remains in doubt, this will be because the means to this end are often unclear. But whenever the causal tendency of acts is clear, utilitarians will be able to discern the acts they should successively do in order to improve the world's balance of happiness over unhappiness.

This task is not one for the faint-hearted. First, it is dauntingly long, indeed interminable. Second, it may at times require the sacrifice of happiness, and even of lives, for the sake of a greater happiness. As our control over the means of ending and preserving human life has increased, analogous dilemmas have arisen in many areas for utilitarians. Should life be preserved at the cost of pain when modern medicine makes this possible? Should life be preserved without hope of consciousness? Should triage policies, because they may maximize the number of survivors, be used to determine who should be left to starve? All these questions can be fitted into utilitarian frameworks and answered *if* we have the relevant information. And sometimes the answer will be that human happiness demands the sacrifice of unwilling lives. Further, for most utilitarians, it makes no difference if the unwilling sacrifices involve acts of injustice to those whose lives are to be lost. Utilitarians do not deny these possibilities, though the imprecision of our knowledge of consequences often blurs the implications of the theory. If we peer through the blur, we see that the utilitarian view is that lives may indeed be sacrificed for the sake of a greater good even when the persons are not willing. There is nothing wrong with using another as a mere means provided that the end for which the person is so used is a happier result than could have been achieved any other way, taking into account the misery the means have caused. In utilitarian thought, persons are not ends in themselves. Their special moral status derives from their being means to the production of happiness. Human life has therefore a high though derivative value, and one life may be taken for the sake of greater happiness in other lives, or for ending of misery in that life. Nor is there any deep difference between ending a life for the sake of others' happiness by not helping (e.g., by triaging) and doing so by harming.

Utilitarian moral theory has then a rather paradoxical view of the value of human life. Living, conscious humans are (along with other sentient beings) necessary for the existence of everything utilitarians value. But it is not their being alive but the state of their consciousness that is of value. Hence, the best results may require certain lives to be lost – by whatever means – for the sake of the total happiness and absence of misery that can be produced.

Kant and respect for persons

Kantians reach different conclusions about human life. Human life is valuable because humans (and conceivably other beings, e.g., angels or apes) are the bearers of rational life. Humans are able to choose and to plan. This capacity and its exercise are of such value that they ought not to be sacrificed for anything of lesser value. Therefore, no one rational or autonomous creature should be treated as mere means for the enjoyment or even the happiness of another. We may in Kant's view justifiably – even nobly – risk or sacrifice our lives for others. For in doing so we follow our own maxim and nobody uses us as mere means. But no others may use either our lives or our bodies for a scheme that they have either coerced or deceived us into joining. For in doing so they would fail to treat us as rational beings; they would use us as mere means and not as ends in ourselves.

Study questions

1 What is the formula of the end in itself?
2 What is the difference between treating a person as a means and treating a person as a *mere* means? Construct a simple example that illustrates the difference.
3 Explain the difference between the requirements of justice and beneficence in Kantian ethics.
4 Discuss some of the specific requirements that Kantian duties of justice place on us in times of famine. Explain why these requirements are

clearer in the cases of those who live with or near famine than in the cases of those who live far from famine.

5   Why does a Kantian give famine relief "high standing" among our duties of beneficence?
6   What is the difference between Kantian theory and utilitarian theory regarding the evaluation of intentions and results?
7   Contrast utilitarianism and Kantian views about the value of human life. Construct an example that illustrates the difference.

For further study

This selection has excerpts, sometimes simplified in wording, from Onora O'Neill's "The Moral Perplexities of Famine Relief" in *Matters of Life and Death*, edited by Tom Regan (Philadelphia: Temple University Press, 1980), pages 260–98. For more on her approach, see her "Lifeboat Earth," in *Philosophy and Public Affairs* 4 (1975): 273–92; her *Faces of Hunger: An Essay on Poverty, Justice, and Development* (London: G. Allen and Unwin, 1986); and her *Acting on Principle: An Essay on Kantian Ethics* (New York: Columbia University Press, 1975). For the view that O'Neill rejects, see Peter Singer's "Famine, Affluence, and Morality" (*Philosophy and Public Affairs* 1 (1972): 229–43).

Related readings in this anthology include Kant (whose theory O'Neill supports); Brandt, Mill, Singer, and Smart (who defend utilitarianism, which O'Neill rejects); and Rawls, Ross, Slote, and Williams (who attack utilitarianism).

J. BAIRD CALLICOTT
The Land Ethic

J. Baird Callicott, an American philosopher born in 1941, is important in environmental ethics. He is the author of *In Defense of the Land Ethic*.

Callicott analyzes and defends Aldo Leopold's influential "land ethic." The scientific foundations for this view are found in Darwin's theory of evolution, while its philosophical foundations are found in David Hume's sentiments-based moral theory. Callicott argues for extending our moral sentiments to include concern for the environment.

As you read the selection, ask yourself whether Callicott has made a convincing case that the environment has moral value in itself. Are we part of an ecological community with moral value? Or, do only humans (and perhaps other individual sentient beings) have moral value?

Introduction to Leopold's article

"The Land Ethic" has not been favorably received by contemporary academic philosophers.[1] The professional neglect, confusion, and (in some cases) contempt may be attributed to three things: (1) Leopold's condensed prose style in which an entire conceptual complex may be conveyed in a few sentences; (2) his departure from the assumptions and paradigms of contemporary philosophical ethics; and (3) the unsettling practical implications to which a land ethic appears to lead. "The Land Ethic," in short, is abbreviated, unfamiliar, and radical.

"The Land Ethic" opens with a charming evocation of Homer's Greece, to suggest that today land is just as enslaved as human beings then were. A glance backward to our distant cultural origins, Leopold suggests, reveals a slow but steady moral development. If moral growth and development continue, future generations will censure today's environmental bondage as today we censure the human bondage of three thousand years ago.

Leopold points out that "this extension of ethics, so far studied only by philosophers, is actually a process in ecological evolution." We may understand the history of ethics in biological as well as philosophical terms. From a biological view, an ethic is "a limitation on freedom of action in the struggle for existence."

The origin and growth of ethics

How did ethics originate and grow in scope and complexity?

The oldest answer in living human memory is theological. God (or the gods) imposes morality on people. Western philosophy, on the other hand, is almost unanimous that the origin of ethics has to do with human reason. We are moral because we are rational.

An evolutionary natural historian cannot be satisfied with either of these general accounts. Any supernatural explanation of a natural phenomenon is ruled out in principle in natural science. And while morality might *in principle* be a function of human reason, to suppose that it is so *in fact* would put the cart before the horse. Reason appears to be a recently emerged faculty. It cannot have evolved in the absence of complex linguistic capabilities which depend, in turn, upon a highly developed social matrix. But we cannot have become social beings unless we assumed limitations on freedom of action. Hence we must have become ethical before we became rational.

Darwin turned to a moral psychology consistent with a general evolutionary account of ethical phenomena. A century earlier, David Hume and Adam Smith had argued that ethics rest upon feelings – which, to be sure, may be amplified and informed by reason. Since in the animal kingdom feelings are far more common than reason, they would be a far more likely starting point for an evolutionary account of the origin and growth of ethics.

Darwin's account, to which Leopold alludes, begins with the parental and filial affections common, perhaps, to all mammals. Bonds of affection between parents and offspring permitted the formation of small, close kin groups. Should the affections bonding family members chance to extend to less closely related individuals, that would permit an enlargement of the family group. And should the newly extended community more successfully defend itself, the inclusive fitness of its members would be increased. Thus, the "social sentiments" would be spread throughout a population.

Morality, as opposed to mere altruistic instinct, requires, in Darwin's terms, "intellectual powers" to recall the past and imagine the future, "the power of language" to express "common opinion," and "habituation" to patterns of behavior deemed to be socially beneficial. Even so, ethics remains firmly rooted in moral feelings or social sentiments which were naturally selected by the advantages for survival.

The protosociobiological perspective, to which Leopold as a natural historian was heir, leads him to a generalization. Since it "has its origin in the tendency of individuals or groups to evolve modes of co-operation, ethics rests upon a premise: that the individual is a member of a community of interdependent parts."

Ethics and community are correlative. This simple principle constitutes a powerful tool for the analysis of moral natural history, for the anticipation of future moral development (including the land ethic), and for systematically deriving the specific precepts of a land or environmental ethic.

Extending ethics to the environment

Anthropological studies reveal that the boundaries of the moral community are generally coextensive with the perceived boundaries of society. Darwin paints a vivid picture: "A savage will risk his life to save a member of the same community, but will be wholly indifferent about a stranger." Tribespeople are at once paragons of virtue "within the limits of the same tribe" and enthusiastic thieves, manslaughterers, and torturers without.

Human societies have grown in extent and changed in structure. Today we are witnessing the painful birth of a human supercommunity, global in scope. Interestingly, a corresponding global human ethic – the "human rights" ethic – has been articulated. Most educated people today pay lip service at least to the ethical precept that all members of the human species, regardless of race, creed, or national origin, are endowed with certain fundamental rights which it is wrong not to respect. As Darwin wrote:

> As man advances in civilization, and small tribes are united into larger communities, the simplest reason would tell each individual that he ought to extend his social instincts and sympathies to all the members of the same nation. This point being reached, there is only an artificial barrier to prevent his sympathies extending to men of all nations and races.

According to Leopold, the next step is the land ethic. The "community concept" has propelled ethics from the savage clan to the family of man. "The land ethic simply enlarges the boundary of the community to include soils, waters, plants, and animals, or collectively: the land." The overarching thematic principle is "that land is a community." Once land is popularly perceived as a biotic community – as it is perceived in ecology – a correlative land ethic will emerge in the collective cultural consciousness.

Human society, Leopold argues, is founded upon mutual security and interdependency and preserved only by ethical constraints. Since the biotic community exhibits an analogous structure, it too can be preserved only by analogous limitations on freedom of action – that is, by a land ethic. A land ethic, furthermore, would be automatically triggered in human beings by ecology's social representation of nature. Therefore, the key to the emergence of a land ethic is universal ecological literacy.

Scientific foundations of the land ethic

The land ethic rests upon three scientific cornerstones: (1) evolutionary and (2) ecological biology set in a background of (3) Copernican astronomy. Evolutionary theory provides the conceptual link between ethics and social organization and development. It provides a sense of "kinship with fellow-creatures" as well, "fellow-voyagers" with us in the "odyssey of evolution."

Ecological theory provides the community concept – a sense of social integration of human and nonhuman nature. Human beings, plants, animals, soils, and waters are "all interlocked in one humming community of cooperations and competitions, one biota." The simplest reason should tell each individual to extend his or her social instincts and sympathies to all the members of the biotic community.

Although Leopold never mentions it, the Copernican perception of the Earth as "a small planet" in an immense and hostile universe contributes to our sense of kinship, community, and interdependence. It scales the Earth down to a cozy island paradise in a desert ocean.

The most salient feature of Leopold's land ethic is what Kenneth Goodpaster has called "moral consider-ability" for the biotic community:

> A land ethic changes the role of *Homo sapiens* from conqueror of the land-community to plain member and citizen of it. It implies respect for his fellow-members, *and also respect for the community as such.* (emphasis added)

Nonhuman natural entities, first appearing as fellow members, then considered as species, are not mentioned in the "summary moral maxim" of the land ethic: "A thing is right when it tends to preserve the integrity, stability, and beauty of the biotic community. It is wrong when it tends otherwise."

By this measure, not only would it be wrong for a farmer to clear the woods off a 75 percent slope, turn his cows into the clearing, and dump its rainfall, rocks, and soil into the community creek, it would also be wrong for the federal fish and wildlife agency, in the interest of individual animal welfare, to permit populations of deer, burros, or whatever to increase unchecked and thus to threaten the integrity, stability, and beauty of the biotic communities of which they are members. Ethical consideration of individual members is preempted by concern for the integrity, stability, and beauty of the biotic community. The land ethic is holistic with a vengeance.

Moral value of the environment

Mainstream modern ethical philosophy has taken egoism as its point of departure and reached a wider circle of moral entitlement by a process of generalization: I am sure that *I* am inherently valuable and thus that *my* interests ought to be taken into account by "others" when their actions affect *me*. My own claim to moral consideration, according to the conventional wisdom, rests upon a psychological capacity – rationality or sentiency – which is valuable in itself and thus qualifies *me* for moral standing. I am forced grudgingly to grant the same moral consideration to others.

If the criterion of moral consideration is pitched low enough – as in Bentham's criterion of sentiency – a wide variety of animals are admitted to moral entitlement. If the criterion is pushed lower still – as in Albert Schweitzer's reverence-for-life ethic – all minimally conative things (plants as well as animals) would be extended moral considerability. The contemporary animal liberation and reverence-for-life ethics are direct applications of the modern paradigm of moral argument. But this model provides no possibility for the moral consideration of wholes – of threatened *populations* of animals and plants, endangered *species*, biotic *communities*, or the *biosphere* in its totality – since wholes have no psychological experience.

Hume, Smith, and Darwin diverged from the prevailing model by recognizing that altruism is as fundamental in human nature as is egoism. According to their analysis, moral value is not identified with a natural quality present in morally considerable beings – as reason or sentiency is present in people or animals – it is, as it were, projected by valuing subjects.

Theoretically then, the biotic community owns direct moral considerability – because it is a proper object of a specially evolved "public affection" or "moral sense" which human beings have inherited from a long line of ancestral social primates.

Practical principles

Leopold derives several practical principles. "The trend of evolution is to elaborate and diversify the biota." Hence, among our cardinal duties is the duty to preserve what species we can, especially those at the apex of the pyramid – the top carnivores. "In the beginning, the pyramid of life was low and squat; the food chains short and simple. Evolution has added layer after layer." Human activities today, especially those resulting in abrupt massive extinctions of species, flatten the biotic pyramid; they choke off some of the channels and gorge others (those which terminate in our own species).

The land ethic does not enshrine the ecological status quo and devalue the dynamic dimension of nature. Leopold explains that "Evolutionary changes are usually slow and local. Man's invention of tools has enabled him to make changes of unprecedented violence, rapidity, and scope." What is wrong with anthropogenic species extinction is the *rate* at which it is occurring and the *result:* biological impoverishment instead of enrichment.

Leopold goes on to condemn, in its impact on the ecosystem, the indiscriminate introduction of exotic species and the dislocation of native species; mining the soil for its stored biotic energy, leading ultimately to diminished fertility and to erosion; and polluting and damming water courses.

According to the land ethic: Thou shalt not render species extinct; thou shalt exercise caution in introducing exotic species into local ecosystems, in extracting energy from the soil and releasing it into the biota, and in damming or polluting water courses; and thou shalt be solicitous of predatory birds and mammals. Here in brief are the moral precepts of the land ethic.

The land ethic and respect for humans

The land ethic implies neither inhumane nor inhuman consequences. Being citizens of some nation does not mean that we are not also members of smaller communities – cities, neighborhoods, and families – or that we are relieved of the moral responsibilities attendant upon these memberships. Similarly, our recognition of the biotic community does not imply that we do not also remain members of the human community – the "family of man" or "global village" – or that we are relieved of the attendant moral responsibilities of that membership, among them to respect universal human rights and uphold individual human worth and dignity.

As a general rule, duties correlative to the inner social circles to which we belong eclipse those correlative to the rings farther from the heartwood when conflicts arise. Consider our moral revulsion when zealous nationalists encourage children to turn their parents into the authorities if their parents dissent from the doctrines of the ruling party. A zealous environmentalist who advocated war, famine, or pestilence on human populations in the name of the integrity, beauty, and stability of the biotic community would be similarly perverse. Family obligations in general come before nationalistic duties and humanitarian obligations in general come before environmental duties. The land ethic, therefore, does not cancel human morality.

Nonhuman members of the biotic community have no "human rights," because they are not members of the human community. As fellow members of the biotic community, however, they deserve respect. How exactly to express respect is a difficult question.

Fortunately, American Indian and other traditional patterns of human-nature interaction provide rich models. Algonkian woodland peoples, for instance, represented animals, plants, birds, waters, and minerals as persons engaged in mutually beneficial intercourse with human beings. Tokens of payment, together with expressions of apology, were routinely offered to beings whom it was necessary for these Indians to exploit. The Algonkian portrayal of human-nature relationships is, although different in specifics, identical in abstract form to that recommended by Leopold in the land ethic.

Study questions

1 How does Leopold's reference to slavery relate to environmental ethics?
2 Explain how Callicott uses evolution to explain why ethics must be based on sentiments.
3 Explain the claim that ethics and community are correlative, and how it points to an environmental ethics. What is the role of sentiments here?
4 Explain how mainstream ethical philosophy extends our concern for ourselves to a concern for other sentient beings. To what extent does environmental ethics follow or deviate from this model?
5 What are the practical principles of the land ethic?
6 Why does the land ethic lead to the principle that we should not render species extinct?
7 How does the land ethic maintain a respect for humans, even as it places moral value on the environment?

For further study

This selection has excerpts, sometimes simplified in wording, from J. Baird Callicott's "The conceptual foundations of the land ethic," in *Companion to A Sand County Almanac* (Madison, WI: University of Wisconsin Press, 1987), pages 186–217. For more on Callicott's view, see that work and his *In Defense of the Land Ethic* (Albany, NY: State University of New York Press, 1989).

Related readings in this anthology include Hume (to whom Callicott appeals in basing ethics on sentiments); and Mill, Ross, Singer, and Smart (whose views require us to give intrinsic moral consideration to other individual sentient beings – but not to aggregates like endangered species or biotic communities).

Note

1 Callicott discusses "The Land Ethic," an essay by Aldo Leopold that proposes that we see ourselves as members of a valuable ecological community. Leopold (1887–1947) worked for the US Forest Service and was a Professor of Wildlife Management.

INDEX